D1598096

BETWEEN KANT AND KABBALAH

SUNY Series in Judaica:
Hermeneutics, Mysticism, and Religion
Michael Fishbane, Robert Goldenberg, and Arthur Green,
Editors

BETWEEN KANT
AND KABBALAH

An Introduction to Isaac Breuer's
Philosophy of Judaism

ALAN L. MITTLEMAN

State University of New York Press

Published by
State University of New York Press, Albany

For information, address State University of New York
Press, State University Plaza, Albany, N.Y., 12246

Library of Congress Cataloging-in-Publication Data

Mittleman, Alan L.
     Between Kant and Kabbalah : an introduction to Isaac Breuer's
philosophy of Judaism / Alan L. Mittleman.
        p. cm.—(SUNY series in Judaica)
     Bibliography: p.
     Includes index.
     ISBN 0–7914–0239–8.—ISBN 0–7914–0240–1 (pbk.)
     1. Breuer, Isaac, 1883–1946. 2. Orthodox Judaism—Germany.
I. Title. II. Series.
BM755.B66M58   1990   89–34101
296.8'32'0943—dc20   CIP

10 9 8 7 6 5 4 3 2 1

CONTENTS

Preface   vii

1. From Frankfurt to Jerusalem   1

2. A Critique of Human Experience   25

3. Creation and Revelation   73

4. Law, Nation, History, and Redemption   124

5. Toward a Critical Appreciation of Isaac Breuer   175

Notes   189

Bibliography   217

Index   223

PREFACE

In this study, I have endeavored to present Isaac Breuer's philosophy of Judaism. The eminent Israeli critic Baruch Kurzweil, in an important essay on Breuer, offered a kind of warning to those who would study him. Just slightly less forbidding than "Abandon all hope, ye who enter here," it reads, "Only one who is enlightened by the rich sources from which his soul drew will attain to an understanding of his personality and work. But as for these, their portion is sealed beyond repair. Heaps of ruins cover the others." Kurzweil, in effect, consigns Breuer to a bygone world, a world that has been submerged in the Shoah and suspended by the founding of a democratic, secular State of Israel. On the one side, the impressive synthesis of Judaism and German high culture that Breuer achieved may be of no more than historical interest. On the other side, Breuer's hope for a theocracy, a "Torah State" in the land of Israel, came to an end in 1948, if not before. The intellectual difficulties of interpreting Breuer, coupled with the apparent impossibility of building upon his thought in a living fashion, have worked to discourage a serious study of his contribution.

Yet all who have been engaged by him, sympathizers as well as harsh critics, have recognized intellectual and spiritual greatness in the man and his work. Among his critics, Gershom Scholem noted the lack of a critical analysis of Breuer and pointed out that such an estimation of that "able thinker" would be desirable. Professor Rivka Horwitz, who related this story, has herself called for and contributed to a philosophical presentation of Breuer's achievement. She noted that without the studies of Maurice Friedman and Nahum Glatzer, Breuer's contemporaries Martin Buber and Franz Rosenzweig might not have found an audience beyond their own milieu.

I am unable to say whether Breuer's greatness equals that of his two noted contemporaries, for I am uncertain how such things are to be measured or indeed whether it falls to us rather than to history to do the measuring. I am able to say that Breuer's philosophical acumen, rigor, erudition, and comprehensiveness compare quite favorably with Buber's and with Rosenzweig's. I imagine, without hard evidence, that his learning in the sources of traditional Judaism, including Kabbalah, far exceeded theirs.

I would argue that Breuer is a philosopher for the latter half of the twentieth century. In Jewish terms, he is a philosopher of the post-Enlightenment age, a philosopher of the dialectic of Enlightenment. He has realized the disillusioning restlessness of modern reason and has abandoned all aspiration to achieve a harmonious accord between it and Judaism. The pretensions of Enlightenment reason, which still live on in science, are exposed. Reason is enculturated. It is someone's story. The Jewish response to reason is necessarily a response to culture, to another's story. The ground on which the Jew stands and out of which the response must come is bordered by the Jewish story. Consciousness of the perimeters of this ground and loyalty to it are prerequisites for a proper philosophical response.

That response comes as an assertion of Jewish Being, of Jewish will, of willing the powerful reality of the Jewish story in dialectical tension with the stories of modernity. Telling both, while trying to maximally live one, was Breuer's way. The metaphysical richness of the Jewish story, on Breuer's account, is hard to match. Breuer will continue to offer tradition-minded Jews a depth of unabashed yet disciplined metaphysical reflection seldom found in today's climate.

For all of this critique of historicized, enculturated reason, however, Breuer never takes flight into irrationalism. He does not propose the triumph of the will, but rather the education of the will. Although nourished by the well-springs of Kabbalah, he is dismissive of mysticism. Nor does his metaphysically grounded stance as a "national Jew" turn into another romantic nationalism. Despite the utopianism of his political vision, he holds to a severe self-criticism that deflates political enthusiasms. His tense, dialectical wrestling with philosophical reason and his critical approach to politics make him a philosopher of Orthodoxy free of any tendency toward fundamentalism. His thought does not lend itself to anticultural reaction and fundamentalist nationalism. Yet, in him much of modern Orthodoxy also comes to an end. He stands between the poles that characterize present Orthodoxy. Neither wholly open to modernity, owing to a typically modern disillusionment, nor wholly closed to modernity, owing to his very being as a German Jew, Breuer may be an antidote to an Orthodoxy in a quandary.

For these and other reasons, it seemed eminently worthwhile to me to undertake a systematic presentation of Breuer's work. My hope is that this study will stimulate interest in Isaac Breuer among English-speaking people and raise his sometimes obscure thought to a level of higher (alas, not perfect) clarity. Of course, this study ought not to be a substitute for reading Breuer's books. It is a *vade mecum* or, as the title makes plain, an introduction. It is also necessarily an interpretation.

I take Breuer to be a serious, philosophical thinker, not an ideologue using philosophy for nonphilosophical purposes. As such, I have presented Breuer's thought in a philosophical manner. Although attending to biographical and historical concerns, my mode of presentation is primarily philosophical exposition. I have for the most part bracketed my own critique out of the exposition, reserving it for the final chapter.

I also take Breuer to be a systematic thinker. He sometimes announces that he is presenting a "system of Jewish thought." In most of his mature works, he deals with issues of epistemology; philosophical anthropology; legal, social, and political theory; and philosophy of history. He relates all of these philosophical discussions to his Jewish theology in a direct manner. I have tried, accordingly, to isolate the key systematic elements and organize them in a coherent exposition, shorn of the literary and often polemical contexts in which they originally appear. Thus a high degree of selectivity was required in deciding what to present. Some learned readers will, no doubt, prefer less intensive treatments here, more intensive treatments there. Yet, *kav l'kav, tsav l'tsav,* I hope that I have given the shape of the whole with fidelity.

Breuer built on his earlier work as he progressed. There were some radical shifts and transformations in both his thought and his life, but generally he progressed by reiteration and nuancing. Capturing the steady nuancing of a thesis has proved very difficult in the context of an introductory work, where the broad outlines must be sought. I have tried to present the basic thesis in most instances, indicating its course through some of Breuer's other writings. This is especially true of Breuer's Hebrew works, *Moriah* and *Naḥaliel.* Written in a lucid Hebrew style, they are popularizations that represent, not so much new views, but new applications of what he had already determined. Accordingly, I treat his German works, which are, at any rate, less accessible to his potential audience, as basic sources and his Hebrew works as elaborations. All translations, unless otherwise noted, are my own.

I could not have concluded this study without the gracious assistance of Professor Mordechai Breuer, Isaac Breuer's son, of Bar Ilan University. His criticism of an early stage of the manuscript as well as his own magisterial study of German Orthodoxy have been invaluable. I must also thank Professors Paul Mendes-Flohr and Rivka Horwitz for their many comments and overall enthusiasm. Needless to say, responsibility for any misinterpretations is strictly my own.

My inexpressible gratitude goes to my wife, Patricia, for her unfailing support, and to my sons, Aryeh and Joel, for their patience. I dedicate this book to the memory of my father, Joseph Mittleman, who taught me that to judge another, one must attempt to stand in his place.

FROM FRANKFURT
TO JERUSALEM

To be sure, the Jews attempted a dialogue with the Germans,
starting from all possible points of view and situations, de-
mandingly, imploringly, and entreatingly, servile and defiant,
with a dignity employing all manner of tones and a godfor-
saken lack of dignity, and today, when the symphony is over,
the time may be ripe for studying their motifs and for attempting a critique of their tones.[1]

From the time of Moses Mendelssohn until the Nazi catastrophe, the Jews of the German-speaking lands entered and participated with extraordinary vigor in their newfound German culture.
In less than two centuries, they became both shapers and victims
of that culture, both architects and sacrificial offerings of modern
Europe. "Sacrifice" need not evoke the ultimate horrors of the final period from 1933 to 1945. A kind of sacrifice began in the Men-
delssohnian era itself. What the Jews lost in the process of the

Emancipation and acculturation was what Gershom Scholem calls "Jewish totality."[2] Isaac Breuer, in similar language, often called it "the Torah's claim to totality" (*Totalitätsanspruch der Thora*). The change in civil status the Jews experienced in the late eighteenth and nineteenth centuries brought about the dismantling of the all-encompassing religious civilization of medieval Judaism, which already was in decline from internal upheaval and external change; the dismantling occurred with the full complicity of the Jews themselves.

The rich inscape of the traditional culture and its structured society of legal and communal institutions could not compete with the new social and economic opportunities offered by a society undergoing a process of secularization. By the middle of the nineteenth century, the last legal disabilities hindering the Jews had fallen in Germany, but the work of articulating a suitable religious and national identity—indeed, the search for a new form of all-embracing community—had hardly begun. Henceforth, whether the Jew opted for Heinrich Heine's or Abraham Geiger's, Samson Raphael Hirsch's or Leopold Zunz's, solution, he was faced with a problem. Judaism, which unlike the disabilities did not disappear, had to be related to German culture, to *Deutschtum*; indeed, to modern humanity as such. Judaism had to both fit into a context and become a fit context.

As Scholem points out, the "Jewish symphony" played in Germany seldom if ever became a German-Jewish harmony, a German-Jewish dialogue. Not that the Jews ever failed to be passionate about finding a conception of and a role for their Judaism in the German scheme of things, nor that individual Germans rose to an appreciation of Jews as Jews. Rather, a genuine willingness by the one people to accept the other people as an equal was never apparent. Individual dialogues never became a national, historical dialogue. "Whether they sell pants or write books," the historian Theodor Mommsen wrote, "it is their duty to put aside their peculiar ways and, with a determined hand, to remove the obstacles between them and their fellow citizens."[3]

In the Jewish attempt to work out an appropriate relationship between Judaism and German culture, between *Judentum* and *Deutschtum*, the two terms of the relation were entirely open to novel definition. 'Judaism' need not bear any relation to what, for centuries, the Jew had understood his tradition to be. Nor need *Deutschtum*, for that matter, have anything to do with the German sociocultural reality. That one could adduce a parallel between the great luminaries of the German classical period and the Hebrew prophets, those universalistic geniuses of religion, in itself could strengthen the edifying myth of a German-Jewish community of spirit. Like any myth, however, it is unclear under what circumstances this one could have been proven false.

The belief in an abiding inner symbiosis of Jew and German supported a style of reasonably self-confident Jewish life, which protected itself from disproof by an elusive insularity. Jacob Katz has written that the Jews, although appearing to belong to the German middle class, in fact formed their own society, a somewhat insular subgroup. "The entry of Jewry as a collective into the body of German society, a process which began in the later eighteenth and early nineteenth century, did not mean real integration into any stratum or section of it."[4] However great the energy the Jews expended on convincing themselves of their Germanness, they failed to convince, in their hour of need, the only ones who mattered.

This study is of the "tones and motifs" of one "German Jewish" thinker, Isaac Breuer (1883–1946). "German Jewish" is properly placed in quotation marks, for although Breuer wrote in German (with obvious relish), and was a doctor of German law, devoted to Kant (in fact, a member of the *Kant Gesellschaft* until his departure from Germany), and committed to a community that was historically committed to Germany, he was not one of those who could be said to have attempted a dialogue between German and Jew. Although not a Zionist (he was a lifelong opponent of Zionism), he believed that Jewish history was at the point of its consummation and that that consummation required total dedication to upbuilding the land of Israel. He was emphatic in rejecting the German-Jewish symbiosis espoused by the members of his own community in Frankfurt am Main. One can hardly imagine a Jewish thinker who was more in Germany, without being of it.

Yet in it he was. Although born in Papa, Hungary, he moved to Frankfurt at an early age, where his father, Salomon Breuer, became rabbi of the *Israelitische Religionsgesellschaft* (IRG). His father was the son-in-law of Rabbi Samson Raphael Hirsch, the first rabbi of the IRG. Hirsch was a leading figure in nineteenth-century German Jewry. He is credited with facilitating an intellectual synthesis whereby orthodoxy and full participation in civic society became tenable. Hirsch was the author of the celebrated *Nineteen Letters*, which relates an imaginary correspondence between a perplexed youth and a young rabbi. The rabbi guides the questioner through his doubts toward a modern philosophy of Judaism. Hirsch expressed his mature thought in an elaborate compendium on the meaning of the commandments of Jewish law, the *Horeb*, as well as in commentaries on the Pentateuch and Psalms.

Hirsch is also remembered for a more controversial contribution to Jewish life, one that forms the immediate background of Isaac Breuer's social world. In 1848 a group of traditional Jews in Frankfurt prevailed upon the government to allow them to organize their own independent religious society. They were alarmed by the progress of Reform Judaism in Frankfurt and sought, if not secession from the community (*Gemeinde*)—membership in which was mandatory for all Jews—at least a degree of autonomy. In 1851 Hirsch left a successful and important post in Nikolsburg, Moravia, and answered the call to assist the fledgling society.[5] Hirsch immediately set out to make his community as independent of the liberal-dominated *Gemeinde* as possible, establishing a modern school (to compete with the liberal "Philanthropin") and a synagogue. But the separatists were still obliged to be taxpaying members of the *Gemeinde* and so to contribute, against their wishes, to the maintenance of non-Orthodox institutions. In 1876, after decades of work, Hirsch succeeded in having an act passed by the Prussian *Landtag* that permitted groups to secede for religious reasons from their church or Jewish community in order to found alternative, legally valid institutions. Henceforth, there were to be Orthodox members of the community who participated with their Reform brethren in a common overarching structure, and those who followed Hirsch on a path of nonparticipation and noncooperation. Although the separatists succeeded in achieving state recognition for their independent community, their problems were compounded when the *Gemeinde* established subsidiary institutions for its more traditional members, those, that is, who did not opt to secede.

The law of secession (*Austrittsgesetz*) further divided the already splintered wings of German Orthodoxy. The legal sanctioning of the incipient schism was greeted with bitter controversy in its day and still evokes strong feelings. Hirsch believed that liberal Jews, and Orthodox who would cooperate with them in a common institutional framework (*Gemeinde-Orthodoxie*), were the original separatists, and that his community and the few elsewhere in Germany that followed its lead restored the Jewish community to its original health.[6] Although not entirely disagreeing with Hirsch over the principle of complete autonomy for the Orthodox, the leading halakhic authority in Germany, R. Seligmann Bamberger (the "Wurzberger Rav," 1807–78), took issue with aspects of Hirsch's policy. The crisis of legitimation engendered by this intra-Orthodox controversy continued to occupy members of the separatist community down to its demise.

According to Isaac Breuer's own testimony, his life in a sense began with the story of his community. His autobiography, *Mein Weg* (My Way, 1946), completed just four months before his death in 1946, begins with the memory of his father passionately defending the independence of the IRG. Breuer relates his origins to his community's story, submerging his own individuality, as it were, into the narrative of his people.[7] In these early childhood memories, Breuer recalls his father declaiming the responsibility of every Jew to turn his back on the Reform community. In the true community of Torah, there is room for the unobservant, the non-Orthodox; there is room for sympathy and tolerance for all kinds of Jew. But there is neither room nor tolerance for a community that as such rejects the sovereign authority of Torah. This nationalization of Torah as the binding, contemporary law of Israel, with direct application to social structure and boundaries and direct implication for the objective value or disvalue of empirical forms of Jewish community, Breuer terms the "Frankfurt Principle." It is no accident that Breuer begins his autobiography with an essay on the implications of this principle for social judgment and ideological orientation, for it has shaped much of his thought. If he is to be taken at his word, it shaped his earliest understanding. His tendency toward framing sharp dichotomies, such as Jew/Gentile, general history/Jewish history, creation/nature, and Israel/galut, perhaps derives from the sharp dichotomization implied by the Frankfurt Principle.

From 1890 to 1898, the young Isaac Breuer attended the school founded by his grandfather Samson Raphael Hirsch. His teacher was his maternal uncle Dr. Mendel Hirsch, son of the founder. The educational ideology of this institution embodied the orientation displayed in Hirsch's many writings. Hirsch's own pithy summation of this culture-affirming orientation was drawn from the Mishnah: *Torah im derekh eretz*, Torah and the way of general culture.[8] The curriculum was divided among Hebrew language and Jewish religious instruction; European languages, history, science, and mathematics; and German language, history, and literature. Breuer admits to having failed to absorb the full benefit of his grandfather's ideal.[9] His secular studies did not move or impress him as deeply as his biblical studies with Mendel Hirsch and his Talmudic study in his father's house and, eventually, Yeshivah.

The portrait he leaves us of his own childhood depicts an almost idyllic world of civil peace, material prosperity (or at least sufficiency), and intense, traditional piety. His home was saturated with Talmudic learning as well as a peculiarly Jewish-national consciousness.[10] The Talmud was daily studied as the living law of a nation in exile. Breuer often alludes to his father's (and mother's) acute sense of living in exile and to his parents' intense yearning for Zion. His parents' passion was expressed in ritual moments of joy, on Passover for example, and of mourning, as on the Fast of the ninth of Av. These memories left a profound impression on him.

He was also oriented, while young, by his father's manner of interpreting Hirsch's philosophy of Torah and general culture. Although Salomon Breuer earned a doctorate in philosophy at Heidelberg, Breuer believed that he never again picked up a secular book.[11] He was thoroughly, if somewhat atypically, immersed in the world of traditional learning. Thus the revolutionary attitude of Isaac Breuer's own generation, typified by a turn away from the comfortable piety of *Torah im derekh eretz* and a turn toward a radical renewal of "total" Judaism, Breuer learned at home. Although he soon emerged as a rather harsh critic of his own community, he never directed his criticism toward his own upbringing. He portrays his family life as the kernel from which his mature thought and action naturally developed. From his father's prophetic doubt about the permanence of the Emancipation to the large map of the land of Israel on the wall of his study, the essential elements of his attitudes and values were shaped at home.[12]

This early childhood idyll was punctured, it seems by a sense of exceptionalism. Because of his father's role as rabbi and, moreover, his own early attraction to Talmudic learning (*Lernen*,) he became aware of himself as a solitary figure. By his own account, it was not until his intense involvement in a university student society (the *Bund Jüdischer Akademiker*) that he mastered his innate tendency toward solitude.[13] This tendency nonetheless remained a feature of Breuer's public persona as he matured.

Breuer seemed destined for solitariness, "Einsamkeit" as he called it, from an early age. He was marked by a singularity of values. As a schoolchild, he feigned participation in the singing of a patriotic song. While others sang "I am a German . . . ," he moved his lips;[14] he knew in a fundamental sense that he was not. He also acquired while young a sense of the fragility of economic well-being. The stream of mostly poor Hungarian and other Eastern European boys who came to study at his father's Yeshivah moved him away from his immediate, bourgeois Frankfurt peer group. He studied with the older boys in the Yeshivah after his own school was over and was deeply troubled by the poverty from which they evidently emerged.[15] He often walked alone along the banks of the Main on moonlit nights virtually tormented by the realities of poverty and class, indeed by the servitude of man to economic conditions. Suspicion, not respect, greeted wealth in the Breuer home. Undoubtedly, the strong orientation toward socialism in Breuer's social thought, his vigorous praise of labor and the proletariat, as well as his manifold and relentless critique of the bourgeoisie, stem in some measure from these early experiences.

The self-portrait that emerges from Breuer's own recollections of his early years is quite engaging. He appears as an extraordinarily devoted son, a loyal follower of his father. Although deeply convinced of the rightness of the Frankfurt Principle, he seems without self-righteousness. Although intellectually invulnerable, he appears to have been emotionally vulnerable, aware of his own failings, and often the butt of a self-deprecating, mordant humor.[16]

Despite his own condemnation of individualism, Breuer reveals himself to be an individualist. As Baruch Kurzweil observed, Breuer sought to subsume his individuality into a putative national pattern of ideal Jewishness, to be nothing more than an "imperishable Talmud-Jew." What he achieved, however, was the status of a misunderstood individualist. The pathos of his singularity appears early in *Mein Weg* but is mitigated by the impression of stunning vitality and wit.[17]

Breuer's early intuition of a tension between the "classical" Jewish values and mores of his father's house and the values and mores of the complacent IRG is not an isolated phenomenon. His discontent (*Unbehagen*) fits in well with the mood of the years before the First World War. The turn of the century brought a sense of a dawning new age but also a cultural pessimism about prevailing forms of social life. The general culture experienced a turn against established authority and norms. Young intellectuals, full of contempt for the petit bourgeois ideal of *still und ruhig Leben*, searched for new forms of communal life, free of the alienation, rationality, and metaphysical impoverishment of the present.[18] This general sense of cultural discontent, heightened by a sense that the age was capable of fundamental spiritual and social change, penetrated Orthodox Jewry no less than it did the sphere of assimilated Jews such as Franz Rosenzweig.[19]

For some Orthodox youth of Breuer's time, the third generation of the neo-Orthodox synthesis, Samson Raphael Hirsch's principle of compatibility between Torah and German culture seemed less a luminous ideal than a fait accompli in which they were trapped. German culture itself no longer called forth unqualified appreciation. Enlightenment and philosophical idealism had given way to empire and materialism. Although Jews had done well, political anti-Semitism introduced a new, alarming dissonance. German-Jewish, *Torah im derekh eretz* compatibility appeared to some of Breuer's cohorts to have had the ironic result of precipitating a loss of Jewish wholeness, a progressive enervation of Jewish energy and soul. Of course the Law was still practiced publicly and privately within the IRG and German Orthodoxy as a whole, but Hirsch's rational-symbolic theology preempted the mysterious depth-dimension of the commandments. Orthodox youth read Hirsch's *Horeb* before they learned, if they learned at all, a *blatt gemore.* Although few were willing to say that Hirsch's legacy led to a spiritual *cul de sac,* many felt the need for a theological progress beyond Hirsch. A new intellectual formulation, derived from a radical, unmediated encounter with all of tradition, was sought. One of a number of Orthodox youth moved by these currents, Isaac Breuer called this quest for a new direction "Neu orientierung" (new orientation).[20]

The youthful advocates of this "new orientation" engaged in radical, multilayered religious, social, and political critique, directed, with all due respect, at inherited ideas and attitudes. On the religious level, they attacked observance justified on the basis of psychological, aesthetic, or habitual grounds in the name of theocentricity. Nothing less than full conviction of the divinity of the Torah would do. Pinchas Kohn (1867–1941), a lifelong, intimate friend (as well as a spirited opponent) of Breuer, called for a revision of the neo-Orthodox attitude toward Kabbalah. This remarkable rabbi, who after earing a Ph.D. in philosophy in Berlin studied Sanskrit at the University of Vienna, exposed Breuer to Jewish mysticism on the eve of the First World War.[21] Nehemiah Nobel, the communal Orthodox leader in Frankfurt who was to exercise so decisive an influence on Franz Rosenzweig, also represented the turn toward Kabbalah evident at this time. From a very different angle, Martin Buber's poetic representations of Hasidism and Gershom Scholem's early researches attest to a diffuse quickening of interest in buried mystical traditions.

The religious thrust of the new orientation, characterized as a demand for Jewish totality and integrity won through a new encounter with the powerful, original sources of Judaism, marks Breuer's entire endeavor. The dogmatic side of Breuer's project can be understood as an attempt to provide a post-Hirschian (but by no means anti-Hirschian) framework for full-blooded Jewish religious life. Breuer sought to augment, if not displace, the *neo* component of neo-Orthodoxy by anchoring elements of old Orthodoxy. Kabbalah is one phase of this reorienting, repristinating movement.

Another is the thoroughgoing deconstruction of reason or, more broadly, of modern intellectual Kultur. The attempt to posit an ontologically fundamental reality of Jewish Being over all forms of time-bound and culture-conditioned intellectual artifacts and praxis mirrors a general turn away from a culture of rationalism now perceived as sterile. Rosenzweig's dependence on the late Schelling, with the priority of Being over reason, reflects the same critical and constructive momentum.[22]

The abiding elements in Breuer's thought of social and political critique and construction also derive from the mood and spirit of new orientation. Breuer was deeply impressed, while still in the Yeshivah, by Theodor Herzl (1860–1904). Not yet a bar mitzvah, Breuer found Herzl's and Max Nordau's speeches "breathtaking."[23] While Herzl shocked both Reform and Orthodox Jews "to death" with his bold call to national consciousness and activism, Breuer heard a profound, if profoundly distorted, confirmation of what he had always known. His very first published writing, a story entitled *Jerusalem* (1903), presented a thinly veiled Herzl as its main character.[24] Breuer found in Herzl a figure of grandly tragic-heroic proportions. Herzl's primordial love of Zion and national consciousness, issuing as a *cri de coeur* from the depths of a Jewish soul otherwise banished to the wilderness of assimilation, confirmed the orienting, primal power of Breuer's own *ahavat Zion* and *ahavat Israel*. Herzl tore the mask off every "German citizen of Mosaic faith" and articulated Breuer's almost innate sense that Jews live in exile and that the exile must end.

Herzl represented radical historicity. Breuer had earlier discovered in himself a fascination with history at an age when other boys read adventure stories.[25] His disposition to understand the Jewish people in the context of a real, textured history, more or less transparent to a divine telos, was further catalyzed by Herzl's historical activism. For Breuer, as for others of his generation, Zionism opened up the heady possibility of history making. Such historically located activism seemed to be the highest realization of the people-forming (*Volksgestaltend*) potential of the Torah itself.

But Herzl was also a tragic figure. Divorced from Torah, Herzlian nationalism was a horrible perversion of the immanent Jewish totality, a veritable *yetzer ha-ra* unchecked by the countervailing good inclination. Owing to the power of the genuine historical current that surged through him, Herzl was nothing less than a prophet. He was, however, a false prophet. His real greatness was also his tragic flaw.[26] Had Herzl been a mere politician, had Zionism been a mere political movement, some accommodation with it would have been possible. Breuer believed however that Zionism and its prophet were much more. Zionism was a pseudo-Judaism, a distorted surrogate drawing strength from the inherent national consciousness of primordial Judaism. Zionism played a providential role by shocking Jews back to recognition of the unity of their national-religious Being. This unity had been masked and bartered away by generations of post-Emancipation life. But Zionism arrogantly made off with this crucial, if now renegade, element. Thus Breuer's call to Jewish totality becomes a call to full national-religious consciousness, such that the power of Zionism can be historically productive and its "poison" can be, at the same time, neutralized.

As we will see, Breuer's "Zionist" anti-Zionism, expressed with relentless ideological precision in dozens of articles and books, destined him to a most paradoxical situation. He applied the Frankfurt Principle of noncooperation and boycott to both secular and religious Zionists, utterly repudiating the latter for replacing God's Torah with a human nationalism. He rejected the religious Zionist movement (*Mizrachi*) not because of its activities but because of what he took to be its inner logic. On the other hand, the *haredi* Orthodox, both Western and East European, had little or no appreciation of his sense of historical moment, as his long, troubled relationship with Agudat Israel clearly illustrates. The providentially productive poison of Zionism never left his veins, making him a kind of *haredi* Herzl in search of a movement.

Zionism therefore provided a lifelong opponent as well as a model and inspiration for his own thought and activism. Constrained by his principle neither to join nor to cooperate with Zionist organizations, he was nonetheless wholly in agreement with some fundamental Zionist principles and policies. The theme of responding to the historical moment, of rising in a mass movement of return to the "national home," runs like a scarlet thread through many of his works. Yet the majority of the traditional audience to whom he directed his energy seemed unable to distinguish his orientation from Zionism as such and unable to grasp why settling the Land constituted anything more than one mitzvah among others of equal weight. Breuer's, one might say, obsession with the inherent demand of the historical moment represented too radical, indeed modern, an orientation for the *ḥaredim*, who looked upon history as a textureless duration, lacking in novelty and significance.

Exposure to Zionism at an early age gave a particular cast to Breuer's *Unbehagen*. The contemporary critique of bourgeois life, rationality, civilization, and alienation, in which Breuer participated, turned in his thinking to a constructive project of raising a world-historical consciousness among the Jews such that they would be fit to act within the emerging world-historical reality. The Frankfurt community, which he understood to be a kind of reification of the social archetype of the eternal, divine Torah, served as his model for the world-historical movement (the "organized people of Torah") he sought to engender. Thus, discontent with the static, bourgeois, privatized piety he encountered in his youth, he was nurtured by his intuition of a world-historical ideal.

From his youth, Breuer turned to history to grasp the framework for the actual realization of Judaism. During his Yeshivah years he deepened his conception of history, coming to understand it in philosophical fashion as the history of consciousness. Although the principal actors in history are nations, history is also, Breuer learned, the history of reason, of humanity realizing itself in its ideas. The Torah, which aims to rule over the Jewish nation-in-history, also aims to rule over Jewish persons. While clarity about the historical process is necessary, clarity about human nature is also essential in order, dialectically, to understand the Torah. Breuer was therefore determined to take up the study of philosophy, which he understood to be both the history of reason and the existential situation of humans per se.

While still in the Yeshivah, Breuer prepared for matriculation exams in order to enter the university. Beginning in 1902, he attended the Universities of Giessen (–1904), Strasbourg (1904–06),

Marburg and Berlin (1906–09), and then Strasbourg again, where he completed his doctorate in law, which he earned in 1912. Hearing lectures in classical, medieval, and modern philosophy, literature, art history, and German grammar, Breuer finally came to the theory of knowledge *Erkenntnistheorie,* which interested him more than other domains of learning.[27]

Kant emerged for him as the premier philosopher of the *conditio humana.* In Kant, Breuer found a lifelong source of nourishment as well as an object of critical opposition. He set to the study of Kant with the same intensity he applied, as a Yeshivah student, to Talmudic commentaries. Lectures were of no use. He worked hard on the primary texts himself, making Kant his own.[28]

Breuer credits several thinkers of the Neo-Kantian school whom he encountered at the university with direct influences on his own thinking. Kuno Fischer (1824–1907), Wilhelm Windelband (1848–1915), and Heinrich Rickert (1863–1936) contributed to his understanding of the nature of values and the subject/object distinction.[29] Breuer claims, however, to have had no attraction to Hermann Cohen (1842–1918), a leading luminary of the Neo-Kantian school. While at Marburg, Breuer was indecisive about attending Cohen's lectures and apparently decided against doing so.

The issue between Breuer and Cohen is significant. Although Breuer appreciated Cohen's definitive standing within Judaism as a source of pride and inspiration to many young Jews such as Rosenzweig, he saw Cohen as having reconstructed Judaism within a Kantian framework. Cohen's Kantianism set the interpretive horizon for his Judaism. The Kantian "religion of reason" provided the standard for what Judaism exemplifies. Breuer, on the other hand, believed Judaism to be singular, divine, and extracategorical. Kant is required, to understand the human condition into which Judaism enters. However, Kant must be read "Jewishly"; Judaism must not be read with Kantian spectacles. Clearly, the hierarchy of Torah and *derekh eretz,* Torah as that which wants to sublate and transform *derekh eretz,* establishes Breuer's basic method.[30]

Breuer claims to have read Kant in order to defend a Judaism of which he was utterly convinced, not to settle any adolescent doubts. It was not his aim to explicate Judaism philosophically, but to grasp the human condition through its own instrument, such that the divine counterpoint of Judaism could resonate even more clearly. He therefore limits philosophy's role. Philosophy both clarifies the human condition and embodies it, insofar as it is the history of reason. Kant's thought is a symbolic representation of the human drama. The drama is ultimately a tragedy. Philosophy is the summit of human wisdom at the same time that it is the abyss of human despair. Whether this position represents a dogmatic delimitation of philosophy or an arguable extension of Kant's own critique will be explored in the next chapter.

Breuer entertained a number of ideas regarding a choice of profession. His father seems to have wanted him to choose the rabbinate, but Breuer did not want his relationship to Judaism to be affected by "professional" considerations. (He also thought it "fatal" to have constantly to prepare sermons.) At length he chose law, the usual resort, he relates, for those who can't make up their minds.[31] Although he could not follow his father into the professional rabbinate, he promised him that he would use his intended profession in the service of Judaism. Some of the writings considered below were prepared to fulfill this promise.

Breuer had distinct views about the nature of law before he began his university studies. As we have seen, he considered Jewish law to constitute the living matrix of his nation's life. Law preceded nation and aimed at forming and reforming it in order to express inherent legal ideals. As Breuer began his studies at Strasbourg, he was distressed to learn that many of his teachers were former Jews who had a dismissive, if not contemptuous, attitude toward Jewish law. His first instructor, Otto Lenel (formerly Levy), dismissed Jewish law as an antiquarian concern. Breuer, convinced of the relevance of his Yeshivah study to his preparation for matriculation, had asked Lenel whether he would be willing to assist him in making the case that six years of Talmud study in a Jewish *Hochschule* ought to count toward university credit. Lenel's brusque dismissal was distressing to Breuer, particularly since the former's expertise was in Roman law, hardly an area free from the taint of antiquarianism. This early encounter convinced Breuer of the inherent risks of legal study at the university.[32] He sensed that jurisprudence might be more difficult to contain than philosophical study, for Judaism, being law, might be vulnerable to contemporary theoretical or comparativist perspectives.

Breuer went through his legal studies with one eye on the Talmud and the other on contemporary legal theory. He brought the two into a critical conversation with each other. Breuer's legal studies exposed him to a wealth of philosophical-jurisprudential systems, historical-comparative issues, and political-economic concerns. While he grappled to comprehend the nature of law in general, he continuously sought to demarcate the boundary be-

tween Jewish law and the human legal experience as such. As he
gained solid grounding in contemporary philosophies of law, he dialectically constructed a philosophy of Jewish law, which—like his
epistemology—bears both the marks of German influence and a
sharp, dichotomizing opposition to the prevailing secular norm.

Three intellectual impressions from his academic experience
seem particularly decisive for his Jewish legal theory. The first is
that positive law has an ideal moral aim. Natural law theory was
fully discredited in academic circles, but Kantian notions of practical reason provided some moral orientation for law. Breuer writes
about law, both general and Jewish, in a strongly teleological vein.
The second impression he acquired is that fundamental skepticism, *aporia*, about justice was prevalent in the jurisprudential
world. Breuer was taken by the Socratic style of his teacher, Fritz
van Calker, during his time at the University of Berlin. All the
fundamental questions—for instance, What is the justification for
punishment? What is a mental state? Do we have free will or does
determinism prevail?—seemed open-ended. He was astonished
at how little certainty was available in matters that ultimately
affected people's lives in the most serious ways.[33] This dearth
of theoretical certainty about fundamental principles coexisted
alongside a thoroughly pragmatic attitude. The law functions
smoothly—criminals are put to death, for example—despite the
fact that no one is sure why or if that extreme action is justifiable.
The gap between theoria and praxis troubled Breuer and indicated
to him that grave confusion prevailed in modern law. Talk of justice remains lip service, if not—under the theoretical circumstances—incoherent babble. His theory of Jewish law attempts to
present a system in which theory, ends, and positive rules cohere.

A third impression, derived chiefly from his teacher Paul Laband (another former Jew), concerns the relation of law to the
State. Laband made the State the goal of law. Breuer's massive critique of the inherent totalitarian dynamic of the State, a recurrent
theme in his work, derives from his earliest study of law and politics. He feared a law in service to, not transcendent vis-à-vis, political legitimation. His Jewish thought draws a sharp line between
the transcendent (as well as transcendental) Torah and the Jewish
State. The State is a creature of the preexistent, cosmogonic law,
not the other way round. Breuer's absolutizing of Jewish law, removing it from all possibility of subjection to national Jewish sovereignty, represents a sharp reaction to what he saw as an essential
flaw in contemporary legal theory. Unclarity about principles, the
demise of natural law theory due to the Copernican Revolution of

modern thought, and the impotence of aims such as justice before
an autochthonous positivism all delivered law over to the State,
which—freed of all self-restraint by its conquest of law—becomes
a totalizing monstrosity. The brutal course of modern history sub-
stantiated this framework, but elements of it were already in place
before the First World War.

Breuer entered the university expecting to be a loner, it
seems. In 1903 an Orthodox student association, the *Verein Jüdischer Akademiker,* was founded in Berlin, and Breuer helped to
found a chapter in Strasbourg. In the summer of 1906, several such
chapters joined and formed the *Bund Jüdischer Akademiker* (BJA,
Union of Jewish Academics).[34] Breuer was completely taken up
with enthusiasm for this student movement and occupied important positions in it, even after he graduated. The BJA provided him
with both like-minded and loving peers and an organization in
which to learn the arts of public speaking and movement building.
He credited the BJA with a decisive influence on the formation of
his character, crediting his wife with the remainder.[35]

The BJA, like the Zionist societies with which it was in conflict and the various societies of the German youth movement in
general, offered an intensive, totalizing environment of fellowship
and ideological coherence. More political and at the same time
more spiritually charged than student organizations in, for example, the United States, the German youth movement celebrated
the psychological-spiritual situation of youth as a value in itself.
The BJA, although mindful of continuity with the older generation
(its founders chose the term *academic* rather than *student* so as to
include older scholars in an advisory capacity), also took the student experience seriously.[36] Without the constraints of practical
responsibilities, political tempers could flare and utopian enthusiasms could, and did, flourish. In the romantic revival of the pre–
World War I period, the youth movement expressed its *Unbehagen*
in back-to-nature excursions, drama, song, nationalist ritual, and a
cult of athletics, drinking, and dueling.[37] The BJA, as a principal
organ of German Orthodoxy's new orientation, also served as a vehicle for youthful discontent and spiritual experimentation. Its
members' commitment to traditional Judaism, of course, precluded some of the enthusiasms of the German or even the Zionist
societies. Nonetheless, essential traits of idealism and rebellion
were embodied in the movement.

What pertains to Breuer is the self-professed aim of the BJA to
fill its members with affirmative, philosophically grounded Jewish
life. The Jewish *Akademiker* was to transcend the habitual obser-

vance of *orthopraxy* and arrive at a theocentrically grounded Judaism. The "harmonious development of all the powers of life," nurtured through Talmudic learning and directed toward full Jewish self-consciousness, was the hope of the BJA.[38] Breuer's quest for Jewish totality or, more precisely, for a philosophy expressive of and insistent on Jewish totality was enlivened by and exercised on the BJA. His lifetime of activity in Agudat Israel, indeed his entire endeavor to shape an ideological movement embodying the ideals of the Torah as he understood them, seems, in a sense, to be an effort to recapture the heady sense of possibility, the idealism, and the responsive atmosphere of the BJA. Breuer's wistful praise for that organization and his solemn attestation of undying loyalty to it at the very end of his life supports this thesis.[39]

As Breuer learned philosophy and law at the university, his concurrent involvement with the BJA afforded him an immediate Jewish context in which to translate his secular studies into an incipient Jewish philosophy. The spiritual perplexities of his friends, particularly their felt need for a rigorous and defensible belief in which to ground their religious observance in a post-Hirschian era, stimulated Breuer's creativity. Some of Breuer's important books come from this period; others reflect the expansion of views already formed at this time. *Lehre, Gesetz und Nation* (Doctrine, Law and Nation, 1910), *Die Rechtsphilosophischen Grundlagen des Jüdischen und des Modernen Rechts* (Legal-Philosophical Foundations of Jewish and of Modern Law, 1911), and *Der Begriff des Wunders im Judentum* (The Concept of Miracle in Judaism, 1916), as well as a number of articles written in Orthodox journals, emanate from the crucible of his student experience.[40] Other works, such as *Die Welt als Schöpfung und Natur* (The World as Creation and as Nature, 1926), *Der Neue Kusari* (The New Kusari, 1934), and *Moriah* (1944), address, as it were, an imaginary BJA audience. *Moriah*, a systematic exposition in Hebrew of Jewish metahistory, was in fact conceived in 1906 as Breuer's sketch for the educational program and philosophy of the BJA, of which he was in charge.[41]

In 1913, Breuer finished his legal studies and internship as a junior barrister and became a lawyer in Frankfurt. The "paradisiacal" period of Jewish life under the Kaiser was soon to end.[42] In July of 1914, Breuer traveled through Switzerland in high spirits following his engagement to a Belgian Jew, Jenny Eisenmann, whom he married in 1916. Switzerland seemed as earthly paradise to him: a peaceful, cultured land where people of different nationalities could live together in the same state. When news first reached him that Austria and Russia were mobilizing their armies, he could not seriously believe that war was possible. As it became clear that conflict was imminent, he went to a museum, sat in front of a favorite statue, and wept.[43] Upon returning to Frankfurt, Breuer was classified as a *Landssturmmann*, a reservist, and— much to his amazement—quickly mobilized.

Throughout the war, Breuer kept an, as yet, unpublished diary, *Ich und der Krieg* (The War and I, 1915–18). He dedicated the work to his grandchildren, a striking act of faith for a man not yet married, in order to tell them the truth about the war. He wanted them to have access to an utterly disenchanted account of events, freed from the propaganda, illusion, and disinformation of state and press. In this private correspondence, Breuer expressed impassioned opposition to the war, seeing it as an absolute evil. Although at the outbreak of hostilities he flirted with defending German war aims, he soon came to see all parties as co-conspirators in a vast rebellion against God.[44] He saw in the war the absolute degradation and dehumanization of man. States came forward and seized the historical process, revealing the impotence of law and culture. The State knew no restraint. It mocked the cherished ideas of civilization and caught up all men in its senseless, avaricious grasp.

Breuer's incipient tendency toward a highly negative characterization of the State was fully crystalized by his experience of the war. He came to believe that the war was not an episode—an aberration in the midst of history—but an epiphany of the true character of history.[45] He experienced the war "historically"; that is, he sought to grasp the world-historical *gravitas* of war. He refused to view it as a private man, a philistine. He wanted to determine how the world war fit into the process of the world per se.

During the war, Breuer wrote *Judenproblem* (The Jewish Problem, 1918) and *Messiasspuren* (Traces of the Messiah, 1918) as well as numerous articles. *Messiasspuren* expresses his conviction that the war initiates a new epoch in history: the period of the birth pangs of the messiah.[46] The people Israel's response to this epiphany of history as rebellion, depravity, and slaughter must be an active messianism. Israel's unique history must be driven to its conclusion. The Jews must become self-conscious and rise to their own metahistory from the somnolence of general history into which they have been lulled by the Emancipation. The war, properly grasped, destroys all illusions. The war is not about the rationalizations with which the diplomats blind their populations. The war is about the removal of the divine presence from history (*siluk Shekhinah*) and the possibility of drawing God near once again (*kiruv Shekhinah*).[47]

The issuance of the Balfour Declaration in 1917 by the British government amplified Breuer's sense of messianic possibility. He understood that declaration from the side of *Völkergeschichte* (the history of the nations) to require response from the side of *Metageschichte* (the divinely charged history of Israel). It was impossible, after the war, to return to ordinary bourgeois life. The Jew, unlike the modern philistine, must now live on the world stage where dichotomized streams of history now surge toward each other.

Shortly after the war, when both Jew and Gentile indeed tried to return to the *still und ruhig Leben* of prewar times, Breuer wrote *Die Idee des Agudismus* (The Idea of Agudism, 1919). In this work he synopsized his active, practical messianism in the form of a program for Agudat Israel, the world Orthodox movement. The Agudah had been formed in 1912 in Kattowitz (Katowice) in Silesia. Breuer attended with his father, a principal figure in the movement. The Kattowitz conference brought together leading German Orthodox rabbis and traditional luminaries from Eastern Europe. The latter were reluctant to enter into a self-consciously political movement, but they were disturbed by the gains Jewish secularists, socialists, and Zionists were making in Eastern Europe. The interests of the masses of Orthodox Jews could not go unrepresented in the volatile political arena. The German Jews provided the organizational know-how to get such a "world movement" started.[48]

Breuer was involved with Agudat Israel throughout his life, serving on its World Executive, traveling twice on its behalf to Palestine, and speaking for it across Europe and America. From the external point of view, Breuer was a well-known Agudist leader, a member of an elite, who was often in the public eye. From Breuer's own point of view, however, he was in a continuous state of tension and estrangement from the Agudah. The bulk of his autobiography concerns the thirty years of loyal opposition to, running argument over, and disappointment with Agudah policies and personalities. His sharp criticism of Jacob Rosenheim, the president of Agudat Israel and a member of the IRG, pervades *Mein Weg*. The intensity and duration of Breuer's ideological feud with Rosenheim is hardly less fundamental than his rejection of Zionism.

Breuer's discontent with Agudat Israel passed through several stages. At first, he and his father argued that the nascent movement must take a separatist orientation similar to the Frankfurt IRG. The large Polish representation found this German (and Hungarian) idea quite foreign, however.[49]

After the issuance of the Balfour Declaration, Isaac Breuer, deeply convinced of the messianic import of that historic event, turned his entire endeavor toward convincing the Agudah to concentrate on development of the national home. His Agudism envisioned the movement as a mighty Orthodox counterweight to Zionism. The Agudah was to become a world-historical movement of national-religious Jews, the organized people of the Torah, wholly dedicated to building the national home in Zion. Armed with this self-conception, Agudah would, in fact, represent all Jews on the world stage, whether they were aware of the movement's leading role or not.[50] The official raison d'être of Agudat Israel, however, was considerably less focused, if not less radical. It saw itself as seeking to solve the problems of the time in the "spirit of the Torah." Breuer was criticized by other Agudah leaders as "Palestinocentric." It was not clear to his critics why he seemed to elevate a preoccupation with Zion over other pressing concerns. To his critics (including his closest friend, Pinchas Kohn), settling the land of Israel represented one mitzvah among 612 others. While Breuer did not deny this fact, he did reject the static framework that the numerical calculation of mitzvot implied. He saw in the ahistorical, local political orientation of Agudah precisely the kind of privatization of consciousness and philistinism he so deplored in Frankfurt. Not surprisingly, he attributed much of the blame for Agudah's static, intercessory *shtadlan*-like approach to Jacob Rosenheim, whom he believed never understood the activist cast of the work of Samson Raphael Hirsch or, therefore, his own orientation.

Breuer considered leaving Agudah at some points. His "Palestinocentric" ideology brought him isolation for the most part and, at times, public humiliation and embarrassment. He did not leave, however, because he found in Agudah's static, ahistorical worldview an accurate, if lamentable, mirror of Orthodoxy as such. He found a tragic irony in the fact that Zionism grasped the reality of history better than Orthodoxy and that, at present, Zionism was better able to act in history than the proper representatives of the Jewish people. Breuer did try to cultivate a force parallel to the Agudah, its loosely affiliated worker's movement,

Poalei Agudat Israel, and—after his *aliyah*—his own organization, *Brit Emunim.* Little came of Breuer's efforts to build these organizations into effective forces, however. Ultimately, despite his own acute sense of failure, Breuer remained with Agudat Israel out of loyalty to his beloved organized people of the Torah.

The name Breuer gave to his own ideology was "Thedaism" (*Thedaismus*), derived from the Hirschian slogan *Torah im derekh eretz* and Breuer's own nuance: *derekh eretz Yisrael.*[51] "Torah and the way of the land of Israel." This slogan, which Gershom Scholem mocked for its deficient Hebrew grammar, captured an essential thrust of Breuer's thought. As Breuer read Hirsch, Torah was to dominate and transform culture, *derekh eretz.* In this epoch, Torah must inform and transform the culture of the nascent national home in the land of Israel. Eventually Breuer used this nuance of Hirschian activism to justify a pragmatic cooperation with the Zionist Organization and Jewish Agency and a scaling-down of his theocratic politics to a plan for nurturing a Torah-informed society.

Breuer made his first trip to Palestine in 1926. Representing the Agudah, he negotiated with the British attorney general, Norman Bentwich, on behalf of the traditional Orthodox community in Jerusalem. Breuer's mission was to intervene in a dispute between that community and the Zionist authorities. In 1925, he had published *Das Jüdische Nationalheim* (The Jewish National Home), which focused on the malevolent (from Agudah's perspective) dealings of the Zionist establishment with the "Old Yishuv." The leader of the old Orthodox community of Jerusalem, R. Joseph Chaim Sonnenfeld (1849–1932), contacted Agudah's World Executive in Frankfurt for assistance in developing a separatist community that would not need to relate to the Zionist presence. Breuer fully believed in the desirability of establishing a Frankfurt-like community in Jerusalem, but he also wanted something more: a united Orthodox front, composed of independent communities across Palestine. He envisioned the legal establishment of an activist Orthodox movement that would counter the "united front" of the Zionist establishment.[52] Breuer indeed won the promise from Bentwich that he would work for the right of a separate, Frankfurt-style community if at least 25,000 potential members could be organized. Nothing came of this, however.

Breuer had fully identified with the struggle of the Old Yishuv to remain aloof from the Zionist transformation of Palestine and worked hard to secure the complete legal independence of their community. But he experienced a certain disillusionment with the Old Yishuv during his first contact with it. He had initially framed R. Sonnenfeld as a Samson Raphael Hirsch for Palestine. What he actually encountered, however, was a leader and a community simply wanting to be left alone. Instead of an activist, Hirschian attitude, he found an insular, negative, and sectarian disposition.[53] Accordingly, Breuer's identification with the Old Yishuv, as with Agudat Israel in general, became increasingly troubled. Breuer reinterpreted the Frankfurt Principle in accord with the new reality of the land of Israel. Not separatism, but the socially revolutionary and transformative power of the Torah, becomes the dominant theme in Breuer's last phase.

When Breuer returned to Palestine to assess the economic situation of the Orthodox for the Agudah in 1933, R. Sonnenfeld's successors became angry with him because he went to visit Rav Abraham Isaac Kook, chief rabbi of Palestine (1865–1935). Kook validated secular Zionism through a highly mystical, original, religious philosophy. While disagreeing with Kook over his assessment of the eschatological justification of secularism, Breuer was in deep agreement with Kook's sense and appraisal of history. He found in Kook a metaphysically enlarged awareness of the immanent messianic dimension of history. He was thus intellectually closer to Kook than to the leaders of the Old Yishuv, whom he had now successfully alienated.[54] It is arguable that Kook influenced his thinking in a moderate, pragmatic direction.

Breuer relates in his autobiography that he knew that during his second trip he would move to Palestine. The Sabbath after his arrival, he had a powerful, illuminating experience (*Erlebnis*) in a Tel Aviv synagogue.[55] As Sabbath approached, Breuer felt swept along by a mass of humanity streaming toward the synagogue. He was overwhelmed by the current of Jews from all over the world, praying, singing, weeping, and demonstrating a depth and immediacy of Jewish passion such as he had never experienced in Frankfurt. The contrast between Tel Aviv and Frankfurt—the unruly, ripe potential of the former and the disciplined if narrow actuality of the latter—filled him with both hope and sadness, enthusiasm and deep melancholy. Hitler had already come to power, and Breuer no longer had any hope for the further development of German Orthodoxy. There had not been, nor was there to be, a "new orientation." The *Zeitgeist*, as it were, had now passed to Tel Aviv.

Yet even before Hitler, Breuer was resigned to the fact that Jewish totality was impossible to achieve in Frankfurt. His synagogue *Erlebnis* made acutely clear that, while the "legal" form of Frankfurt was correct, the content of Jewish life in Frankfurt was drastically circumscribed by the reality of the diaspora as such. Torah could not fill every aspect of existence. Although Breuer rejected the implication of his community's legal name, *Religionsgesellschaft*, "religious society," he had to admit that in the diaspora the degeneration of Judaism into a "religion" was irresistible. Frankfurt had correct form but deficient content. In Tel Aviv, however, the human raw material was overfull, while the legal form of the Torah State was not even on the horizon. Breuer was riveted by the intensity of the contrast and turned with fervor to the messianic potential of life in the old-new land.

As Breuer sat in the synagogue, he was struck by the man praying with high emotion at his side. The man was a simple worker, still dressed in his weekday work clothes. This too was a stark contrast to bourgeois Frankfurt. The proletarian nature of Orthodoxy in Palestine, as in Poland, fascinated Breuer. Breuer had read Karl Marx on his own at the university and maintained an intellectual affinity for a humanistic socialism throughout his life. Marx was for him a kind of Kant of economics. Although sharply critical of Marx's dehumanizing materialism, Breuer nonetheless found in his critique of capitalism an echo and a root for his own cultural *Unbehagen*. At any rate, Breuer was much concerned with the economic laws of the Torah and construed their underlying thrust in a socialist direction. Much of his "code," *Naḥaliel* (1951), is devoted to an interpretation of the halakhot of agriculture, commerce, and tithing as means to achieve an ideal, socialist society. In practical terms, Breuer found it impossible to advance his economic idealism in the diaspora and conceived of his task in Palestine, rather like a labor Zionist, in strongly economic terms. Breuer reposed much hope in the instinctive socialism of the observant Jewish proletariat and sought to cultivate an indigenous worker's movement (*Poalei Ha-Ḥaredi*) that would exemplify his ideals. The economic success of Orthodox Jews, he believed, would be the best propaganda for the sovereignty of the Torah over the economic sphere.[56] The stress on the practical problems of developing an economic infrastructure among Orthodox *olim* was perhaps another moderating influence during his final phase.

In 1933, Rav Kook had cautioned him that Frankfurt-style separatist communities had no role in present-day Palestine. Kook would oppose their erection. While affirming the wisdom of Hirsch's policy in its time, according to Breuer, Kook rejected it for his time, trying to persuade Breuer of the sacredness of pan-Jewish cooperation. Although not entirely convinced by Kook's argument, Breuer was open to his perspective. Alienated from the Old Yishuv and now committed to realizing his Thedaism through his own *alivah*, Breuer had to find his own way in the years ahead. He never abandoned his dream of a Torah State, but he shifted toward a realistic policy of developing an incipient Torah culture and society that would bore from within and eventually transform the anticipated secular Jewish state into a Torah State.[57] By the end of his life, he concluded a provisional peace with Zionism and worked to secure the rights of traditional Jews within the emerging polity. Far from a betrayal of the Frankfurt Principle, this was, he believed, an epochal opportunity to apply the Torah to "natural," in this case Jewish, humanity as a people-and culture-forming norm.

On March 2, 1936, the Breuer family arrived in Palestine. Breuer's last decade was spent in work for Agudat Israel as director of its Palestine Central and its fund for Agudist settlement, *Keren Ha-Yishuv*. Owing to the same sorts of controversy over ideology that he experienced in Europe, he decided (after an Agudah fund-raising mission to the United States in 1940) to relinquish his paid position and return to the practice of law for his livelihood. Breuer had to learn English and sit for exams. In 1942, four years before his death, he became qualified to practice law under the British Mandate.

During his years in Palestine, Breuer mastered spoken and written Hebrew, composing two full-length books in it. He started a synagogue in Jerusalem and developed a following of emigré students. He continued to promote his agenda within Agudah and conducted sensitive negotiations for the Agudah with both the Jewish Agency and the British authorities.

In his last year, Breuer represented the Agudah before the Anglo-American Committee of Inquiry. Breuer's testimony reveals the principled yet pragmatic orientation that remains his paradoxical legacy. Although representing "independent" Jewry, Breuer explained to the committee that his presence demonstrated solidarity with all Jews and basic agreement with the Jewish Agency that an open immigration policy was an urgent necessity. The year was 1946. The Holocaust had brought about a strong will to cooperate across ideological lines. Breuer advocated a position of power-sharing with Zionists in a reorganized Jewish Agency.[58] Breuer wanted free immigration for all Jews, regardless of religious orientation. He urged the committee to recommend a political solution that would guarantee security for all Jews and indicated that he would not oppose a sovereign Jewish state, although he did not consider it an absolute necessity. Significantly, Breuer framed his argument both on the basis of the internal, historical dynamic of Judaism and on the basis of "absolute Justice." Breuer continued to hold out hope, after Auschwitz and despite his own almost gnostic theory of history, for the rule of international law, if not to say sanity. Breuer was sanguine not only about the possibility of justice for the Jews, in line with the Balfour Declaration, but also about the prospect for the development of a Torah society in a Jewish state. He steered the Agudah into the policy of cooperation that eventually led it, after his death, to join the government of the new state of Israel.

Breuer's singular way was one of paradox. He was modern, down to his dying hope in international law and the possibility of justice, yet antimodern in his dualism. He was anti-Zionist in every way except for his radical "Zionist" commitment to developing the national home in the land of Israel. He was a scrupulously disciplined metaphysical thinker in search of a proletarian mass movement. A logician and a novelist. A German by culture in self-imposed exile while still in Germany. Breuer was suspended between Kant and Kabbalah; eschewing the way of synthesis, he embraced the existential tensions of his conflicting loyalties. To the intellectual product that emerges from this tension we now turn.

◆ 2

A CRITIQUE OF HUMAN EXPERIENCE

BEYOND THE "RELIGION OF REASON"

One could begin the study of Breuer's philosophy with an investigation of either his epistemology or his philosophy of history. Both were fundamental disciplines for him, each revealing much about the underlying tragedy of human existence. Epistemology provides a critique of existence in its individuated dimension, while philosophy of history critiques collective existence. Both inquiries reveal that humanity is divided against itself and against its Creator.

This study begins with epistemology because Breuer gave such discussion considerable weight in his overall system. Breuer's penchant for epistemology is one of the distinguishing characteristics of his work. Although he was not alone among Orthodox Jewish thinkers in attempting to ground his thought in an epistemology (Rav Kook did so in an early work), he is unique in the intensity, rigor, and sophistication with which he pursued his task.[1]

In *Die Welt als Schöpfung und Natur, Der Neue Kusari*, and another major German work, *Elischa* (Elisha, 1928), Breuer proposed a complex thesis on the nature of human perception, knowledge, and will. The thesis is reiterated in his Hebrew works, *Moriah* and *Naḥaliel*.[2] The attempt to anchor his philosophy of Judaism in a multifaceted epistemology is evident in all phases of his creativity. Consequently, an understanding of his epistemology—and of his reasons for doing epistemology—is necessary for any comprehensive grasp of his thought.

Before exploring his basic thesis, we must inquire into his reasons for venturing into the terrain of epistemological theory (*Erkenntnistheorie*) in the first place. His reasons for placing so much emphasis on this branch of philosophy tell us much about his results.

In one of his earliest studies, *Lehre, Gesetz und Nation*, (1910), Breuer makes a general remark about *Lehre* (doctrine, or philosophical-theological discourse in general).[3] Why should Orthodox Jews bother about such discourse, he asks. Would it not be sufficient to speak only about the Law (*Gesetz*)? Breuer fears that the attempt to define a Jewish *Lehre*, to isolate an "essence of Judaism," sounds suspiciously like the preoccupation of liberal theologians. He answers, in effect, that modernity gives the Orthodox Jew no choice. In the bitter spiritual conflict of the last century, for example, the great teachers of the era were forced to speak the language of *Lehre* in order to defend the integrity of the Law. Straying into the risky hinterland of philosophical-theological discourse is not a concession to religious liberalism; rather, it is a form of polemical counterattack.

It is significant that Breuer should have begun his first theological essay with such a disclaimer. Perhaps he simply meant to raise an initial caution against the easy identification of his essay with the liberal "Essence of Judaism" literature, represented most enduringly by Leo Baeck's volume of the same name. In that genre, philosophy was used to sift a conceptual essence of pure Judaism from the presumably impure accretions and forms that the religion acquired in the course of Jewish history. Breuer's caveat, however, represents more than a minatory remark. It reveals a deep ambivalence about the practice of philosophy and a defense of his own engagement in it.

A full two generations after Samson Raphael Hirsch opened up a way for traditionalists to participate in secular culture, some uneasiness remained. Not, however, because secularity was still foreign, but because it was too familiar. The argument over the place of secular culture, *Deutschtum*, had long been settled in Orthodox Jewish life in Germany. It was still divisive in Eastern Europe, of course, and an aggravating factor in Breuer's relationship with Eastern European members of the Agudah.

The ambivalence toward philosophy already apparent in *Lehre, Gesetz und Nation* does not disappear. In as late a work as *Moriah* (1944), Breuer laments that his generation cannot choose between the way of philosophy, that is, the way of dialogue with other cultures, and the cultivation of a pure Jewish inwardness. He implies that he has been forced to stand in the intellectual give-and-take of the age. "But happy is the generation that has a clear choice between these alternatives"; he ends that thought with the suggestive phrase, The wise will understand (*Ha-maskil yavin*).[4] This almost wistful observation occurs at the end of his discussion of the work of Maimonides, the premier figure in Jewish history in the reconciliation of philosophy and Judaism.

Breuer gives Maimonides his due for demonstrating a "perfect harmony" between reason and revelation. Much to Maimonides' credit, although he was devoted to Aristotle he remained relatively independent of him in decisive ways. Breuer esteems Maimonides not only for his sound philosophical construction but also for his sound attitude toward philosophy. "It is not fitting for human reason to judge the Torah, but on the contrary, for the Torah to judge human reason."[5]

Maimonides' harmonization of philosophy and Torah was impossible to sustain. In the hands of his successors, his philosophy shattered the "unity of the Jewish personality." Breuer locates the cause of the Maimonidean controversy—the protracted debate over the place of philosophy and secular learning in Judaism during the century after Maimonides' death—in the "abnormality" of diaspora life. The harmony of philosophy and Torah that Maimonides had achieved had not developed under the watchful eyes of "the sages of Israel" under normal conditions of landedness and statehood.[6] Breuer quotes with full approval the text of R. Solomon ben Adret's ban on the study of philosophy. He leaves no doubt as to which side of the Maimonidean controversy he would have taken.

Two Jewish thinkers contributed most immediately to Breuer's specific form of ambivalence toward philosophy: Judah Halevi and Samson Raphael Hirsch. Given Breuer's cautious distancing from Maimonides' paradigmatic attempt to harmonize reason and revelation, it is no accident that he turned to Halevi as a model for his own project.

Judah Halevi (ca.1075–1181), although he lived before Maimonides, may be taken as a paradigmatic critic of Jewish rationalism and as an exemplar of the Jewish tradition in which Breuer locates himself. Halevi was a poet and a philosophical critic of philosophy. "Turn aside from mines and pitfalls," he wrote. "Let not Greek wisdom tempt you, for it bears flowers only and no fruit. . . . Why should I search for bypaths, and complicated ones at that, and leave the main road?[7] If Maimonides and his followers can be taken to maintain that Torah and philosophy fulfill one another, and that philosophy is a necessary part of the life of Torah, Halevi and his "followers" can be taken to hold that the two are categorically different, in fact opposed.

In Halevi's view, philosophy is a fragmentary introduction to Torah. Human reason cannot attain to meaningful truth without divine revelation and prophetic tradition. Maimonides' perfect man has achieved the telos of his being by the practice of mitzvot and by scientific study. Man perfects himself. Halevi, on the other hand, sees this movement as divinely initiated. The prophet, who as perfected man occupies the highest level in the hierarchy of nature, is filled by divine grace with the *inyan elohi*, the divinely endowed capacity to achieve truth.[8] For Halevi and consequently for Isaac Breuer, disciplined effort in the sciences will not secure the desired, saving gnosis. Only loyal adherence to the community in which the divine dispensation has historically been available gives man the possibility of truth.

Halevi's subordination of philosophy, secular learning, and culture to revelation and the inherent truth of the revelation community finds a strong echo in Samson Raphael Hirsch. Hirsch, of course, did not reject culture and reason: he embraced them warmly. But he did order them in an Halevian manner. Culture and contemporary rationality depend upon Torah for their own fulfillment.

Hirsch was unequivocal in both his blessing of modern German culture and in his insistence upon full, traditional observance of the Law. His motto enunciated the reality of a new eclecticism: *Torah im derekh eretz*, "Torah with the manners of the land."[9]

Urging full Jewish participation in the life of the surrounding society, Hirsch nonetheless insisted that only as loyal, Law-affirming traditionalists (*Gesetztreue*) could Jews make a patriotic contribution.

In order to win assimilating Jews back to observance and to offer a coherent ideology to those who already were, at least in a sociological sense, observant, Hirsch recognized the necessity of turning to philosophy. In his *Horeb* (1837), he developed a philosophical interpretation of the mitzvot.[10] In general, the mitzvot are to be understood as symbolic devices directed toward education in virtue (*Bildung* in the Enlightenment sense). Like medieval rationalists such as Saadiah and Maimonides, Hirsch sees the discipline of Jewish life as a medium for moral education and human perfection. But unlike those rationalists and similar to Halevi, Hirsch held that Judaism had to be understood in terms of categories inherent to Torah. Judaism was a totality (*ein All*) that had to be grasped in terms of its own laws and not in terms of some rational ends.[11]

Following Halevi, Hirsch begins with revelation as a fact of history and rejects metaphysics or natural theology as a starting point for understanding Judaism. The life of reason distinguishes man from animal, but only the life of Torah can turn natural man (*Mensch*) into Jewish man (*Mensch-Yisroel*). The Jew represents the entelechy of human being, the highest type of man. With Halevi, Hirsch conceives of the universe as a vitalistic hierarchy. All creatures have a function, all were created "according to their kind."[12] The function of the universe *in toto* is to serve God. Insofar as only human beings are conscious, and of them only Jews are conscious of God's revealed Will, the Torah, only the Jew is consciously involved in divine service. The Jew represents the pinnacle of creation.

Halevi's prophetic man has become Hirsch's *Mensch-Yisroel.* Unlike Halevi's prophet, though, Hirsch's paradigmatic Jew flourishes in secular culture. Secular culture gives him the opportunity to learn new strengths and skills to augment his mission. Halevi's prophet yearns for Zion as the place where the people Israel, the "heart of the nations," can become well once again; the Hirschian Jew yearns to become whole in the German diaspora.

Both Hirsch and Halevi severely qualify the value of natural humanity, which lives by the light of a reason that is untutored by revelation. Judaism must not be manipulated to conform to the canons of this reason. For both thinkers, thinking about Judaism begins with revelation, not science; with the history of Israel, not metaphysics. Judaism begins not in the garden but at Sinai, and we know about Sinai from reliable tradition, not from metaphysical speculation. Judaism consists primarily of laws, not of doctrines, that create and train the *Mensch-Yisroel* to execute his function of cosmic service. The basis of these laws is factual, historical revelation, and therefore in order to understand their character, one must appeal to Jewish history and not to nature. Nature does reveal some evidence of God's will, but God's presence is most fully disclosed in Jewish history.[13] Nature and Torah present separate orders of facticity. Each is an organon intelligible in terms of its own laws. Just as a fact remains a fact in nature even when the scientist cannot understand it, so too does a fact remain such in Torah. Thus, the laws of the Torah are not always accessible to reason (such laws are known as *ḥukim*), but they remain law. If one wants to understand Judaism and live the life of the *Mensch-Yisroel*, one must rationally set aside natural reason and live in obedience to the historically revealed Torah.

Hirsch offers a peculiar hybrid theology. He rejects rationally deduced natural theology but does not then turn to faith alone. He minimizes the value of faith, emphasizing the factual, historical nature of revelation. He also rejects the mystical tradition and its transference of the implications of ritual observance to a transcendent order. The result is a rationalistic, Enlightenment conception of religion as a medium for moral *Bildung*, without any component of natural religion.

One hesitates to call Hirsch either a Maimonidean or an anti-Maimonidean. Like Maimonides he accepted culture and science, but unlike Maimonides he deemphasized the competence of reason. He denied philosophy access to ultimacy, linking ultimacy with God's revelation in Jewish history.

Breuer has to be seen as a follower of his grandfather Hirsch. The ambivalence that we find in Hirsch toward philosophy reemerges in Breuer, owing to Breuer's conviction of the primacy of revelation over reason and of the revelation people over natural humanity. Some quotations from Breuer's autobiography, *Mein Weg* (1946), document this ambivalence:

> Blessed is God who has given his wisdom to Kant! Every authentic Jew, who with serious and honest effort studies the *Critique of Pure Reason* will say "amen" from the depths of his heart. "Follow not after your heart and your eyes." [Num.

15:39] In Kantian terms: "Follow not after the evidence of your inner and outer experience," Lest you become unfaithful to God. The entire Kantian epistemology gives to this fundamental sentence of the Torah the necessary and sufficient commentary.[14]

I studied Kant as a Jew. From the first moment, I suspected, I knew, that I would find in his arsenal the weapons to defend the holy terrain of the Torah, her nation, and her Jewish personality against the increasingly audacious grasp of the "spying emisaries" (*Kundschafter*) of our time. I used Kant to defend against the "heart and eyes" without proscribing or diminishing respect for them. Without them, the unity of the Jewish personality would be negated and splintered. For our Torah is the "Torah of life."

Kant became a weapon for me . . . not a light for the perception of Judaism. I did not carry Kant into Judaism.[15]

The enthusiasm for Kant in the first quotation suggests a Maimonidean cohcrence between philosophy and Torah. It is as if the God who created Kant preordained a harmony between Kant and Torah, such that Kant can be read as a *perush*, a commentary, on Torah. But the second quotation qualifies the first. Here a Halevian tendency emerges: Philosophy is used to critique reason and its current cultural sword-bearers:—bible critics, materialists, historians, and others. Philosophy can not be fully assimilated into Judaism, nor should it be. Breuer does not bring Kant's banner into the fold of the faithful in order to make Judaism over into Kant's image, but only to build a fence around the Torah.

I did not make the whole position of Judaism dependent upon Kant. In order to understand the spiritual foundations of our present epoch, Kantian training is absolutely necessary. The fundament of the Kantian *Critique* is still firm. Should a completely different epoch arise that bursts this fundament, I am certain that divine authority will allow another Kant to arise whose research will once again secure the truth of the Torah. Not the Torah, but my books might then be outdated.[16]

Breuer's use of philosophy, then, seems primarily strategic. He employs philosophy in general, and epistemology in particular, as a tool. The question that must be considered then is, Does

Breuer in fact have a real philosophy, or is it all, as a critic of his once alleged, a brilliant escape?[17] Given the strategic, polemical mode of his thought, should we take his philosophy seriously or see it, as Zvi Kurzweil does, as philosophy that has degenerated into ideology?[18] In Kurzweil's view, Breuer has developed a rigid, authoritarian apologetic for his polemics, in effect a pseudophilosophy. To pose this question opens up a semantic, cultural, even political Pandora's box with respect to the meaning of 'philosophy' and 'philosophizing.' Professional philosophers argue constantly about whether their colleagues are also professional philosophers or whether, perhaps, they are mere literary critics. One of Breuer's chief influences, Arthur Schopenhauer, entertained similar doubts—to put it mildly—about Hegel. The question as to what counts as *bona fide* philosophizing is too loaded with presuppositions to be easily, if at all, settled.

It is evident to any close reader of Breuer that he at least took his philosophical task very seriously. He pursued his work with rigor, subtlety, and fidelity to contemporary standards of discourse within his idiom. His ultimate rejection of secular philosophy as a self-sufficient framework is based on a solid philosophical construction. That is to say, Breuer's doubts about philosophy are philosophical doubts.

The question of whether or to what extent Breuer is a "real philosopher" reflects, it seems, a Jewish perplexity as to what constitutes real Jewish philosophy in the present age. From an external point of view, that of the historian of German thought, for example, Breuer fits quite naturally into the Kantian renaissance of the *fin de siècle*. Friedrich Niewöhner treats Breuer as one of a number of Jewish neo-Kantians without any doubts about his status as a philosopher.[19]

In this study I treat Breuer as a real philosopher, albeit one with a polemical agenda and a popularizing style. I also treat him as a philosopher within a tradition, actually within a number of traditions both German and Jewish. The question as to whether Breuer is a living philosopher, whether, as Jacob Levinger states, he "should . . . be studied by every student . . . specializing in the Jewish thought of modern times," is closely bound up with the status of the philosophical traditions in which Breuer worked.[20] Zvi Kurzweil believes that Breuer is not a compelling contemporary thinker owing to diminished Jewish interest, in the latter half of our century, in organizational affiliations and ideologies.[21] Assuming that Breuer's though transcends organizational apologetic, a more pertinent issue is whether the Kantian tradition remains compelling, such that one of its outstanding Jewish exemplars can still speak to us today. More broadly, we might ask whether Breuer's stance as a sharp, internal critic of modernity retains a meaning for both religious modernist and religious postmodernist alike? The issue of Breuer's contemporaneity will be addressed in the final chapter.

Given this general account of Breuer's relation to philosophy, what is his motive for doing epistemology? First, Breuer wants to overthrow the modern preeminence of understanding (*Verstand*) and reason (*Vernunft*) as arbiters of religious meaning. He wants to take Judaism outside of the bounds of reason alone, not by a leap of faith or a plunge into mystical absorption, but by so delimiting the bounds of reason that very little human meaning can subsist therein. There is a postmodern impulse at work in his epistemology. He wants to dismantle religion within the limits of reason alone. He wants to destroy the contemporary Jewish mythos of Judaism as a religion of reason. The alternative is not a religion of unreason, but a religion that transcends reason. Breuer wants to lay the groundwork for a metarational religious commitment by offering a critique of reason such that one must reasonably go beyond to find ultimate meaning. He discovers meaning in the willed deed, in the choice of the whole being for Torah, rather than in the ratiocination of the partial being alone.

Beyond this initial abridgment of the scope of understanding and reason lies another, more subtle, purpose. Breuer is concerned about the social reality of reason. He wants to rule out the ontological and moral primacy of individuals. He wants to use epistemology to get beyond into society, state, and history. A critique of the pure human experience will reveal the poverty and incompleteness of the individual's experience. By treating what in the language of the time was called "the problem of individuation" (*Individuationsproblem*), Breuer will accomplish several theological ends. If it were the case that individuals as such do not have primary ontological value (which is not to say that they have no moral value, only that they are inferior in value to some other entities; for example, to the mystical collectivity of Israel (*knesset Israel*) and the Torah), then the demands of individual subjectivity count for little. Obedience to the Law does not require subjective conviction for its normativity. The individual conscience might opt for some version of Judaism other than Orthodoxy, but that conscience is categorically disqualified from making relevant, correct judgments of value. Breuer's commitment to understanding Judaism as a religion of Law (*Gesetzreligion*) militates against giving a primary role to individual subjectivity.

If individuation were to lack ontological value, then a culture that prizes individuality would be open to a fundamental critique. If individuality were a disability or a malaise rather than of fundamental worth, then much of the contemporary culture that presupposes the ultimate value of individuality could be shown to be radically confused. Liberal bourgeois *Zivilisation* would be found to sin against some more elemental, nonindividuated unity. If individuality were a malaise, then contemporary secular civilization would be a paradigm of human alienation as well as of alienation between man and God. The assimilated Jewish adherents of this culture, who in Breuer's view include the Orthodox as much as the Liberals, would be found to sin against the true culture of unity: the ideal collectivity governed by Torah. So goes Breuer's logic. This far-reaching assault on the modern bias toward individualism was already noticed by Baruch Kurzweil in his seminal essay on Breuer in 1943.[22] At a later point we must discuss whether Breuer, by abandoning the individualism of the liberal Enlightenment, came too close to the illiberal ideologies of the opposite pole of the Enlightenment's dialectic.

Breuer is deeply convinced, then, that the individual must transcend both his rationality and his personal subjectivity and seek a unity with a transcendent Jewish collectivity, defined by Torah. Rationality and individuality carry the individual to the brink of despair. He must choose to shed his individuality in the unity of *knesset Israel*, through accepting the yoke of the Law.

Epistemology will point out the inherent tragedy of the individual experience. It will also reveal an archetypal, tragic flaw in the experience of humanity per se. Breuer will argue that reason—outside the circle of revelation—culminates in a hopelessness that deepens the tragedy of individuation. Humanity, outside of Judaism, has only reason in its paradigmatic form of philosophy for guidance. Therefore humanity is by nature alienated from ultimate, metarational meaning. Reason points the way toward its extrarational entelechy, but cannot, by definition, give that fulfillment any content. Philosophy is emblematic of the tragic human situation, of humanity crying out for salvation that must come from beyond itself. Philosophy is an icon, an isomorph, of the human tragedy. Thus philosophy stands to Torah, and humanity to Israel, as introduction to conclusion. Breuer is more like Rosenzweig than Cohen here, more like Halevi than Maimonides; philosophy and Torah, far from being compatible, are deeply incompatible, yet they need one another. Humanity needs Israel for its salvation, but Israel needs humanity for its *raison d'être*.

A NEW *KUZARI*

Turning now to an explication of Breuer's basic thesis on epistemology, we begin with the comprehensive account in *Der Neue Kusari*. This work, like Judah Halevi's original work, is cast in the form of a philosophical dialogue. It will be helpful to look at the literary structure of the book and to contrast it with the original *Kuzari*.

Halevi's *Kuzari* relates the story of the spiritual struggle of the legendary Khazar king. The king begins a search for religious truth because he has a dream in which he is told, "Your thoughts are good, but not your deeds."[23] The king decides that he must seek the true path and invites a philosopher, a Christian divine, and a Muslim sheikh to illuminate him on their respective doctrines. The king is able to detect flaws in all of their approaches and finally turns—with no real hope—to a representative of the "despised" religion, a rabbi. To his astonishment, he discovers that the Jew's tradition is the true one. The remainder of the *Kuzari* follows the rabbi's exposition of Jewish teaching to his newly won convert.

Breuer's *Der Neue Kusari* proceeds according to the same pattern. Young Alfred Roden (formerly Rosenstock) had been raised in a cultured, bourgeois, and carefully deracinated German-Jewish home. After a carefree youth, he entered a brooding, troubled adolescence. He began to question whether life has meaning—whether life is able to generate meaning out of itself, or whether meaning comes from beyond. He started to dwell on God. God had previously been an empty boundary concept (*Grenzbegriff*) for him. Lacking moral and existential repercussions, 'God' was a mere limit of human knowledge beyond which, and about which, nothing could be said.[24] But as human existence (*Menschsein*) became increasingly void of meaning for Alfred, the idea of a knowable, consequential, transcendent reality became more and more compelling to him. He turned to the Bible with fascination and disgust. It seemed to presuppose everything and prove nothing. Having been driven by his restless search into nausea and ennui,

Alfred finally heard a dream voice say, "Your striving is good but your deed is not."

This exhortation surprised Alfred. As a cultured youth who had drunk deeply at the well of popular Kantianism, he had always believed that only the will was good and that the deed was of little value. Requiring now an education in the possibility of the deed, of correct action, he turned to investigate the significance of his hitherto irrelevant Jewishness (*Judesein*). He did so with the hope that he would discover a pattern of correct action validated by transcendent reality.

Alfred turned in dialogue to his father, to a liberal rabbi, and finally to a secular and religious (*Mizrachi*) Zionist. Each dialogue is richly detailed and full of vigorous argumentation. Breuer presents not dialogical straw men but figures who hold credible principles. Although ignorant of the truth, Alfred, like the Khazar king, was able to perceive logical weaknesses in each presentation. The liberal rabbi holds that the Jew's highest duty is to honor God's name among his fellow human beings. The essence of Judaism is identical with civic responsibility and virtue. At heart, religion in general and Judaism in particular is an *Erlebnis:* a subjective experience of nearness to or absolute dependence upon God. Religion as an objectified, historical phenomenon is spiritually sterile. Only the lived, radically individual experience of religiosity (*Religiosität*) affords spiritual authenticity. Liberal Judaism is precisely the process whereby the eternal, subjective core is threshed from the time-bound, objectified husk.[25] After probing, Alfred rejects this view. It seems to him that *Erlebnis* signifies nothing other than a recrudescence of one's own feeling (*Gefühl*). The objective, normative structure of correct action for which Alfred was searching could not be found in subjective religiosity.

Alfred's dialogue with the Zionists is equally unsatisfying. The secularist Zionist glories in a Jewish nationalism that seems to Alfred little more than the vision of a Bismarck in Hebraic colors. The elevation of the nation as an end in itself seems to him a contradiction of the idea of Judaism that is beginning to emerge for him: a nation ruled by God's law, a national experience of submission to a Sovereign higher than the nation. The religious Zionist, hoping to supplement and correct the limited vision of his colleague, argues that the Jews are a nation whose purpose lies in the fulfillment of Torah. But Alfred discerns that this addition of Torah onto nationalism entails an ironic, if fatal, distortion of Torah. By cooperating with the secularist in the name essentially of the secularist's concept of nationhood, the religious Zionist tacitly acknowledges that his ultimate value is nationalism rather than Torah. He has allowed Torah to become a matter for personal choice; he chooses it and the secularist does not. By so doing he has robbed Torah of its normative, objective status and, like the Liberals, reduced it to a subjective *Erlebnis.*

Thus Alfred concludes that for all of his dialogue partners Judaism resides in a subjective experience. None of them attained a concept of Judaism as an objective, shared reality with a decisive, transcendent source. All of them remained trapped by modern notions of religion as primarily a subjective and personal phenomenon, bound up with private experience and choice. Alfred had, through the exercise of reason alone, arrived at the formal requirements for what Judaism must be, without having any idea of its content.

As Alfred happened one night to be reading the Book of Leviticus, chapter 26, he had an astonishing experience. It became clear for him in a breathtaking instant that this chapter, with its prophecy of Jewish exile and punishment for disobedience, perfectly described the course of Jewish history. It was as if the voice of the Almighty were speaking directly to him. The text revealed the sense of the "Jewish phenomenon in all of its immeasurable, puzzling complexity."[26] The extent to which these words so accurately predicted the path of Jewish history convinced Alfred that the words must come from God. As he tried to understand the implications of this *Erlebnis,* he determined that, unlike the religiosity of the Reform rabbi and the religious Zionist, this experience has its origins in an external reality that has been internalized.[27] The true *Erlebnis* is a recognition of Jewish history as the place where God is at work in the world. This *Erlebnis* intuits the reality of the Jewish people as a "metahistorical" miracle.[28] Other allegedly religious experiences derive from psychological sources such as feeling or occur as rational experiences of nature in the form of metaphysical awareness. Natural experiences are products of the individual's feeling, understanding, or reason. They not only are derived from an immanent source but are limited and doomed to ephemerality.

Our inward life is a fleeting, fragmentary process of dying away *(Erstorben)* rather than truly living *(Erleben).* Only when the whole being takes into itself an external, transcendent objectivity (rather than casts an apotheosis of itself from its own depths) does it achieve a synthesis of all of its capacities. The acceptance of the

Sinai covenant, and the acquiescence of feeling, will, understanding, and reason to Sinai's normative objectivity, would constitute such a synthesis. Furthermore, in that Sinai speaks to a nation, the individual who is engaged by the distinctly Jewish *Erlebnis* sheds individuality and takes on instead the historical personality of his people.

On the basis of this personal revelation, Alfred determines that his life, indeed, that Jewish life, must be fully conditioned by the laws of the Torah in order to be genuine and valid. In short, he discovers a community where the Torah—at least in theory—governs every aspect of individual social existence: the *Israelitische Religionsgesellschaft*. For all of its human failings, this community was accepted by him as the only legitimate address of Judaism in Germany.

In the second half of *Der Neue Kusari*, Alfred has become a teacher and an inspiration for the native members of the IRG who are dispirited and perplexed. He has the unique perspective of a *ba'al teshuvah*, a "returnee" to tradition who has experienced total alienation and total repatriation. His radical transformation enables him to speak from a depth unknown to those whose religious experience is merely that of unreflective culture-religion. It is conceivable that this character may have been inspired by Franz Rosenzweig or by Nathan Birnbaum, returnees to tradition whom Breuer knew personally. At any rate, it expresses the traditional valuation of the *ba'al teshuvah*: repentance is superior to habitual piety. "The place the penitent occupy, even the perfectly righteous are unable to occupy." (T. B. Berakhot 34b.)

The discussion about epistemology is one of the discourses Alfred delivers to his fellows in the IRG. The occasion for it is that a young man, Weiler, who is outwardly pious has lost his faith in the existence of God and in the divine origin of the Torah (*Göttlichkeit der Thora*).[29] He comes to Alfred hoping to be given philosophical proof of these doctrines. Only then will he be able to practice the law with a whole heart. This invitation gives Alfred the opportunity to decipher the meaning of his own *Erlebnis*.

The dialogue begins as Weiler asks for proof of the existence of God and of the divinity of the Torah. Alfred suggests that proof is not as desirable as it seems. What of those believers who based their faith on the ontological argument for the existence of God? Kant demolished both the argument, quite properly, Breuer implies, and their faith.[30] Proofs offer only the illusion of certainty: as philosophical styles change, proofs disappear in the wreckage of old paradigms. But Weiler's anxiety and despair are too deep to be so easily parried. Alfred must now justify his denigration of philosophical proofs by philosophical argument. He advances three arguments, which we may consider logical, epistemological, and moral arguments.

The first argument concerns the logical nature of proofs per se. Proofs are based not on pure deductive logic but on logic applied to experience. Logical procedures allow us to extend our knowledge outward from a center grounded in experience. In the activity of proving, something that is not yet known is related to something already known: something as yet "unconditioned" by the logic of our conception of it becomes conditioned. This is all well and good for objects that make no claim to being unconditional, but how could God and Torah, which by definition are Absolute and unconditioned, become conditioned? Clearly, God and Torah are not dependent upon or derivative from anything; rather, everything is derived from and dependent upon them. That is what we mean when we speak of God and Torah.

> All of these proofs led the unknown back to the known. Now how could unconditional truth be unconditional if it must first itself be proved, that is, must first be led back to [some other] unconditional [facts]? Whoever would prove the divinity of the Torah, denies its unconditionality, denies its character as truth in itself. If the divinity of the Torah is an unconditional truth, then it cannot be an object of a [philosophical] proof. It is itself the highest authority for any proof, the highest means of proof for the derivative truth of all other things. . . . A proven God is a de-divinized God. A proven Torah is a dethroned Torah.[31]

In this argument, Breuer uses Kant's concept of the 'unconditional'. In the *Critique of Pure Reason*, the unconditional (*das Unbedingt*) accounts for the origins of concepts of pure reason. Such concepts are in no way empirically derived. They are prior to all experience.

> If the concepts of reason contain the unconditional, they are concerned with something to which all experience is subordinate, something to which reason leads in its inferences from experience and in accordance with which it estimates and

gauges the degree of its empirical employment, but which is never itself a member of the empirical synthesis.[32]

Breuer uses *unconditional* in this distinctive, technical sense. He identifies Torah and God with the Kantian unconditional in terms of a logical equivalence. Torah and God are exempt from the "empirical synthesis" of experience. They stand above all experience as standards for reason and understanding. Furthermore, Torah and God, as unconditional, are the transcendental (that is, nonempirical) conditions by virtue of which the world in all its conditionality is possible.

In his second argument, Breuer puts the case epistemologically, focusing on the relationship of the knowing subject to its object. To prove something renders that thing fully intelligible to reason and subjugates it to the understanding (*Verstand*). God and Torah, however, are precisely those forces that shape and define the understanding. God is the creator of the understanding. Torah is that which gives the understanding a normative context in which to operate.

> Who advances the proof? Indeed, is it not the understanding? Now if it were the case that the knowledge of God and of the divinity of the Torah were the result of a proof directed by the understanding, then God and the Torah could not count as the Absolute. The understanding alone would have to count as the Absolute. The understanding would be judge over God and Torah, and the claim of the Torah to give direction to the understanding would be a ludicrous presumption.[33]

Those who try to prove the existence of God and the divinity of the Torah are guilty of a category mistake. To attempt to assimilate God and Torah to the category of things that can be subordinated to the understanding is to misunderstand their very nature and status.

It does seem in both of these arguments that Breuer is simply begging the question by offering as definitions of God and Torah the very assumptions he is asked to defend. This problem, however, is most likely an inheritance from Kant and entailed by the form of argument employed: the transcendental deduction. Kant himself has often been interpreted in such a way as to make him appear to beg the question against, for example, David Hume. It seems that Kant tries to refute Hume by pressing claims that, if Hume were correct, could not be right.[34] It also appears that

Breuer begs the question by pressing definitions of God and Torah that are precisely what his opponents find controversial and in need of defense. There is some of this question-begging in both Kant and Breuer, but both share a more "subtle line of attack."[35] Kant's defense of the transcendental deduction is that his premises are actually presupposed by his opponents. Breuer employs this line of reasoning as well. The premises set by philosophy are themselves erroneous because they ignore truths about the world on which, in fact, the assertions themselves depend. This is ultimately due to the fact that they stem from an order of being and experience that is distanced from God. Philosophy is trapped within the tragedy of history: it aims at promise, but it does not know fulfillment.

Relating God and Torah to the Kantian 'unconditional' removes these realities in crucial ways from the experiential context of perception and knowledge. Before long, Breuer will blend the Kantian *an sich* with the kabbalistic *ein sof* to explicate the foci of Judaism. Judaism is not offensive to reason, but it transcends reason. In the language of Breuer's last work, *Naḥaliel*, it "circumcizes" reason. Consequently, the encounter that God and Torah demand exceeds the competence of rationality alone. God and Torah require the devotion of the whole being. One of Breuer's aims in developing an epistemology is to portray the nature of this whole being. After the critical delimitation of reason, epistemology runs into anthropology.

In the first argument, Breuer demonstrated how the logical characteristics of God and Torah exempt these concepts from the logic of proof. In the second argument, he showed that the normative relationship between understanding and Torah invalidates the former's pretensions of dominance over the latter. In the third argument, Breuer considers man's relationship to God and Torah as an explicitly moral one.[36]

When one wants a proof, presumably one wants the best kind of proof: mathematical proof. In mathematics, the full rigor of logic is apparent. Mathematics consists of an application of the laws of our thought (*Denkgesetze*) and the forms by which we structure our intuition (*Anschauungsformen*) to a system of symbols. Humanly speaking, however, the operations of mathematics leave us wholly unfree with respect to accepting or rejecting their conclusions.

> Over and against mathematics, we find ourselves, so to speak, in a situation of complete nonfreedom. If we do not

want to abandon our entire thought and intuition, we must
believe in [the validity of correct mathematical] statements.
Such statements are, indeed, nothing other than applications
of the laws of our thought and of the forms of our
intuitions.[37]

It follows that Judaism cannot be analogous to mathematics, for
the fact is that Judaism, like good and evil and unlike mathematics, is chosen in freedom. If Judaism were somehow inherent in us,
if it were revealed to us in an *Erlebnis* running from our own
depths outward, then we would be angels and not men.

Thus if the groundwork of Judaism were provable in a mathematical fashion, then it would simply be innate to us. We
would not be men, but angels. Nor would being Jewish constitute a life-determining task. It would be, I would say, a natural given. The freedom of man concerns itself, however, not
only with good and evil, but also with truth and falsity insofar as the latter are related to the former. The sentences of
mathematics have nothing to do with good and evil. The cognitive groundwork of Judaism, however, is immediately concerned with good and evil. If man has [the power to make]
the decision for good or evil, then he must also possess freedom of choice with respect to God and the divinity of the
Torah. Trust in God and in the divinity of the Torah is itself
the result of a supremely moral act.[38]

Judaism must be recognized as transcendent and objective: a
reality that must be freely chosen. Extrinsic to the epistemic,
moral subject, Judaism can in no way be derived from the structure of the subject's own mind. Judaism is in this way similar to
good and evil in that a decision of the person to assent, act, and
obey is required. It is after all true that one must struggle to bring
one's whole life into harmony with the Torah. Breuer here uses a
transcendental deductive argument to state what must be true of
Torah in order for that empirical, psychological-sociological fact to
be true.

The relegation of mathematics to the realm of unfreedom,
and the underlying emphasis on the necessity of a transrational
choice, suggests Breuer's reliance on a thinker somewhat more
"existential" than Kant, Arthur Schopenhauer. Breuer relies on
Schopenhauer for the main premises of his epistemology. This is

not surprising. Kant is the arch critic of the pretensions of reason, but he nevertheless esteems the life of reason and locates man's freedom and dignity within it. Schopenhauer, however, places a greater value on sense perception and understanding than he does on reason. Reason is at the farthest remove from immediate connectedness with the world of things-in-themselves. Consequently, the life governed by agencies other than reason is more authentic. Ultimately Schopenhauer's elaborate metaphysics of will entirely depreciates the axiological value of reason. Breuer's dismissal of mathematical reasoning is strongly reminiscent of Schopenhauer's discussion of mathematics in book I, paragraph 15, of *The World as Will and Idea*.[39] There, Schopenhauer condemns the abstractness and remoteness of mathematical reason vis-à-vis the immediate quality of sensory experience and its first-level synthesis in the understanding. He argues that the man of genius is disinterested in mathematics, for his genius arises directly out of ontological connectedness with the world of things-in-themselves.

Breuer uses Schopenhauer's post-Kantian critique of reason in order to frame an argument against the pretensions of philosophy. Put positively, Schopenhauer's call for the commitment of the whole being to a certain style of metaphysically aware life (in his case, a life of denial of the will) is transformed by Breuer into a decision by the whole person to accept and interiorize the Torah revelation. Breuer calls for a radical engagement of the whole person with a world that reason cannot fathom: the world of things-in-themselves (the *Welt an sich*). This engagement, with its corresponding acceptance and interiorization of Torah, is actualized not by reason but by will.

THE GERMAN BACKGROUND

Breuer's exposition reveals a subtle appropriation and critique of much modern German philosophy. Before proceeding with our exposition of his epistemological thesis, it will be useful to sketch his philosophical sources. While Kant lies in the background and in the methodological approach, Schopenhauer is the main influence on Breuer's epistemology.

Schopenhauer considered Plato and Kant to be his masters, and in a sense *The World as Will and Idea* is an attempt to harmonize and synthesize both of them. Plato and Kant affirmed that the world presents itself to us as a more or less impenetrable veneer, but a veneer nonetheless. For Plato, the sensory world in which we conduct our lives is like a shadow play on the wall of a cave. The real world is the world of the Ideas that are imperfectly actualized in our domain. For Kant, whose theory requires no such hypostasis, it is perception, understanding, and reason—the apparatus out of which the phenomenal world is constructed—that shape a lawful cosmos the inner nature of which is permanently mysterious. Objects are always objects of interest for some subject whose own laws of thought and perception define the form in which the objects are given to him. What the things are in themselves is by definition unknowable, for knowledge is precisely that which organizes our experience of objects in their givenness.[40]

Schopenhauer inherits and accepts the fundamental dichotomy between thing (*Ding*) and thing-in-itself (*Ding an sich*): between phenomenon and noumenon. In the first book of *The World as Will and Idea* he describes the world under its phenomenal aspect: the world as representation or perception (*Vorstellung*). It is important to stress that the world under this aspect is our, that is, someone's perception. Talk of objects necessarily entails talk of subjects. Every object exists if and only if there is a subject, every percept if and only if there is a perceiver. The relationship is biconditional. The subject becomes aware of itself as subject only if it experiences an object, and the object has ontological status only if it is "called into being" (as a *Vorstellung*) by a subject.[41] The transaction that occurs in this process of perception (*Erkenntnis*) is satisfying and serene.[42] Breuer develops this thought in a dogmatic direction: man as perceiver acts in *imitatio dei*. Man the perceiver calls a world (the *Vorstellungswelt*) into being in lordly serenity. Under this aspect, man is a cocreator with God.

What composes and orders man's world is his understanding (*Verstand*). The understanding receives its data from the body and registers changes in the body. Strictly speaking, body is the immediate object of the perception facilitated by the understanding.[43] Under the transaction of perception, however, we have no special knowledge of our bodies; body is perceived as an object (or set of objects) among objects.

The world as perception is not mysterious or anything other than what it seems to be. The cement that holds it together, the principle by which the understanding operates, is "sufficient reason" (*Satz vom Grunde*). Schopenhauer rejects Kant's thesis that the understanding operates in terms of distinct categories. He postulates a single fundamental modality that appears in various forms in terms of the context of its employment. The principle of sufficient reason may appear as space, time, matter, or concepts: that is, may appear as the connectedness of representations under these employments.[44]

While the understanding is a first-order synthesis, in terms of the principle of sufficient reason of the data tendered by the body, reason (*Vernunft*) is a reflection, abstraction, and generalization of the results of the understanding. Reason is that extension of the process of understanding that operates in terms of sufficient reason with concepts (*Begriffe*). Whereas the higher animals have understanding that operates in them as it does in us, we alone have reason. Reason, which often operates intermixed with understanding, appears in purest form in language and mathematics.

We need not enter into greater detail into Schopenhauer's argument. But we must notice a value judgment underlying his assertion, which is crucial for Breuer. Schopenhauer, while retaining Kant's two-tiered model of understanding and reason, inverts their value. For Kant, reason is still the domain of freedom and the source of man's dignity. Reason in its practical employment enables man to achieve the good will. In Schopenhauer, however, reason is disparaged in favor of the more primal capacity of understanding. Schopenhauer, active during the Romantic period in German thought, sees reason as much farther alienated from nature than is understanding. (Indeed understanding is also alienated from nature insofar as it receives its impressions "second hand" from the body. It is just not removed to the same degree as reason.[45]) Just as when one puts a mirror in front of a mirror one experiences both a sense of expansion and confusion, so too does the reason lead to endless new terrain and an endless loss of bearings. If reason is the crown of creation, it is also a crown of thorns. This premise leads Schopenhauer to the second half of his thesis, the notion that the will *is* the thing-in-itself or *Ding an sich.* Schopenhauer believes that we do have available to us a form of awareness that is not a priori alienated or mediated. It remains to be noted that the reason, owing to its remoteness from both the representations and the things-in-themselves, has a tragic character for Schopenhauer. This critique of reason fits in well with Breuer's purpose of moving Judaism beyond the realm of a now truncated rationality.

Another benefit of Schopenhauer's devaluation of reason concerns the value of science. Schopenhauer relegates the entire project of science to the work of understanding and reason, which is to say that the domain of science is "merely" the world as representation and its rational organization into concepts. Science is therefore deprived of fundamental ontological comprehension of the things-in-themselves and is thus inferior to other practices, such as art, that fully grasp the metarational reality of the *Ding an sich*. Breuer uses this inversion of reason to argue against those who, in the name of science, assail Torah through theories of evolution, cosmology, Bible criticism, and so on. Although Breuer does not follow Schopenhauer into granting art a special status as a *sensus numinus*, he does mark off an *an sich* character for Judaism that science cannot touch. Breuer, as a neo-Orthodox Jew, cannot reject science, but he can and does try to limit its scope and pass a critical judgment on its ultimate worth.

Reason and its projects are trapped in a fragmentary, limited apprehension of reality, which Schopenhauer, following the Scholastics, terms the "principium individuationis."[46] The *principium individuationis* is the factor that accounts for the metaphysical condition of individuation in which Being finds itself over and against what is assumed to have been an original condition of unity. Schopenhauer is very much concerned with how one can break through the *principium individuationis*. He argues that we are able to break through the order of perception governed by the principle of sufficient reason when we become aware of ourselves as will. Life might have been nothing more than a display of perceptions and the world nothing more than an order of representations. If we were disembodied intellects, this is indeed how the world might seem. But it is not the case. We are aware that this network of representations is grounded in something other than itself. We experience ourselves not just as a constellation of percepts but in a direct, unique way: we experience ourselves as will (*Wille*).[47] Will implies that our immediate, actual experience provides a content to the representations, which are now understood as merely the veneer of the world. From the point of view of the world-as-representation, we are not able to say what the content of a representation is. We are merely able to say how these perceptions are related to one another. Science is able to chart the causal relations between representations, but science reaches its limit when the question of what representation *in se* is.[48] The world of which science speaks is a seamless "veil of Maya" apparently clothing nothing. When we become aware of ourselves as will, however, we know that this veil is not the whole story. Here philosophy has a role to play in ascertaining that the will and the merely stipulative *Ding an sich* are identical.[49] Schopenhauer makes the bold metaphysical assertion that the entire natural and human world, the entire cosmos, comprised as it is by representations, has as its inward nature the will.

Schopenhauer is a monist insofar as he postulates a single underlying unity. Although this unity is a fundamental fact, life is lived in the *principium individuationis:* to be is, in part, to be a phenomenon, to be an individual. To be is to offend against transcendental unity (*Einheit*). But ironically, it is precisely the will, whose "objectification" constitutes the world of phenomena, that offends against itself. For the cosmos is nothing other than will, both pure and objectified. Will, although one, is also, through its objectifications, divided against itself. The will is thus in constant struggle against itself. Consequently, the world is ultimately absurd, aimless, and tragic. To be conscious of will is indeed to become related in a nonmediated or nonalienated way to the world in itself, but it is a troubled, restless world that has thereby been entered. This theme is picked up in Breuer's last book, *Naḥaliel,* where Breuer speaks of the storms of creation (*sa'arot ha-briah*) in which the human will finds itself entrapped.

What possible response is there to the tragedy of being? Schopenhauer offers two responses. As suggested above, it is possible to experience in perception a certain serenity. When we really perceive or contemplate something, we experience a sense of quietude, release, and self-sufficiency. This experience is impossible, however, in normal perception, which is usually tied to willing. Aesthetic perception and contemplation (*Erkennen*), on the other hand, momentarily frees us from the knot of the will. Aesthetic perception is will-less perception. When we perceive without willing, we detach the perceived objects from the context of causality. The object transcends the world of representations, and the subject transcends the normal order of perception cum willing, becoming a pure, knowing subject. The artist who achieves aesthetic perception transcends the *principium individuationis,* sheds his own individual, epistemic features, and becomes a universal subject who perceives objects that have become universal Ideas. Here Schopenhauer's vein of Platonism comes to the surface. The Idea (*Idee*) represents a universal, necessary grade of the objectification of the will, the system of which constitutes the world. To perceive an Idea is to discover in the midst of a mere representation the inner nature of the world, that is, the will without the attendant inner conflict of the world. Such is the form of transcendence that the true artist achieves. The common man, however, can never free his perception from his self-centered concerns. His experience of the world remains locked in the *principium individuationis.*[50] This Platonizing doctrine of Ideas is fully developed by Breuer in *Naḥaliel.*

Although Schopenhauer greatly esteems the artist, he believes there is yet a more royal road trodden by the saint.[51] The saint may be a Christian, a Hindu, or a Buddhist (but not a Jew). All of these religions resolve into the same wisdom: the renunciation of the will. In the life of the saint, the momentary transcendence of the artist has become a permanent state. The saint confronts the restless, struggling will to live that impels his being and the entirety of Being, and he renounces it. He realizes that the will that is fractured into the *principium individuationis* and masked in the veil of Maya is nevertheless one will. The sufferer and the one who inflicts suffering are both objectifications of this one will. The will still contradicts and struggles with itself in the eyes of the saint, but now this contradiction and struggle are looked upon with passivity. The ontological conflict has not been solved; it has been abandoned. The saint refuses to live the life of will and by so doing becomes, at last, free.[52]

The large themes of Schopenhauer's system—critique of existence grounded in epistemological analysis, salvation through the acceptance of tragedy, rejection of individuation, and affirmation of a salvific, rather gnostic *Einheitslehre*—find their way into Breuer's philosophy with significant adaptations. Some of these adaptations are due to Breuer's "judaization" of Schopenhauer's post-Christian philosophy, while some derive from Nietzsche's treatment of Schopenhauer.

Nietzsche was influential in the popularization of Schopenhauer. While Schopenhauer directed his critique to the existential dilemma of the individual subject, Nietzsche broadened the problem of individuation into a problem of culture. For Nietzsche, the individual reluctance to renounce the will becomes a shared pathology of cultural self-deception. Primordial unity has been shattered by inauthentic, "Apollonian" culture. Rather than confront the tragedy of his existence, man flees from existential horror into gorgeous illusion, rationality, civilization. The god Apollo rises to mastery in the ancient Greek world where this drama was first played out. With his rise, the god of tragedy, Dionysus, is banished. Apollo drapes a veil of unknowing over the world. Man is caught in the cage of his own reason, fearful of Dionysus and the primordial *Einheit* he represents. Civilization, the work of Apollo, is an anti-Dionysian evasion.[53]

For Nietzsche, the problem of individuation points toward a critique of culture. It remained for the generation of Breuer's contemporaries to develop Nietzsche's social critique into a blueprint or at least a ground rule for a new kind of society. Breuer has a certain affinity with these neo-Romantic thinkers who provide some of the conceptual vocabulary for his mystical conception of Jewish collectivity.

An abiding concern during the period around the First World War was the possibility of creating an organic, unitive, spiritually authentic community (a *Gemeinschaft*) out of the sterile rationality of modern society (*Gesellschaft*). Men such as Martin Buber, Gustav Landauer, Julius and Heinrich Hart, and the publisher Eugen Diederichs created model communities (for example, the *Neue Gemeinschaft*, a club at the University of Berlin in which the first four men were active, and the Sera Circle at Diederich's home in Weimar) in which such utopian expectations could be experimentally enacted.[54] Following Schopenhauer and Nietzsche, these neo-Romantics held that the very epistemic apparatus of modern man militated against experiencing life as unity. Scientific perception and thought not only chain man to apprehend the world in causal terms but play into the unseen and sinister hands of a materialistic, overly rationalized society that celebrates the *principium individuationis* by an emphasis on individual rights, privacy, and capitalist competition. The analytic attitude of science and the alienation inherent in the *Gesellschaft* are dialectically related. Apollonian-Socratic man, whose experience remains chained to the laws of rational thought and who rejects the possibility of unitive experience (*Erlebnis*), has fashioned a society that perpetuates his spurious form of consciousness.

As suggested, much of Breuer's program of new orientation must be seen against this cultural background. It is also necessary to view Breuer's treatment of *Erlebnis* against this current as well. In *Der Neue Kusari*, Alfred was critical of the Reform rabbi's view that religion was an *Erlebnis*, but when he finally realized the truth about Judaism he did so by an *Erlebnis* as well. An *Erlebnis*, albeit, of a special kind. His *Erlebnis* came from beyond himself, in contrast to the typical *Erlebnis*, which surfaces from within.[55] By retaining the term and redefining it, Breuer critiques the contemporary philosophical culture in which the term had its use. What exactly was that use?

An *Erlebnis* amounts to an experience of the noumenal, which contrasts sharply with the normal experience (*Erfahrung*) of phenomena. A contemporary delineation of these two types of experience was developed by Wilhelm Dilthey. Dilthey argued that the knowledge of man, and hence the human sciences, is available to us by a means different from knowledge of physical objects (and hence that the human sciences have a method and structure different from the physical sciences.)[56] Between objects, we must infer causal relations, whereas within our own lived experiences we "live" causality. We must reason about why a stone falls, but we live through and thus know directly why we, for example, are distraught when we experience something dreadful. Thus there are two kinds of experience: *Erfahrung*, which provides mediated knowledge, and *Erlebnis*, lived experience, which provides immediate—and, typically, self-referential—knowledge. Dilthey extended *Erlebnis* to explain our knowledge of the inner states of others. We can have fairly direct knowledge of other human beings given the fact that we express our inner states. Our knowledge of another's sadness, for example, while not as immediate as the knowledge of our own sadness, is yet knowledge of an order different from the theory of electromagnetism. The ability to have lived experience of another mind (*Nacherlebnis*) provides epistemic grounding for the human sciences (*Geisteswissenschaften*).

Dilthey did not intend his concept of *Erlebnis* to apply to nature insofar as he marked off a legitimate domain for the natural sciences, that is, a domain in which *Erfahrung* is appropriate. Clearly a romantic fusion of *I* and *All* lies beyond the border of a Diltheyan *Erlebnis*. That is, however, the direction in which Dilthey's students, the members of the *Neue Gemeinschaft*, developed his concept. Taking a more Nietzschean tack, they devalued the causal, *Erfahrung*-type experience and privileged the more intuitive *Erlebnis*. Unlike the common man, they depreciated the worth of sense experience, and unlike the scientist they refused to grant reality to sense data alone. For Dilthey's students, the inner lived experiences of intuition and feeling reveal true reality, while perception and cognition fragment the real unity of being. Here, unlike both Schopenhauer and Nietzsche, the content of this doctrine of unity is nothing but the flux of pure feeling (*Gefühl*) alone. Breuer's contemporary, the neo-Romantic philosopher Karl Joel, wrote:

> Perception is a breaking apart, a forming, a separating, and then again a joining together. The unity of the spiritual and

the sensual, of the subject and the object, is experienced in feeling. The divisiveness of perception is broken by the welling-up, even the overflowing, of feeling. Whoever eats of the tree of perception divorces himself from the paradise of feeling.[57]

The theory of the neo-Romantic *Erlebnis* is a secularized, salvific gnosis that goes beyond both Schopenhauer's saintly renunciation and Nietzsche's Dionysian ecstasy; for the first time, it is something that can be enacted communally. In the case of Eugen Diederichs and his Sera Circle in Jena, the development of a community (*Bund*) of those who can together achieve *Erlebnis* drew its inspiration from the German mystical circles of the seventeenth century. Such a *Bund* was intended by Diederichs to nurture the spiritual elite of a renewed German national community.[58] The parallels with Breuer's cultivation of a theocentrically oriented, elite community of university students (the *Bund Jüdischer Akademiker*) are striking. Breuer's university career brought him to Berlin, a center of this kind of thinking, during the period before the First World War, but his actual familiarity with these figures can only be conjectured. It is clear that all of these streams of German philosophy play upon Breuer's epistemology, critique of culture, and philosophy of religious experience. With these thinkers in the background, we are now in a position to analyze Breuer's doctrine.

EPISTEMOLOGY AS TRAGEDY

The opening discussion of the literary development of *Der Neue Kusari* led to Breuer's assertion that proof and, in the broadest sense, reason, are irrelevant to the *Erlebnis* of Judaism. Instead of reaching truth through philosophical demonstration, Breuer asserts that ultimate truth must be willed (*erwollt werden*). Breuer coins a new expression for the kind of willing he has in mind, *Erwollnis*, which parallels existing usages such as *Erkenntnis* and *Erlebnis*. *Erwollnis* is to designate a certain kind of willing, a dimension of the process of willing that discloses something ontologically fundamental, just as *Erlebnis* indicates a certain kind of ontologically disclosive life-experience.

Erwollnis describes a mental act of willing (*Willensakt*) whereby the *I* maintains itself in the face of its perceptions, prevents itself from getting lost in its perceptions, and at the same time certifies the presence of a world that is not its perceptions but a thing-in-itself. By invoking this alleged aspect of the will, Breuer hopes to prove that the very thing that the *I* must do to continue to be is relevant to the affirmation of the truth of Torah. Ultimate truth is a matter of the will, of the *I*'s will to live rather than of its ability to reason.

In *Der Neue Kusari*, Alfred's dialogue partner, Weiler, bridles at the assertion of a connection between truth and will, which seems to him to imply that one can arbitrarily will the truth of something. Does this not mean that truth is dependent upon desire? If the Torah is not true in some conventional sense of the word *true*, then what responsible person would dedicate his life to it?[59] Ought we not wait for proof of our religious "truths" before we will or choose them? Is this not what human beings normally do: conclude the processes of perception and cognition (*Erkenntnis*) and then determine their wills to do *X* or *Y*?

> Weiler: How can I will what I do not first perceive? The will is blind if the eye does not first enlighten it.[60]

To meet this objection, Breuer advances an argument for the dependence of perception on will, which introduces the whole apparatus of Schopenhauer into his thesis. If it could be shown that willing has ontological priority, that Being is most fundamentally a matter of willing and not of perceiving and cognizing, then the approach to Torah through the will would be more primary than the approach through reason. Breuer uses Schopenhauer's emphasis on the fundamental nature of willing and the will's relatedness to the essence of Being. Far from slavishly following Schopenhauer, however, he relates perception and will in an original way.

According to Breuer, perception (*Erkenntnis*) implies a subject, an *I*, perceiving an object correctly.[61] Perception necessarily involves an *I*; perception is always someone's perception. It is also true that the subject's own body and internal states are objects of perception, so the question arises, What then is the *I*? Where is the *I* to be found?[62] When all of the objects of perception are stripped away, it is not the case that nothing is left; rather, a self-consciousness remains. The *I* perceives and knows that it perceives, yet the *I* is neither perceived nor known. The knowing subject is indeed unknowable, but it becomes aware of itself in the act of perception (*Erkenntnisakt*). In perception, the perceiving subject becomes alert to its own being, but were it not for the presence of objects to perceive, the subject would be nonpresent, nonapparent to itself. "And self-perception? It means that the percipient is able to perceive himself in and through the percept as that percept is his percept. Every perception is simultaneously self-perception."[63]

Breuer has followed Schopenhauer here but has also broken new ground. Schopenhauer maintains that the body is a representation for the subject, an object among objects in the world. But Schopenhauer, of course, goes on to emphasize that the subject is aware of a deeper and unique connectedness with its body: The rush of representations that the subject receives from its condition of embodiment has a content, namely, the will. The subject becomes aware of itself as a thing-in-itself.[64] Breuer agrees that the subject is different in kind from its world of objects, but he will not yet give the subject a real content. The I-in-itself (Ich an sich) will not simply equal the will. Breuer prefers to speak functionally rather than substantively about the I, Kantian that he is. Eventually, however, he will relate the deepest, inner nature of the I not to the will but to creation. The I will discover that its innermost being is God's own possession. The reality of divine transcendence signals one break that Breuer must make with Schopenhauer. He cannot accept a monistic cosmos in which no radical distinctions between God and creation are possible.

Prima facie, then, we cannot know about the innermost nature of the I, but we can say what the I does. The I is the principle by virtue of which perceptions always occur as someone's perceptions. The I is the transcendental condition for perception. Furthermore, the I is that which maintains itself in the midst of perception. I implies the maintenance of the self over and against the rush of perceptions (Selbstbehauptung).

Breuer follows Kant in protesting Hume's conclusion that the I is not a transcendental condition for perception but merely a product of perception. "The I is no mere sum!" (doch keine Summe!) he exclaims.[65] The rush of inner and outer perceptions "want" to constitute the subject, but something, the I, prevents them from doing so. This assertion is not exactly proven, but Breuer appeals to experience. Is it not the case that we find ourselves in the condition of being or having selves over and against the world that we perceive? The function of the I in asserting itself against the world, while in the midst of receiving the world, Breuer terms "will." "I is the function of self-maintenance in the manifold of outer and inner perceptions. This self-maintenance, this continual positing of self by virtue of which alone the total, constantly changing [field of] perceptions are my perceptions, I call 'will.' "[66]

Breuer has taken Schopenhauer's view of the subject that exists as an individual in a body—that is, the subject as "objectified will" (which is therefore in constant need of asserting itself against every other will)—and transferred the need for this assertion to the process of perception itself. In Breuer, the incessant struggle for identity is going on within the subject as such, while in Schopenhauer the struggle occurs between subjects. By this move, Breuer imports the tragedy of existence into the very operations of the epistemic subject, further enhancing the thesis that salvation must come from beyond.

The primal function (Urfunktion)—but not the primal essence or substance—of the I is will. Willing is the I's confrontation with its perceptions, such that it is not lost among them but is continuously asserted against them. Were it not for this ongoing act of will, the subject and its objects would collapse into one another. Thus, this movement of the will—Erwollnis—renders possible the process of Erkenntnis. Breuer has, by his own lights, demonstrated the dependence of perceiving on willing and has refuted the conventional view of the matter.

Given the fact that perception and cognition (Erkenntnis) is tied to self-maintaining willing (Erwollnis)—"Perception and willing are one"—Breuer elaborates on the implications of the relationship.[67] If the primal function of the I is to maintain and assert itself before the field of perceived objects, how is it that the I enters this field at all? What sort of union is possible between I and object? Given that the I is not an object, and therefore that no object is an I, what kind of correlation can there be between two so utterly disparate elements? In brief, how is knowledge of things possible?

> If I posit the I outside of the world of things, then how does it come about that the I perceives the things? For they would indeed be outside of the I. If I posit the I within the things, then there would be only the I without remainder. [It seems as if] either the I is broken by the otherness of the things, or the things dissolve themselves in the illusions of the I. Either the I stands helpless before the sealed-off world, or the I devours that world and stares into emptiness. Either the non-I is nonperceptible, or it does not exist at all.[68]

In Breuer's view, two possible relations between the *I* and its objects must be ruled out. The *I* cannot be fully exclusive of objects, but it cannot be fully inclusive of them either, consisting only of a sum of objects. The *I* must preserve its transcendental uniqueness, *and* the world must retain its ontological independence. Both radical empiricism and absolute idealism are ruled out. Empiricism reduces the *I* to a sum of sense data, and idealism robs the world of an extra-egoistic reality. For Breuer, unlike Kant or Schopenhauer, this extrahuman givenness is a sign of the createdness of the world.

In Breuer's rejection of a thoroughgoing idealism, the influence of Schopenhauer again appears. Schopenhauer could not allow idealism of a Fichtean sort. Fichte argued that the *I* is actually the cause of objects. Schopenhauer, however, argued that causality only applies to the domain within the subject or to the domain within the realm of objects. It cannot apply between domains. Within the subject, motive *A* can affect motive *B*, and within the world of objects, object *C* can affect object *D*, but no such causal relation can hold between *A* and *C*. Fichte errs in believing that the object is an effect of the subject, while the empiricists err in believing that the subject is an effect of the object. A third error is that of Hume, who believes that the whole topic of causality is illusory and irrelevant. Schopenhauer calls the two versions of the former error "dogmatism" and the latter "skepticism." Both of them are category mistakes in that they try to place causality where it does not belong.[69]

The true view is that subject and object are both a priori necessary. Object and subject presuppose one another, before the principle that governs either of their internal transactions (the principle of sufficient reason) is in place. The dialectical necessity of subject and object implies for Schopenhauer that a fourth possibility, commonsense realism, cannot work. The commonsense realist holds that objects have an independent existence in the world before we perceive them in the form under which we perceive them, and so—when we perceive an object—nothing appertains to that object other than what we have perceived. If, however, there is a biconditional relationship between the two (subject if and only if object), then both are necessarily deprived of any autonomy vis-à-vis the other. Subject and object are intrinsically connected. This premise leads to Schopenhauer's thesis that the representation—the form under which we know the object—is already in the subject, but that there remains something we do not know: the

Ding an sich. All that one knows of objects is the object as *Vor-stellung.* We can trace the existence of an object as representation to its ground of knowledge, that is, to the way in which we know it as a representation, but we cannot carry it to its 'ground of being.' We cannot locate the ground of being in either the object or the subject. Fichte, in talking about the *I* as a ground of being, is a counter-Copernican reactionary and the advocate of a new medievalism.

Breuer follows Schopenhauer in the assertion that all the sub-ject knows of objects is the object's representational nature and that this is already a mentalistic entity. Breuer makes much of the *Ding an sich,* which we cannot, by definition, *know,* but which we can nonetheless intuit. For Breuer, to lose the *Ding an sich* would be to abandon the world as a givenness (*Gegebenheit*), that is, as something other than man, as something created. There is a natu-ral theology here, in that epistemic analysis, by revealing the pres-ence of the *Ding an sich,* reveals a formal sign of God's activity as Creator. Breuer's theory of creation, which may be seen as a meta-physics grounded in epistemology (again, a parallel of Schopenhau-er's procedure), will be treated in the next chapter.

In answer then to the question, How does the *I* know—"con-nect" with—its objects? Breuer answers that the aspects of the ob-ject that the *I* knows as well as the *I* itself are already so formed as to relate to one another. His description of this relation is poetic. Alluding to the sexual connotation of the verb *to know* in Genesis 4:1, Breuer describes the art of knowledge as a procreative cou-pling, creative not of the object per se, but of a union between the preexistent and mutually dependent *I* and its object.

> To put it figuratively: I love my percepts because I cannot exist without them. They are, as one says, "my everything." But I can only love them as long as I am. My percepts return my love as well, because they cannot exist without me. Hence I must, while devoting myself utterly to my percepts, for my sake and for theirs, yet again maintain myself over and against them. My percepts and I: we are both one and yet two. Indeed, perception is the genuine analogue of true love.
>   Weiler: "And Adam knew Eve."
>   Alfred: So it is. Out of this single sentence of Scripture, I gained the most decisive impetus for all of this. Great is the Torah![70]

The *I* and its representations are as lovers. They are paradoxical beings who are discrete entities but who need, in order to be lovers, to come together. Were they to remain together, however, they would become some *tertium quid* and no longer lovers. The moment of establishing unity (*Feststellung des Einsseins*) is cosmogonic: a new world has been born, namely, the world of representations (*Vorstellungswelt*).[71] But immediately, the *I* denies what it has affirmed and rejects the representations as its own determinative content. After oneness comes dichotomization (*Entzweiung*). Breuer's description of the process of perceiving and knowing sounds rather like that of Karl Joel quoted above, "Perception is a breaking apart, a forming, a separating and then again a joining together." But the emphasis and valuation are entirely different. Breuer, following Schopenhauer, finds perception to be a blissful, if quite transient, state. Joel, the neo-Romantic, locates Edenic bliss in the more primal experience of feeling. As we will now see, Breuer comes to precisely the opposite view of feeling. When we turn from perceiving and its corresponding movement of the will, *Erwollnis*, to passion, that is, to the entrapment of the will in the world-in-itself, man loses his sense of harmony and balance, and the full tragedy of the human condition emerges.

Breuer designates the movement of the will that repudiates the representations the "contraction of the will" (*Willenskontraktion*). In the creative, unitive moment of perception the will experiences itself as autonomous, sovereign, and authoritative. This sort of willing represents the highest degree of self-assertion for the will.[72] But the will, of course, must leave this state of extension into the world and retreat into itself to remain whole and self-identical.

Willenskontraktion seems to be a deliberate allusion to the kabbalistic concept of *tsimtsum* (also "contraction"). In the Kabbalah of Isaac Luria (1534–72), stemming from sixteenth century Safed in northern Galilee, creation occurs after God contracts into himself in order to create a space for extradivine being. Luria's cosmogonic myth differed from earlier kabbalistic speculation, which generally held to a Neoplatonic emanationism. Now rather than creation pouring forth out of the divine fullness, creation involves loss, constraint, and retreat.[73] With the concept of *tsimtsum*, the kabbalist was able to account for the absence of God from creation, whereas the earlier cosmogonies implied his presence in a radical way. The Lurianic Kabbalah, following the great trauma of the ex-

ile from Spain, provided a language in which to talk about loss and
tragedy experienced on a cosmological scale. It is at this point that
the allusion fits in well with what Breuer is trying to say about the
radical nature of the human tragedy. The tragedy is cosmogonic
with respect to man's creator-like role vis-à-vis the world-as-
representation. Man's brief experience as creator of an experiential
framework is immediately followed by a melancholy estrangement, a state of exile.

> In the same instance, however, that the *I* wills itself and only
> itself, it willfully renounces its content as that which does
> not belong to it, pushing its content, like a ripened fruit, out
> of itself with an elemental force, and making its content in-
> dependent by an elemental contraction of will as that which
> no longer belongs to it. Pushing it to become a thing that
> stands outside of the *I*, that is, a thing-in-itself, it is now able
> to in the same moment reunite in satisfying, loving percep-
> tion with this stranger to its will; thing-in-itself as, once
> again, a percept.[74]

Breuer argues that in the midst of the act of perception
(*Erkenntnisakt*) the *I* advances to the limits of experience, that is,
to the realm of things-in-themselves. By expelling its content of
phenomena, the *I* becomes aware of a dimension to those contents
that is emphatically other. To repudiate a representation is to encounter its nonrepresentational nature. The serenity of the *I* in
perception, together with its sense of power in willing, suddenly
gives way to a new moment of disharmony and powerlessness. The
will, which has contracted in independence from the representations and which has abandoned them to the unknowable world-
in-itself, suddenly becomes trapped by that world. This state of
entrapment is 'feeling' (*Fühlen*).

Breuer asserts that previous philosophers have been beguiled
by the nature of the bond between *I* and *thing* because they have
misrepresented man as primarily a perceiving being. Because they
conceived of man as most relevantly an epistemic subject, philosophers have believed that the *Ding an sich* had to be intelligible to
that subject on its own terms. The philosophers have failed to recognize that the world addresses man as more than a perceiver and
cognizer. One of the important and obvious pieces of evidence to
support this claim is that the world presents itself to our wills in

the experience of feeling, such that we are stimulated by the world and we respond with desire.

We do not perceive or conceive of feeling, we simply feel it (befühlen). It is true that feeling becomes contextualized in the forms of time and space: we perceive and know that we have had a feeling. But the pristine arousal of feeling is different from the process of the perception of it. Whereas perception occurs in a mediated fashion, feeling is immediate. The *I* perceives a cup of coffee as a collection of sense data. The *I* as will simultaneously affirms itself against the coffee and declares the coffee to be something other than itself. The *I* experiences a momentary bliss in perception as the will simultaneously asserts itself with power, repelling the percept from its own identity. In the very next moment, however, the *I* begins to crave the coffee. This craving (Begehrnis) wells up from some source other than the perceiving *I*. The *I* may subsequently perceive that it craves, and the inner state of craving then becomes an object of perception, but in the first instance craving is *sui generis*.[75] Breuer, again following Schopenhauer's lead (Schopenhauer credited Spinoza with the insight), emphasizes that no account of man can dispense with passion. It will not do to treat man as if he were an angel who does not become entangled in the world of desire. That philosophers are prone to do so, expresses the false consciousness of philosophical rationalism.

After the *I* divorces the representations and recognizes them as things-in-themselves, it finds that it has become entrapped in the world-in-itself. Feeling is a state of enslavement (Knechtschaft) that presents an ongoing contrast to the state of sovereignty (Herrschaft) otherwise enjoyed by the *I*. Breuer is very much concerned to develop this fundamental dialectic of the human experience. Man's most simple and continual experience of lordly freedom continually resolves into its opposite: bondage to the things of this world. The bondage of feeling is the constant consort of the world-generating activity of cognition. This ongoing reality of domination by the noumenal world militates against any naturalistic scheme of freedom. Freedom requires a methodology of willing over and against the coercive pressure of the world-in-itself.

The coercive moment of feeling or craving emerges out of the depths of the *I* in conjunction with a stimulus from the noumenal depths of the object. Breuer calls the source of feeling on the side of the subject the "*I*-in-itself" (Ich an sich). This depth dimension of the *I* is unknown and unknowable, for it is disclosed in a non-cognitive experience. The perceiving and cognizing *I* (*erkennende Ich*) is a "world *I*"(*Welt Ich*): a sovereign, cosmogonic force operating in terms of universally valid laws, which Kant delineated. The feeling *I*-in-itself, however, is a drastically reduced, individuated will tied hungrily to its portion of the world-in-itself. This is the *I* of the *principium individuationis*. Philosophers prefer to write about man as perceiving *I*, for there man appears free. The pathetic, enslaved, feeling *I* seems to be a creature entirely different from the autonomous, perceiving *I*. The free *I* wills itself against its representations. The unfree *I* is, so to speak, willed by the world-in-itself.

> In desire, the *I* loses the freedom that it won in perception. The freedom of the *I* is its self-maintaining disengagement from its content. This disengaging is an act of will. In perception, the *I*'s will detaches itself, but this detached, perceptual will of the *I* is immediately thrown into chains again by desire. In the perceptions of the world qua percept, the world-in-itself—eternally unperceived—arises for the contentless *I*. It arises for the *I* above all, as a subsidiary part of the world-in-itself, that is as body, known only as a percept among percepts, eternally unknown, however, as force, which storms in upon the *I* and its self-maintaining will. And [this portion of the world-in-itself] drags the *I* into the midst of experience— the *I* that in perception was elevated above all experience as the necessary condition for experience—and enslaves, debases, and disfigures it to such an extent that the vast majority of thinkers have not been able to identify this "coffee-craving" will any more with the sovereign free, world-encompassing, world-free, world-law-bearing will of the *I*. . . . Perceiving is willing. Desiring is having to will. Perceiving the *I* wills the world as perception. Desiring, the *I* is willed by the world in itself.[76]

For man to be understood as he actually is, therefore, he must be conceived as a concrete individual. The actual, individuated condition of the *I* stands in stark contrast to the fantastic, world *I* of philosophical imagination. The *I* of feeling is fully idiosyncratic. The *I*'s feeling encounter with the *Ding an sich* is private and unique, wholly unlike the *I*'s dialectical structuring of a world of perception, cognition, concept, and idea. Furthermore, whenever the *I* encounters the *thing*, it is molded (willed) by the *thing*. Its will is entrapped in the world and becomes inflected by the entrapment. Thus it is in feeling that individuation occurs and that the *I* becomes aware of itself as an individual (rather than a world *I*) in a distinct and painful way.

Breuer, like Schopenhauer and Nietzsche, gives a tragic account of individuality. The differentiation of the *I* from all other objects arises out of the will's enslavement to the world-in-itself. Thus individuality is the antithesis of freedom. Individuality is an ontic fall from grace. Individuality entails embodiment.[77] As in Schopenhauer's treatment of body, Breuer initially maintains that, qua representation, one's own body is not different in kind from any other object. If man were exclusively a perceiving *I*, his relation to his own body (if he could be said to have a body as such a being) would be a disinterested epistemic relation. But this is not the case, and therefore the special relation we have to our bodies is not a matter of perception. What remains is will: the specially felt relation of the *I* to its own body must be a relationship of will.

The *I*'s relationship to the particular *Ding an sich* felt as body is unique among its relationships to things-in-themselves. For this *Ding an sich* is the very condition (*Zuständlichkeit*) into which the will is set, and it is by virtue of this condition that the world-in-itself can be given to us at all. From the point of view of perception, body is indeed one representation among many, but from the point of view of will, body is the condition for our world. When the will becomes aware of its conditionality, its embodiment, then it becomes individual.[78] It would appear from this discussion that embodiment is a rather negative condition, but Breuer does not accept this conclusion. In an extensive discussion in *Naḥaliel*, he views Judaism as the only adequate metaphysics of body. The many laws of the Torah dealing with the body, the laws of kashrut, for example, are directed to the reality of embodiment in phenomenologically appropriate terms. Judaism comprehends body, while philosophy and modern culture in general either skirt it or fall, at the opposite extreme, into its absolutization.

Through much of this discussion, Breuer has followed Schopenhauer in the depiction of a metaphysical world picture that specifies an epistemically grounded ontological tragedy. Schopenhauer recommends world resignation, a course that Breuer, who would seize history and rise to mighty acts of national renewal, cannot accept. Nevertheless, Breuer's depiction of the

conditio humana is every bit as bleak as his philosophical men-
tor's. His peculiar coloration of the tragedy is best summed up by
this quotation:

> In the parting of perceiving and feeling, in the parting of the
> active, pure will, which asserts itself in perceiving and in the
> world as perception, from that empirical will that is possible
> in the world-in-itself, lies the entire tragedy of humanity. If
> we were only perceiving beings, we would be—in the eternal
> quiescence of our living will—angels. If we were only willing
> beings, we would be—in our eternal, boundless ensnarement
> by the world-in-itself—animals. If we could perceive and will
> at once, such that our *I* by willing itself could release the
> world from itself, by willing itself could perceive itself inde-
> pendently of the world, could perceive the world not merely
> qua perception but qua world in itself, and could find eternal
> satisfaction of the eternal living will in the perceived world—
> if all of this were true, we would be God. We, however, are
> men.[79]

Breuer's break with Schopenhauer is in a sense a return to
medieval Jewish philosophical tradition. Far from a monism of the
will, Breuer's cosmos makes room for angels and God. The schema
is medieval in the sense that God will be characterized by kinds of
perfection that make sense over and against human imperfection.
As we have seen, God will occupy a place beyond constitutive human limits in a manner that contrasts logically with the logical
characteristics of human being.

The internally divisive nature of man places man at a certain
rank in a vitalistic hierarchy. The animal kingdom is on the one
end, and the angels are on the other. Human being is a synthesis
that has emerged from the thesis of a free epistemic being and the
antithesis of an unfree, feeling being. The next turn in *Der Neue
Kusari* is toward a philosophical anthropology derived in large
measure from medieval Jewish philosophy.

ANTHROPOLOGY AND FREEDOM

Breuer asserts that the human being is composed of three
parts. Before investigating his distinctive view, it will be useful to
get a sense of the development of the tripartite theory of the soul

in Jewish tradition, for Breuer manipulates that tradition and re-models it to accord with an epistemology inspired by Kant and Schopenhauer.

The tripartite view of the soul is derived from Plato and Ar-istotle and adapted by Saadiah, Maimonides, and the *Zohar*. Saa-diah Gaon was apparently the first to give Hebrew designations to the three classical components of the soul. Using three biblical Hebrew terms, he distinguished between *nefesh* (appetite, desire), *ruaḥ* (spirit), and *neshamah* (reason). For Saadiah, these represent three aspects of one entity that has been placed in the body by God.[80] The physical seat of this tripartite soul is the heart, where the three aspects of the soul work together. Saadiah differs from the Platonists, who ascribe different locations to each aspect of the soul, but he follows Plato in understanding these aspects as con-current functions or faculties that complement one another.

Maimonides follows Aristotle and holds that *nefesh, ruaḥ,* and *neshamah* are not complementary and concurrent functions, but rather represent stages of development. *Neshamah* now repre-sents the highest order of man's development. *Neshamah* is the rational faculty, latent in the mind, which communicates with the "active intellect." In the course of time man grows in "acquired intellect" until his reason is able to commune with the reason of God. *Nefesh* and *ruaḥ* are seen as lower stages that must be overcome.[81]

The *Zohar* seems to provide the immediate inspiration for Breuer's version of the tripartite soul. In the *Zohar*, the three as-pects, as in Saadiah, represent distinct spiritual agencies: *nefesh* means "life," *ruaḥ* means "spirit," and *neshamah* means "soul." But, following Maimonides, the three are not coexistent, separate faculties—*ruaḥ* and *neshamah* are latently present in *nefesh*. Ac-cording to the *Zohar*, the adept acquires the capacity of *ruaḥ* and ultimately of *neshamah* through study of Torah, the practice of mitzvot, and research in the esoteric tradition of Kabbalah.[82] This developmental schema is Maimonidean with an important excep-tion. For Maimonides, even the *nefesh* is divinely given and, as such, not identifiable with the natural world.[83] For the *Zohar*, the *nefesh* is animalistic and the cause of sin.

"The *nefesh* has no light within it whatsoever, but receives its light from *ruaḥ*."[84] *Ruaḥ* in turn receives light and being from *neshamah*, which emanates from God. *Nefesh* is that aspect of the soul most closely bound up with the body for the *Zohar*. It pro-vides the instinct for self-preservation and the ability for sensation. "The *nefesh* is the infernal animating force [*hit'orrut tahtonah*]. It is joined to the body and whores [*zanah*] after it. The body grasps her, and she is grasped by it."[85]

The *neshamah*, in the view of the *Zohar*, equips man for his essential purpose: to learn Torah and to perform mitzvot. "Above all the parts of the soul stands the *neshamah*. It is the supernal power by which man knows the Holy One, blessed be he, and obeys his precepts . . . He has put in man a holy *neshamah* in order to instruct man to walk in the paths of the Torah and to obey his precepts, in order that man may be reformed."[86]

The *ruah* is not discussed as extensively in the *Zohar* as are the *nefesh* and *neshamah*. Its function is to sustain the *nefesh* by providing it with some of the light and power of the *neshamah*. This apparatus is taken over into Breuer's anthropology in both *Der Neue Kusari* and *Nahaliel*.

In *Der Neue Kusari*, man is a being who is entrapped, as we have seen, in the world-in-itself. As such, he exists under the aspect of *nefesh*. "Nefesh is the animal form of man."[87] *Nefesh* represents man's unfree, passional nature. *Ruah* represents man's free, autonomous nature as an epistemic subject, a subject not caught in the world-in-itself but enjoying sovereignty in the world-as-representation. Of course, neither the servitude nor the sovereignity of man alone describes his situation. Man is both: a "king-beggar" (*König-Bettler*) as Breuer describes him. This synthesis is represented by *neshamah*.

Breuer comes closer here to the *Zohar* than to the faculty psychology of Saadiah or the developmental psychology of Maimonides. *Nefesh* and *ruah* are applications of the *neshamah*, ways in which the *neshamah* can become actualized.

"Nefesh and *ruah* thus designate the relationality of the *neshamah*. *Nefesh* is its relation to the world-in-itself, *ruah* its relation to the world-as-perception."[88] *Nefesh* and *ruah* are fragmentary expressions of the *neshamah*, which appears now as both the pristine condition of the soul and its normative state.

With the concept of *neshamah* there enters the possibility that man can define himself by defining his relation to the world. (This sort of possibility is entirely foreign to Schopenhauer, of course.) The *neshamah*—the *I* in its a priori condition—can experience life under the twin aspects of *nefesh* and of *ruah*. It experiences freedom in the perceptual encounter and enslavement in the feeling encounter. Man, growing weary of this ceaseless dialectical movement, sometimes declares the experience of freedom an illusion. When he lets go of this aspect of his *neshamah*—the *ruaḥ* experience—he sinks to the level of *nefesh*. *Ruaḥ* is demoted to being an epiphenomenon (*Begleiterscheinung*) of *nefesh*, a light that the will, enslaved in *nefesh*, holds up before itself.[89] The dialectical subject is lost, and only the world-in-itself remains. The moral consequence of this abandonment is this: "So, in the greatest possible enjoyment lies the sense of life—that is the conception of materialism. Man seeks to free himself from *neshamah* through the stupor of enjoyment. He endeavors to ornament the chains of his will with roses, because he is not able to hope to shake them off."[90]

Another alternative presents itself, however. Man can seek to deny *nefesh*, to repudiate the world-in-itself and to dwell only in the world as representation. Man seeks to actualize his *neshamah* as *ruaḥ* alone. The moral consequence of this view is asceticism, the path of renunciation. For Breuer, these two alternatives, practiced with gradation and nuance, represent the only two possibilities open to humans outside of Judaism. Thus the critique of human experience per se leads him to conclude that human beings are utterly unable to solve their own predicament. They lack the fundamental insight required to achieve correct action: the correct ordering of the soul. This correct path, the proper synthesis, is the way of Judaism. "The way of Judaism—the Jewish way. In order to understand it correctly, we undertook this entire excursion into pure humanity, for the knowledge of Judaism has as its presupposition the knowledge of humanity."[91]

In *Naḥaliel*, Breuer develops his philosophical anthropology in relation both to a metaphysics of creation and to the life of the divine commandments. Consideration of these distinctive thrusts must be left to the next chapter. Here it suffices to mention that Breuer continued to develop his model late in life. In his Hebrew work, he wrote of three aspects of the *I* (*anokhi*): the animalistic aspect (*anokhi b'hami*), the perceptual-cognitive aspect (*anokhi-sekhli*), and the ideational aspect (*anokhi ḥazoni*). He interchanges these terms rather freely with three corresponding aspects of human will (*ratzon*): again animalistic, rationalistic, and ideational will.[92] Man shares both his animalistic (metabolic, reproductive, survival-oriented nature) and his perceptual-cognitive aspects with animal forms of life. It is the ideational dimension of his being— the ability to contemplate "nonnatural" ideas, such as freedom, justice, goodness, holiness—that distinguishes humanity. It is the ability to will these ideas, in particular to will the idea of justice (the idea of ideas) in a national, historically efficacious form, that distinguishes Israel from others.

Does this anthropological model point toward a resolution of the tragedy of human existence? How can the dialectically constituted human subject, simultaneously trapped in and sovereign over its two-tiered world, liberate itself from craving and causality?

In order to reveal the solution to the problem of pure humanity, Breuer now refines his thesis on the complex nature of the will. Recalling that the will—in its experience of perception—experiences satisfaction, autonomy, and freedom, and in its experience of feeling undergoes entrapment and slavery, Breuer terms the will that is able to assert itself in the face of the world as representation a "willing will." The will that is entrapped by the world-in-itself he terms a "willed will."

In attempting to understand how it is that the will is simultaneously free and determined, Breuer follows Schopenhauer in holding the view that motives follow upon one another in an almost mechanical way such, that the subject is never free insofar as he is a willing subject. Schopenhauer conceives of the individual's will as a strictly determined succession of states.[93] It only seems to us that we could have acted other than we did. In actuality, choice in an illusion produced by a constitutively inadequate knowledge of our own nature. Schopenhauer was a strict determinist who found his way out of determinism by a metaphysical back door: The will, although struggling against its own self-determination, is nonetheless one within itself. This monism implies that any will reveals or discloses the entire cosmos in itself. Thus Schopenhauer is led to believe that the necessary causal process of the will, going on within the context of an individual's motivation, is a cosmic process. An individual's motivation is a cosmic process. An individual is nature acting in a particular manifestation.[94]

Given these two premises—the causal nature of motivated will and its microcosmic character—Breuer argues that the will in its depth-engagement, its *Erwollnis,* with the world-in-itself is an unfree reflex of that world. The will that is enmeshed in desire for the world-in-itself becomes an unfree piece of that world, dreaming that it is free:

> Your will, which is determined in its quality by the world-in-itself, aroused in its intensity by the world in itself,

decides according to the law of its equality and intensity—
because it can do no other. Ultimately, it is not your will that
decides, but the world-in-itself that decides through the medium of your will. While you mean to will, in truth the
world-in-itself is willing through you. You believe that you
will, but you are willed. . . .

However, the more the willed will—long before the
will's decision—is predestined, on account of its complete
enslavement to the world-in-itself, so much more does it
revel in its supposed dual ability (to apparently undertake or
omit a course of action). Of course, this ability is nothing
other than the reverse side of slavery: it is the arbitrary
choice of the willed will. Precisely because the willed will
can will no other than what it has finally willed, it requires—
in order to appear to itself as will, if only willed will—the
deceptive pretense of "being able to have acted differently."
The freedom of the willed will is nothing other than the illusion of arbitrariness.[95]

Breuer is at one with Schopenhauer in his determinism and
in his conviction that choice is an illusory expression of an underlying unfreedom. Yet the sense the perceiving *I*, as a willing will,
has of freedom is not illusory. The will as an active assertion of
self against the world is indeed free, although only momentarily
so. "The freedom of the will and the self-maintenance of the *I* are
identical."[96]

Thus the will, as willing will, in perception is free, but immediately, as willed will, it is unfree. If it were the case that the
will had a means of asserting itself against the world-in-itself, just
as it asserts itself against the world-as-representation, then it
would be able to achieve an overall freedom. Clearly, however, this
means must not be a denial of the world-in-itself, for we have seen
that that path is an inauthentic failure. The *I* must, as always, be
engaged by the world-in-itself but must now control that world
rather than be controlled by it. This is to say that just as the *I*
"legislates" a law for the world-as-perception by means of which
perception is achieved, so too must it legislate a law for the world-
in-itself.

Yet how could this be done? While the willing will has the
inherent capacity to order and maintain itself over and against the
world of perceptions, the *I* discovers no comparable resources
within itself to apply to the world-in-itself. It has no choice other

than to suffer the contradiction of becoming a willed will. The solution to the problem of will must therefore come, if it is to come at all, from beyond human experience and its inherent dilemma.

The law that the will must legislate, it is now revealed, is the Torah. In order to become free, man must become analogous to God. His will must become a sovereign, controlling will. Unlike man, God perceives and wills at once in a purely assertive way. God's self-maintenance does not occur over and against the world; it is itself productive of the world. God can will without becoming entrapped, which is what man now aspires to do. Insofar as Torah is God's plan for creation, is what molds creation without being molded by it, man—by willing Torah—becomes like God. "Subject, not as creator, but as partner who completes creation: not God, but God's assistant. Not creation of the world in itself, but self-maintenance and self-assertion over and against the world in itself."[97] Torah, the law of creation (Schöpfungsrecht), is what enables human beings to will the world-in-itself in freedom.

For Breuer, the law that human beings must will, to achieve freedom, comes from God. The extranatural origin of this law, which ex hypothesi is beyond the competence of reason or will to discover, casts additional light on the tragic failure of philosophy and on the stark contrast between reason and Torah. The case of Kant is particularly melancholy.

In Breuer's view, Kant's moral theory was an effort to impose a law upon the world-in-itself. Freedom, autonomy of the will, means freedom from entrapment in the passional dimension of experience. Kant sensed that the order that prevails in man as a perceiving, knowing subject represents the true dignity and stature of the human person, and that, in some as yet unknown way, this dignity must be asserted and retained against man's experience of need, craving, and subjugation to desire.[98] Kant exhorted the will that is tangled in the world-in-itself: "Act freely! Act in such a way that the motive of your action could become a generally valid law!"[99]

Breuer reports in Mein Weg that when he first studied the Critique of Practical Reason he was disturbed by the paucity of Kant's results. He found in Kant's categorical imperative a mere shard (Scherbe) of a system of freedom.[100] Kant was unable to reach beyond the mere formal requirements for a law of freedom because he had not stood at the foot of Sinai. He proceeds no farther than the door of Judaism. He has arrived at the idea of a law of freedom but not the law itself. Kant understood that freedom has a legal cast (act in such a way that your motive can become a generally valid *law*), but he promulgated only a transcendental condition for that law. For Breuer, Kant's categorical imperative represents a failed hope. The spectacle of each individual legislating for the universe would be ludicrous were it not tragic. Here Breuer's Schopenhauerian and neo-Romantic background works against Kant's Enlightenment individualism.

What Kant requires is a genuinely cosmic *nomos* (*Kosmonomie*): a law that actually binds and obligates all men, by virtue of which they achieve freedom. What Kant attains is the idea of such a *Nomos*. Kant represents the acme of pure humanity. He is the very icon of humanity's hope and humanity's dilemmatic failure. Thus: "If one wants to know where pure humanity necessarily flows into Judaism, then one may study Kant."[101]

Although humanity and Judaism, philosophy and Torah, are in one sense radically discontinuous, a kind of transition is suggested by Breuer's language. While philosophy ends abruptly before revelation, pure humanity "necessarily flows" (*zwangsläufig mündet*) into Judaism. Breuer is not suggesting that the transition is logically necessary or actually inevitable. What is implied is that the desperate soul of humanity cries out continually for liberation and looks beyond itself, although it does not know where to look. Humanity, whose dilemma is to be enslaved to craving, craves the anonymous freedom that the Jews know as Torah. Man does not want to deny his world or his self, nor does he want to divinize either of them. But without knowing how to will his freedom, how to order his cosmos with a suitable law, he cannot but fall into the most pernicious philosophical, indeed historical-political, error. The promise of humanity searches restlessly for its fulfillment.

We are now in a position to make sense out of Breuer's assertion that one must will the Torah (rather than reason one's way toward it, etc.) and that this particular act of willing solves the problem of man, itself a problem of will. It will be recalled that this assertion was the immediate reason for the entire epistemology of *Der Neue Kusari*. Even now, however, the idea of willing the Torah is hardly free of difficulties, as Breuer's fictitious dialogue partner is quick to point out. For one thing, if the *I* craves freedom and therefore desires to will Torah in order to achieve freedom, has not the *I* embedded itself yet again into the context of unfreedom? If its motive is desire—even desire for the Torah—then the *I* is still wedded to the causality of motives. Furthermore, does not the *I* really require a motive—which is also to say, a reason—for willing Torah? After all, on some level, willing Torah entails an existential choice and a commitment to a certain discipline. Does not one need a reason, in a very conventional sense of the word, to do so?

In answer to the first problem, Breuer asserts that there is a single motive, which so to speak steps outside of the logic of motivation. The willing will is free when its motive is freedom per se. "The salvation of the *I* from resignation to the world as percept and the world-in-itself is the *I*'s sole motive. That is to say, that will is free whose sole motive is freedom per se."[102] Here Breuer would appear to fall back on Kant, whom he has harshly criticized for the vacuity of the concept of freedom. But Breuer immediately qualifies his assertion that freedom is the only nondetermined motive of the free will. The motive of freedom entails a content for that freedom: the Torah. That is to say, acting freely is not just intending to be free, it is doing something—or forbearing from doing something—a mitzvah, which gives concrete expression to the intention. Jewish freedom has a content. Kant's freedom had no content, hence its content by default became the undirected longing and desire for freedom. Longing remains unfulfilled longing: motive remains causally determined motive. This is the tragedy of Kant.

The next stage of the degeneration of freedom occurs in Schopenhauer's formulation. Although Breuer does not refer to Schopenhauer by name, the view that he cites is clearly Schopenhauer's: "Freedom signifies nothing other than the determined renunciation of the motives that storm upon the will out of the world in itself. . . . Freedom, as a motive, can only lead to a complete renunciation of action as a result of the unconditional negation of all motives of the willed will that would lead to action."[103]

Schopenhauer's system culminates in the denial of will altogether. Breuer does not acknowledge this essentially Buddhist alternative as a genuine solution that does in fact free man from the dialectic of will. Rather, he sees it as an inauthentic repudiation of the world-in-itself, inauthentic because it distorts the unity of self and world.

Breuer's solution—the willing of a cosmonomic Torah, the law of creation, onto the world-in-itself qua creation—presents itself as that which facilitates the unity and correct synthesis of self: *neshamah*. The *neshamah* must will the Torah to be free and to arrive at its perfection. With freedom as its motive, how does *neshamah* choose to become a Jewish *neshamah*? Again, does choice have a role here? Does one have a reason to choose? Breuer's resolution of this persistent problem is somewhat a semantic stipulation. Ultimately, the *neshamah* does have a choice between the paths of freedom and slavery, and it has a choice in the sense of the term we conventionally employ. However, it will be recalled that the context in which we normally speak of choice is that of the willed will: the very place where choice is illusory. It now becomes possible to say that the only real choice a *neshamah* can ever make is the transcendental choice between the life of freedom and the life of slavery. True choice commits one to a struggle to live freely by continually struggling to will Torah.[104] Out of this struggle, both the world-in-itself and the *I*-in-itself become dialectically molded into instruments of God's creation plan.

In answer to whether there is reason for the *I*'s willing one way and not another, Breuer asserts, "The decision is beyond comprehension. It does not belong to the comprehensible world of the understanding. There are no further reasons for this decision. Whoever wills freedom becomes free. Whoever wills servitude remains a slave. However—God will judge!"[105] As in Schopenhauer, the decision to remove oneself from the context of causality is an archetypal act: an act at the limits of sense. Breuer's term *beyond comprehension* suggests that the decision does not originate in or appeal to concepts but has its source and meaning in the deepest level of self: *neshamah*. Still, it might be objected that there is too much equivocation here on the concepts of choice and reason. Breuer concludes the discussion by introducing a final substantive point. The *neshamah* desires to act out of love. *Nefesh* typically craves the world-in-itself, loves the world-in-itself, in order to complete itself. Motivation is a state of being willed by the world in order to appropriate the world. Such is the acquisitive love of *nefesh*, whose nature is therefore privation (*Entbehren*).[106] The love of *neshamah*, on the contrary, is desire wanting to complete the world and hence desire without motive. The reason or motive for the *neshamah's* choice of freedom is love.

"The love of the *Neshamah* is desire freed from the world. Love is motiveless desire."[107] Rosenzweig's view of love, which perhaps influenced Breuer, is pertinent here. Rosenzweig held that it is divine love that lifts man from the isolation of his inherent, human individuality. Man is commanded by God to respond to His love with love, which in turn is directed toward the human neighbor. The act of human loving is unique: it is neither teleological nor directed by rational motives. This unique, extracategorical form of action redeems the world, which grows in actuality and life because of love. The radical distinction between loving and other forms of action (which are goal-directed and dependent on motives), as well as the surpassing redemptive significance of love, reminds one of Breuer.[108]

Unlike the *neshamah* distorted into *nefesh* or *ruaḥ* by the poverty of purely human possibilities, the supernaturally guided Jewish *neshamah* responds appropriately to the facticity of the world by giving itself in love to that world. Its completion is achieved in giving, not taking. It gives the world the design that God intends for it, and so achieves the design that God has intended for itself. Thus the fundamental act of the Jewish will is a *tikkun:* an act with both cosmic and self-transforming implications.

"A cosmic significance attaches to every human action. . . . Repentance is return to freedom and, through freedom, to love."[109] This line of argument expresses once again a distinctly kabbalistic motif to Breuer's thought: the life of Torah has both personal/ moral and universal/metaphysical effects. The inner world of humanity, the historical world of the Jewish people, and the creation of the world per se are correlated by the Torah. To this connection between creation and Torah revelation we now turn.

❖ 3

CREATION AND REVELATION

For Breuer, the epistemological analysis and critique of human experience reveals that man is a citizen of two worlds. His divinely given birthright entitles him to live in a world of freedom, but his fate condemns him to endure the world of necessity. Philosophy, especially Kantian philosophy, calls attention to this human dilemma insofar as we understand ourselves, in philosophical reflection, to be both objects within the order of causality, and subjects, whose consciousness presupposes a transcendental freedom. In its attempt to solve the human dilemma on its own terms, philosophy embodies the struggle, hope, and failure of the human communities outside of the Torah community. Philosophy becomes isomorphic with the tragic human situation. Due to the foretaste of freedom found in his own epistemic experience, man is prompted to seek liberation from the world of necessity. Without Torah revelation, however, man is unable to pursue his search in a nomic way. Breuer's "Torah-less" man, like Paul's "first Adam," drives himself deeper into despair and failure by means of the very practices that he imagines will secure transcendence for him. Indeed, insofar as man's medium is society, state, and history—as we will see—he drives himself beyond despair into evil. For his unresolved ontic dilemma moves him to escape into social and political projects that render history a long and cruel rebellion against God, His law, and His people.

Epistemological and anthropological analysis, then, does not lay the groundwork for revelation in any positive sense. The *conditio humana*, as displayed in these analyses, is a condition of privation of meaning. Revelation cannot be validated by recourse to epistemological facts. It is only the kind of being who needs and receives revelation that epistemology and anthropology indicate.

This reluctance to ground revelation in epistemology gives Breuer's thought something of a postfoundational cast. Breuer stresses the inadequacy of philosophical discourse for affirming the reality of revelation, turning instead to the inherent logic of the discourse of the religious community in history. His reliance on Judah Halevi, with his subsequent stress on metaphysical community over reason, contributes to this postfoundational appearance.

The resemblance ends, however, as Breuer moves beyond epistemological critique into metaphysical construction. Here he is very much a foundationalist. He contends that the epistemic, ontic situation of man has its roots in the metaphysical, ontological situation of the world as such. The dualistic character of human being reflects a dualism fundamental to extrahuman reality.

The world presents itself to us as an order of necessity, as nature (*Natur*), which is occasionally punctured by transcendental traces of an order of freedom, creation (*Schöpfung*). Breuer's idiosyncratic use of the term *creation* must immediately be noted. For him, as for Rosenzweig, creation is not primarily an event in time or, strictly speaking, an event productive of time—although it is minimally that—but a continual aspect of the world.

Creation is the world viewed in freedom, from the perspective of God. Breuer uses the term *creation* to mean both an event in *and* an aspect of the world. Creation is, as for Rosenzweig, an ongoing dimension of the world process. Furthermore, creation, although a signifier of divine freedom, is inherently unstable, unfulfilled, and incomplete. Creation requires revelation in order to become stable. We have already seen something of this paradoxical treatment in Breuer's equation of the unfree world-in-itself with creation. Creation is the world in its givenness by God. The divine is immediate to creation. Creation by definition, however, is not God (*Nicht-Gott; lo-elohim*). In this attempt to distinguish creation first from nature and then from God, one finds echoes of the kabbalist R. Menachem Recanati's treatment of the Sefirot. Recanati, who was active at the end of the thirteenth century, argued against the identity of the sefirotic creation with divinity. The Sefirot were not essentially divine, but instrumentalities for divine expression. Breuer read Recanati, discovering him first on the eve of the First World War as he returned from a vacation in Switzerland and stopped to visit his friend Pinchas Kohn in Ansbach. He continued to study this kabbalist throughout his life. Recanati's break with the Zoharic tradition of identifying the Sefirot with the emanations of God and delimiting the sefirotic world to the "garments" rather than the essence of divinity has repercussions in Breuer's complex treatment of creation and nature.[1]

The concept of creation was of crucial concern to Breuer, as the following quotation attests: "Creation: the fundamental concept of the Torah; its entire, governing, central thought. Creation: the overall, unambiguous, determinate essence of Judaism; the formula that carries and clarifies all."[2]

Breuer shaped his thesis in three German works, *Die Welt als Schöpfung und Natur* (1926), *Elischa (1928)* and *Der Neue Kusari* (1934). He brought the thesis to its final systematic expression in *Naḥaliel* (1951). While these successive texts represent attempts to refine and strengthen a basic thesis, *Elischa*—held to be Breuer's most difficult work—and *Naḥaliel* have thrusts different from those of the other two. The aim of the thesis on creation in *Die Welt als Schöpfung und Natur* and in *Der Neue Kusari* appears to be a critique of natural science. As an Orthodox Jew, Breuer rightly recognized modern scientific cosmology to be a threat to the believer's world picture. The defense of the traditional creation account, however modified by its lengthy Jewish *Wirkungsgeschichte*, is a concern of most Orthodox thinkers. The burden of *Die Welt als Schöpfung und Natur* is to develop a metaphysics in which a traditional *creatio ex nihilo* cosmology can coexist with modern scientific cosmology, understood from a Kantian angle. Breuer suggested that this crucial venture represents a prolegomenon to a system of Jewish philosophy, thus indicating the gravity of his project and the extent of his aspirations.[3] Were it not for this announcement of such serious intentions, the leading critic of that work, Oscar Wolfsberg, would not have been so severe in his philosophical critique. Wolfsberg's critique led to a reworking of the thesis in *Der Neue Kusari*.[4]

The different thrust of *Elischa* is due to a different opponent. Breuer takes issue in this work with the tradition of German idealism, especially as that tradition is represented by Fichte. Whereas scientific empiricism implies a world that does not need creation owing to its naturalistic self-generation, idealism presents a world that has been created by a spiritual force, mind. In *Elischa*, Breuer uses the often obscure language of idealism, hence the general difficulty of the work.

Naḥaliel has yet a different object. Its purpose is not primarily polemical but constructive. In this his most traditional work, Breuer presents a philosophy of the commandments. The mitzvot are grounded in creation. They are an ontological therapy, a *tikkun* for an incomplete cosmos. Creation is not yet stabilized against chaos. The mitzvot bring perfection and pacification (*Shabbat*) to creation. *Naḥaliel* presents an enormously detailed exercise in finding the reasons for the commandments and builds on the metaphysical foundation of Breuer's German works. The Hebrew philosophical treatment of creation occasionally relieves the obscurity of the German.

In all of these works, creation is a prolegomenon: a necessary first stage in a process that leads to revelation and then, with human cooperation, redemption. Creation itself is fulfilled by this process. Until its fulfillment, creation bears a strangely ambiguous status. Breuer presents creation in paradoxical ways: as the realm of God's freedom and as the realm of man's bondage. The ambiguity carries over onto another key, related concept, Sabbath. For Breuer, Sabbath represents an almost negative termination of God's free, creative activity and an eschatological limit that man must impose upon a refractory created world.

The theses on creation, while related, lend themselves to separate treatments. Some of the sense of ambiguity is resolved by discerning the different polemical aims at work, but ambiguities do remain. I will present the thesis of *Die Welt als Schöpfung und Natur*, and its refinement in *Der Neue Kusari*, as Breuer's basic text and will turn to *Elischa* and *Naḥaliel* to illustrate the richness of his conception of creation.

THE WORLD AS CREATION AND AS NATURE

What does Breuer mean by creation, and why does he invest this concept with such crucial importance? As stated, 'creation', refers not so much to an event as to an ongoing dimension of reality. The title, "The World as Creation and as Nature," suggests that the world is inherently ambiguous. Furthermore, this metaphysical ambiguity is tied to an epistemic, perspectival ambiguity. There is a dialectical (not a reductive) relationship between *esse* and *percipi*. It would have been safer for Breuer to have asserted that the world is ontologically simple and to have embraced some version of monism—either empirical or idealist—as Schopenhauer did in *The World as Will and Idea*. For Schopenhauer, the world as sense datum resolves, once metaphysical insight is achieved, into the world as will. Breuer however rejects this reductionism. He is committed to a cosmos with multiple levels of reality. This commitment steers him away from Schopenhauer and back to Kant. In addition, it places him within the Jewish mystical tradition, although in a way heavily qualified by his Kantianism.

I have already suggested a similarity to R. Menahem Recanati. Another kabbalist Breuer read was R. Isaiah Horowitz (1555–1630), author of the *Shnei Luḥot ha-Bŕit* (Two Tablets of the Covenant); who was known as the "Shelah." Shelah must have held a particular appeal for Breuer. After serving as rabbi of Frankfurt, Shelah ascended to the land of Israel to fill out his days at Safed, home of Isaac Luria. Shelah's influential book interpreted the mitzvot from the perspective of Lurianic Kabbalah, helping to popularize kabbalistic interpretation among Ashkenazi Jewry. Breuer quotes the Shelah with approval in *Der Neue Kusari*, citing his notion of the multileveled nature of reality.[5] Shelah believed that the biblical discourse treats both of mundane events and of the relationship of God to His creation. The apparent discourse of the text, which runs along an intramundane axis, is in fact an analogy of the real, supernally oriented discourse. For this kabbalist, the language of Scripture has its true frame of reference in the divine realm to which the world of nature alludes.[6]

Breuer assumes such a world picture, as well as such a view of biblical language, but qualifies it with Kantian strictures. The spheres of nature and creation, while real, are not hypostatized. They are related to one another as God's freedom is to His self-limitation. They are, in fact, shorthand expressions for these states of the divine economy. But they are not contradictions of each other insofar as they stand in a relationship of temporal succession (*Nacheinander*).[7] In another sense, they stand to one another in the relation of the intelligible to the empirical: creation is the interior (*an sich*) aspect of nature.[8] By this formulation, Breuer ex-

pressly introduces Kantian language and emphasizes the perpec-
tival element of the creation/nature dichotomy. He frees himself,
as Jewish interpreters have often done, from the biblical picture of
simple temporal succession within the creation process.

Through his use of Kantian concepts such as 'intelligible' and
'empirical', however, Breuer breaks from the mystical-theosophical
tradition. He is unwilling, indeed by the logic of his argument unable, to speculate about the process of creation as such. Creation
as event is unknowable (unerkennbar) insofar as knowledge pertains only to the order of phenomena, and phenomena are the stuff
of nature, not creation. The activity of God on the first six days is
a "creation secret."[9] Our knowledge and the world of which we
have knowledge are born on the seventh day. The order of necessity and lawfulness that knowledge replicates and shapes (i.e., nature), represents what Breuer terms the "Sabbath of the Creator."

Nature is the nonimmanence of God, the withdrawal of God
from divine praxis, such that an autonomous and self-sufficient
world arises. Breuer respects the autonomy and facticity of nature
and is careful to distinguish the knowledge of nature, science, from
Torah. As such, he lays a promising basis for a coexistence (not a
synthesis!) of Torah and science.

> The "repose" of the Creator is the law of nature. Nature is a
> veil, but not an illusory one, because the "repose" of the Cre-
> ator is an authentic reality. "On the seventh day, He changed
> creation into nature and became invisible." Nature is thus as
> true as is the "repose" of the Creator. The law of nature is the
> law of the creation changed into nature; the law of the cre-
> ation out of which the Creator has vanished. The law of na-
> ture is the law of the seventh day, of the birthday of nature.[10]

On the seventh day, God withdrew from his creation and
wrapped his work of six days in Sabbath robes (Sabbathgewand-
ung; Sabbathkleider; malbushei shabbat).[11] This dress poetically
represents the law of causality and the other laws of nature. Nature is born on the seventh day as God simultaneously veils His
work and reveals its opacity to man. Breuer may well have juda-
icized Schopenhauer's veil of Maya, but there are ready Jewish
sources for garment imagery as well. Psalm 104, for example,
speaks of creation with reference to such imagery: "Bless the
LORD, my soul. LORD, my God, you are very great. You are

clothed with glory (*hod*) and majesty (*hadar*), stretching out the light like a garment (*salma*), pulling the heavens like a curtain" (verses 1-2). In his commentary, Abraham ibn Ezra states that the point of the garment is that God's plenitudinous *hod* and *hadar* render man's eyes unable to see His glory, just as a garment prevents one from seeing the person clothed by it. The Sabbath robes, which constitute nature, veil God from man's gaze at the same time that they invest nature with coherence, lawfulness, and autonomy. Similarly, in kabbalistic sources, *garment* (*malbush*) often refers to the form supernal entities must acquire in order to descend into the human realm and reveal themselves to man. Nachmanides uses a verbal form (*halbish*) in his commentary on the creation account to refer to "clothing" matter with form.[12]

Sabbath terminates creation as event and instantiates nature. From the point of view of nature, therefore, Sabbath is positive. From the point of view of creation (*Schöpfungsstandort*), however, Sabbath is rather negative. The function of Sabbath resembles that of the *Ding an sich*: it is not in the first instance a positive reality in itself as much as it is a limit—in this case, a limit of the divine activity. Sabbath is like a shadow cast by the self-limiting, retreating Creator.

The commentary of Samson Raphael Hirsch on Genesis 2:1 sheds additional light on this strangely negative role for Sabbath. Hirsch notes that the opening word in the chapter, *vaykhulu*, has the nuance "[The heaven and the earth] were brought to their destined completion." The root *kh-l-h* in Hirsch's view expresses the concept of striving for a certain end. Sabbath represents a divinely intended entelechy that the created things have at last attained. Consequently, after this stage has been reached, no new creation is possible. Hirsch challenges scientists to point to a single example of a new creation that has occurred in human experience. One cannot be found, he insists, for nature is a realm of maintenance and continuity, not of unprecedented and novel creativity. Since the seventh day, Sabbath reigns over creation. Hirsch quotes a midrash in support of his view: God is known as *Shaddai* because He told His creation, *Dai!* (enough!). Had he not told heaven and earth "enough," they would still be in a state of continuous progressive development.[13] Thus for Hirsch, Sabbath is more than a mere cessation of creative activity; it is a deliberate termination of that activity by means of which a new order, a Sabbath of Creation, arises.[14] This Sabbath provides a kind of *argumentum e silentio*:

the lack of subsequent creation indicates that creation is not autonomous and therefore implies the transcendent presence of a Creator.

For Hirsch, the Sabbath of Creation represents a limit that nonetheless trumpets God's glory. For Breuer, Sabbath tells of God's self-imposed retreat. God's self-limitation leaves nature in its wake. Nature is a seamless, seemingly endless connectedness (lückenlose Zusammenhang) behind which man cannot perceive. Breuer writes of the six days of Creation:

> They are and remain God's six days. Why touch upon this mystery? Perhaps on the first day God did wrestle something out of nothing—the transition from creation to nature was first completed with the Sabbath; indeed, this transition constitutes the essential characteristic of the Sabbath. Not only something out of nothing, but also the formation of the something lies on the other side of the Sabbath and thus on the other side of our knowledge.[15]

Although this severe dichotomization between unknowable creation and knowable nature will serve Torah well in its relation to scientific reason, it is not without its problems for Torah. After all, Torah does not speak of six days of creation in such a way that a report (Schöpfungsbericht) appears to be given of the activity that took place on those days. Could it not be the case that Torah makes available to the Jew a special kind of knowledge, which scientific reason cannot achieve? Or must Breuer insist that reason and knowledge are everywhere one, and that Torah communicates no special gnosis but addresses the will alone? This would appear to be the conclusion justified by our last chapter.

In Die Welt als Schöpfung und Natur, Breuer is content to let the matter of the six days rest behind the veil, but in the revised discussion of Der Neue Kusari he takes up the challenge. His fictional dialogue partner asks him to move beyond his metaphysical generalities of creation qua noumena and nature qua phenomena and grapple with the conflict between the cosmogonies of Torah and science. Science, he points out, does not content itself with epistemological truisms; it gives etiological accounts of individual phenomena: "But regarding this evidence, you cannot come any further with an epistemological way of thinking directed toward the whole. You make it too easy for yourself!"[16] Torah's account must be reconciled with scientific talk about the fossil record and epochs of prehistory. Facile metaphysical generalizations do not do justice to the phenomenology of science.[17]

Breuer confesses that if such a reconciliation were not possible, he would not hesitate to repudiate science, for it is science that must be justified before the court of Torah and not the other way around.[18] This admission seems subtly directed against Maimonides, who affirmed that he would have to revise his conception of Torah were science to present relevant, persuasive arguments. Breuer implicitly rejects Maimonides' controversial position, reiterating his familiar view that understanding and reason must be governed by Torah. They enjoy their legitimacy and autonomy within limits.

In response to the problem of the explicit biblical account of creation, Breuer points to a rabbinic saying. Why was the world created with ten divine utterances rather than one, the Mishnah (*Pirkei Avot* 5:1) asks. It is in order to emphasize the parallel between the creation of the world and the giving of the Torah on Sinai (which commences with the Decalogue). Breuer calls attention to the fact that the account of creation has a moral point. Thus Torah has a logic different from that of science. Science speaks to the understanding, Torah to the will. Breuer suggests that the ten words by which God created the world indicate that the creation is a kingdom of successive orders (*Stufenreich*). The heirarchy begins with undifferentiated matter and climbs toward man, the most differentiated of creatures. Each order of creation includes the preceding orders, thus to destroy any creature is to destroy a microcosm of the whole.[19]

This schema suggests the possibility that each order of creation might have developed out of the preceding order and that, therefore, Torah would be compatible with the theory of evolution. Breuer is ready to entertain the notion that God created an indeterminate something (*Etwas*) out of nothing, and that God's subsequent expression enunciated nature laws that stimulated this *Etwas* to develop according to its inherent nature. The six days then might be considered to have been epochs of great length, a view that already occurs in rabbinic midrashim. By suggesting such an evolutionary view, Breuer comes close to the views of Nachmanides and of Abraham ibn Ezra. Ibn Ezra, for example, held that primordial matter (*hule*)— which was not created by God— developed according to natural law in a sequence of self-generating acts. Similarly, Nachmanides, whom Breuer cites with approval in *Nahaliel*, distinguished between a primordial, pure creation of "what the Greeks call "hule" and a subsequent formation of entities out of that created matter.[20] Breuer thus has some traditional grounds for this attempt to make the biblical creation story congruent with science.

Curiously, however, Breuer's Kantian tendencies quickly reassert themselves. Breuer insists that any talk of a primordial something or of its evolution remains human talk that fails to describe creation as an event. He disallows ibn Ezra's cosmogonical speculations, not because they are controversial but because they are categorically mistaken. Ibn Ezra's hermeneutic, Breuer might say, even though faithful, runs off the logical track because it fails to recognize the epistemological and therefore linguistic limit imposed by the Sabbath of creation. Thus, despite a greater willingness in *Der Neue Kusari* to explore the problems generated by his thesis in *Die Welt als Schöpfung und Natur*, Breuer cannot escape from the severity of his dichotomy.

Given this dichotomy between nature as the world of phenomena and creation as the world of things-in-themselves, what implication does such a schema have for the relation of scientific reason to Torah? Creation is the inner, *an sich*, character of the world, while nature is the seemingly eternal order of causal connectedness: "Creation and nature are opposites but only from the point of view of the understanding. It is not the case that there is perhaps a creation and, next to it, nature. Rather creation and nature correspond entirely to what the philosophers call the 'thing in itself' and 'phenomena' (*Erscheinungen*)."[21]

A major implication of this ontological situation is that the laws of nature that govern the order of phenomena cannot govern the order of things-in-themselves. The understanding cannot help but know the world in terms of natural law (*Naturgesetze*), for it is nothing other than thinking nature (*denkende Natur*) itself.[22] Understanding cannot know the law-in-itself (*Gesetze an sich*), that is, the laws of Creation (*Schöpfungsgesetze*). Following Leibniz and the idealist tradition, Breuer conceives of understanding as a microcosm of nature raised to self-awareness. Insofar as the key to this process is causality, understanding, for all its harmony with nature, is unable to perceive or know creation, for the essence of creation is its acausal disconnectedness (*Zusammenhanglosigkeit*). Creation is the free realm of divine activity and is not bound by the laws of cause and effect. [23]

Modern man conceives of nature as the entirety of the world (*Weltall*). Beyond this order, nothing can be imagined by him. Thus from the modern perspective, the scriptural account of creation is simply false. It does not make sense to say that the world is 5,686 years old (the *anno mundi* year in which Breuer's book appeared). Modern man points to the fossil record and the findings of natural science that indicate a considerably older date for the world's origins. Breuer's reply reveals the main thrust of his effort to find a reconciliation between Torah and science. Those who assert that the world is millions of years old would do better, he suggests, to claim that the world is not "very old" but ageless. Nature presents itself to our understanding as an endless, beginningless chain of causal connections. "Nature is an order of unbroken connectedness. Phenomenon always leads only to phenomenon; the chain is endless or encloses itself into a circle. A beginning is to be found not in nature, only in creation."[24]

Breuer holds that the language of *beginning* and *end*, of *goal* and *purpose*, in effect presupposes creation. The language appropriate to nature is one of eternity and permanence. This view might be traced to Kant, who states in the first analogy of experience that the postulate of permanent substance is necessary to explain the various ways in which we perceive relations in time.[25] Breuer follows Kant in such a way that he takes the natural world to be an eternal succession of events concerning a permanent substance. The isomorphic organ of the world, the understanding, is unable to intuit and predicate of it beginning or end.[26] For Breuer, true notions of beginning and end are not available to pure reason. Reason is incompetent to conceive of the world as other than eternal. The question then of how the world can only be 5,686 years old, rather than millions of years old, is based on a category mistake. The different logics of creation and nature have been muddled.

One cannot compare different numbers of years from the time of creation, because the understanding cannot lead one to creation. The attempt to make creation the first event in a series of subsequently natural events is to distort creation by forcing it into a Procrustean bed of causality. I might note in passing that Breuer would give no sanction, therefore, to "scientific creationism." The logical dissimilarity of creation and nature excludes any pious attempts to harmonize their different languages in a single hermeneutic. Breuer departs from both medieval and modern creationism. For him, both the scientific account and the scriptural account are true within their own frames of reference.

Breuer offers a dialogue between himself and a natural scientist as an example of this newly won compatibility. The two reach a happy accord. The scientist acknowledges that his research pre-suppose the validity of natural law that operates in the closed cir-cle of the understanding, and Breuer announces that he can live with whatever the scientist discovers (which seems to be little more than a case of Platonic *anamnesis*) if the scientist confesses that he can never penetrate to the world of creation.

> Research the world of the resting God, and whatever results you discover in the honest endeavor, respecting the age of the earth and its development in general, will be authoritative for me, providing you emphasize that one condition under which your entire research stands and without which you are blind: the value of natural law. But do not extend the natural law to the world of the creating God. Your science knows nothing, nor could it know anything, of this world. For the natural law, which is God's natural law, veils this world. So let us part in peace.[27]

Whatever victory Breuer seems to have won here, however, is Pyrrhic. He has argued that the natural world presents itself to us in a certain way, but he has not shown why this way is inadequate. True, the world as nature is a world without either beginning or goal, but it is not a self-contradictory or an incoherent world. The only deficiency of a world conceived wholly as nature is that it does not admit of being viewed as creation. Does Breuer beg this question? Furthermore, if the language of creation is categorically unlike the language of nature, which is after all our language, how can talk of creation be meaningful? Why is it not empty?

Some of these questions were anticipated by Oskar Wolfsberg.[28] Wolfsberg claimed that Breuer evaded a genuine con-frontation between science and Torah; that Breuer's system is thor-oughly deductive, descending from dogmatic presuppositions and avoiding a scientific, presumably inductive method; that Breuer's conclusions sound too much like his premises; and that Breuer proceeds with "the arrogance of the dogmatician" who knows ev-erything in advance without a shred of evidence. Wolfsberg be-lieves that Breuer's ostensible engagement with the claims of natural science is actually a "brilliant escape" that protects him in advance from the real conflicts.

There is some truth in this critique, although not entirely for the reasons Wolfsberg stressed. It was not Breuer's intention to pro-mote a grand dialogue between science and Torah. He scrupulously avoided the way of synthesis as a matter of principle. Not wanting to bring the creation traditions of Judaism into conversation with modern science, Breuer addressed himself to the fundamental, logical characteristics, as he saw them, of each system. Thus, methodologically, Breuer is doing metaphysics. The scientific method that his critic expects him to practice is not appropriate to his endeavor. In the preface to his book, Breuer announces that he intends for the work to serve as a prolegomenon to a system of Jewish philosophy.[29] *System*, for such a philosopher, refers to a structure of deductions from fundamental, unshakable premises. For Breuer, these premises derive partly from his "dogmatic" convictions and partly from the inherent problems he believes he has found in contemporary epistemology and ontology. Conviction and philosophical argumentation support one another in his metaphysics. To the extent that Breuer is deductive and systematic, he can hardly be blamed for doing what religious metaphysicians have always done.

What can reasonably be expected is that any metaphysics honestly confront its own dilemmas. The chief dilemma which Breuer's thesis raises is this: By establishing a coherent and autonomous realm of nature, the concept of creation becomes gratuitous. No one other than the dogmatist needs to speak of creation, for nature stands perfectly on its own. This conclusion, however, is intolerable. To accept it would be to doom Torah to the level of an intellectual scandal and thereby depart from all previous Jewish philosophy. However much Breuer tends in this direction, it is a step which he never allows himself to take. As much as he is ready to critique the nature of reason and to delimit its role, he cannot allow Judaism to become divorced from the language of reason. For Torah to turn its back on reason would be a cowardly abdication of its throne.

Breuer does confront his own dilemma. He turns toward the deconstruction of nature, seeking to qualify its autonomy and coherence. There is something about nature as such, not just its beginning or end, that demands the framework of creation. Here Breuer can gain some ground with a traditional argument. In medieval Jewish philosophy this something is the problem of miracles. Jewish philosophy has always had to make sense out of the biblical miracles while holding to the existence of an orderly, coherent natural world. The two alternatives to this dilemma:—Epicureanism, which severed Providence entirely from nature, and Kalam, which associated Providence with every event in nature,—

have seldom been welcome options.[30] Jewish philosophers have had to preserve both the facticity of supernatural miracles and the lawful integrity of an autonomous natural world. The concept of a free divine *creatio ex nihilo*, which gave nature the sort of character in which miracles were possible, linked the phenomenology of the miracle to an argument from creation. As in the Jewish tradition, so too in Breuer: the discussion of miracles falls under the logic of creation.

A useful and important counterpoint to Breuer is found in Maimonides. In his discussion on whether the world is created or eternal, Maimonides rejected the Aristotelian thesis of eternity in part because it left no room for miracles. Maimonides wanted to remain with the Aristotelian framework of a world governed by divine reason possessed of regularity and coherence, but he could not deny certain fundamental, nonnatural novelties: the Red Sea did part, and the Torah was given on Mount Sinai. The problem was that to admit exceptional breaches in the laws of nature would be to imply changes, and therefore defects, in the will of the Lord of nature. It also implied that God was less than omniscient. If indeed God knew the future course of events, then he would not have to alter the contemporary structure of nature in order to bring about the miracle to resolve the particular exigency. Maimonides' answer was already, as he relates, noticed by the rabbinic sages: miracles are not, in fact, disruptions of the natural order necessitated by some historical circumstances; rather, miracles were emplaced in that order at the time of its creation.[31] Nature and miracles are part of the same order of lawfulness; nothing miraculous is contrary to nature. God's reason and will, which govern nature, did not have to change, nor was nature's coherence disrupted by the miraculous. The concept of creation synthesizes miracle and nature into a single comprehensive system.

Breuer differs sharply from Maimonides. From Breuer's Kantian perspective, the question of whether the natural order is disturbed by miracles is the wrong question because it is a precritical question. The emphasis in the analysis of the miraculous ought to be on the experiencing subject rather than on the purportedly experienced object. With this shift in emphasis, Breuer departs from most prior teaching on miracles, though he does preserve certain similarities to Judah Halevi. The disruption of nature just means a disruption in our means of perceiving and hence of constructing nature. A miracle is not the occurrence of some event within the framework of nature yet extracategorical to it—that is absurd. Rather, 'miracle' refers to the perception of some event through some dispensation other than our ordinary perceptual apparatus.[32] Miracles are not, therefore, events in the world that lie "side by side" natural events, differing only in their ultimate origins, as Maimonides would have it. If miracles were only more startling versions of natural events (for example, if the miracle were constituted merely by the fact that the Red Sea piled up into a wall rather than flowed normally), they could not, logically, exist. For the essential characteristic of a miracle is that it lies entirely outside of the system of context created by the understanding. It is not the case that miracles are hard to understand given what we know about the world. Miracles are impossible to understand because they are unassimilable by the understanding. Nor is it the case that their causes are difficult or impossible to determine: they have no causes. "Either a miracle is imperceptible or it ceases to be a miracle the moment we perceive it."[33]

Like creation, miracles are not a part of nature or, strictly speaking, of the experience of causality. Miracles do indeed derive from and indicate the world as creation, but in terms entirely different from those of Maimonides. Although Breuer has departed substantially from prior tradition, his thesis bears certain similarities to Judah Halevi's. Halevi rejected the Aristotelian notion that prophecy comes about through the perfection of the human intellect and through its direction toward the active intellect. He emphasized the movement of God toward man and the activation within man, by God, of a capacity for prophetic perception, a *sensus propheticus* (*ha-inyan ha-elohi*).[34] Breuer reaches the same conclusion. The sort of perception that man needs to "perceive" miracles can only be granted by God. "Whoever experiences a miracle becomes a prophet by reason of this experience. For at that moment he has arrived at a glimpse into the activity of God, which is not granted through means of human perception but through direct observation."[35] Halevi also held that the miracle does not communicate a specific content but discloses a presence. The point of the miracle is not to confirm or assert something but to reveal God. In Breuer, the experience of the miraculous is also sui generis and self-certifying. "The legitimization of the miracle is the miracle itself."[36]

In this special case, the natural world, which is to say our construction through the categories of the understanding of a natural world, is penetrated by a supernatural perception. The world as nature suddenly opens up to the world as creation. (This brings to mind Schopenhauer's doctrine of aesthetic perception, where the world as representation suddenly opens up to an Idea.) One might think that Breuer would make much of this exception to the coherence of nature, but he does not. He might have thought that miracles are too controversial, his thesis notwithstanding, to strengthen the foundation of his theology of creation. More likely, Breuer was led by the logic of his argument to downplay the importance of miracles, but not, say, for Maimonidean reasons. Maimonides deemphasized miracles, and some of his followers denied them altogether for reasons of rationalism. Breuer deemphasizes miracles not to protect rationalism but because of the centrality of what he calls the "historical miracle" (*Geschichtswunder*) of the people Israel. For him, history, not nature, is the scene of God's most perfect revelation. Creation is fulfilled, as we will see, by Torah, by Israel's struggle for Torah in history. Accordingly, the discussion of miracles, while making a point about creation, is not the main emphasis in Breuer's deconstruction of nature.

Breuer's main approach to qualifying the autonomy and establishing the partial incoherence of the natural world is not the medieval problem of miracles, but the modern problem of the *Ding an sich*. Nature does not merely break down in exceptional cases at its borders; it breaks down at the very center of our human experience. The problem of the thing-in-itself, in Breuer's view, has never been solved by the philosophers because it has not been related to creation.

In philosophy, the thing-in-itself remains an essentially negative concept: a limit to our understanding except when it erroneously receives positive content through a muddled inclusion back into the phenomenal world as, for example, a first or a final cause.[37] The attempt to find a content for the concepts results in a confusion of logical categories. For Breuer, the root problem is that the philosophers are unaware of the Sabbath of Creation. They do not "remember the Sabbath" (Exodus 20:8). Breuer implies that because the gentile philosophers do not actually remember Sabbath in an halakhic sense they are unable to understand that the Sabbath, in an ontological sense, prevails over creation. They cannot penetrate through the Sabbath robes to creation, the true content of the thing-in-itself, so they locate the thing-in-itself in nature. Because they are not observant Jews, Kant and Fichte, for example, fail to achieve the ontological insights, the "creation standpoint," that alone could solve the dilemma of the thing-in-itself. Philosophy remains either a formal intuition pointing airily in the right direction or a furious denial of that direction. Promise without fulfillment.

The failure of the philosophers to locate the thing-in-itself in creation leads to a conception of nature as an order of abstract generality, of "mere Being." "Ultimately, nature remains for them the merely existent."[38] The laws of thought describe the laws of Being per se. This conception only makes sense, however, if Being is nothing more than an order of phenomena connected by generally valid laws. Philosophers and scientists can and do speak of that which exists (*das Seiende*) in a logically appropriate way, but they cannot speak of the novel individual events that lie outside of the "generally valid." They cannot speak in their own discourse of the unique experiences of concrete individuals. They cannot speak of "you" or "I." Breuer will argue that creation is necessary to account for the radical individuation of reality.

> [The scientist's] answer is inadequate respecting all that which is unique in existence, that is, respecting unique individuals; their suffering, joy, life and death, their unique beauty and ugliness— their unique pathos; respecting all that maintains itself under the [Sabbath] garment in suffering, billionfold, thus-and-not-otherwise-Being (*So-und-nicht-anders-Sein*).[39]

Breuer's attempt to develop a need for creation as the source of nature relies on Schopenhauer's doctrine of individuation. Perception—the stuff of science—has a generally valid character, whereas willing is atomic, anomic. Will, not perception, relates man directly to the world-in-itself. Breuer believes that he has found a crucial incoherence in the world as nature and therefore in the rational, scientific, discourse that describes that world. Nature and its *Wissenschaften* cannot get from Being to "me." Dilthey might well have said the same. Hermann Cohen, who argued that religion discovers individuality in a way that ethics, due to its universal character, cannot, has a similar line of thought. For Breuer, only a theology of creation can reconcile the general with the personal, the universal with the particular. "Only the teaching of the world as creation and as nature can reconcile the general order of existence with 'me.' "[40]

We have seen in chapter 2 that Breuer regards individuation with deep suspicion. Individuation is a metaphysical and an existential problem, the resolution of which requires a willed act of submission to the cosmic, creation nomos and a corresponding incorporation within the metaphysical peoplehood of Israel, *knesset*

Israel. Asserting that creation is the ground of individuation thereby imputes a certain negative dimension to creation. The instability of creation, its need for fulfillment in revelation and redemption, its claim upon consciousness in the form of craving, and so on, illustrate this negativity. Nonetheless, Breuer remains somewhat ambivalent about individuation. He not only needs it as a crucial philosophical category for his argument, he also has a certain esteem for the distinct, nuanced reality of individual consciousness. While no existentialist, Breuer echoes the protests of a Kierkegaard or a Rosenzweig against all efforts to assimilate the concrete into an abstract, general system. Breuer celebrates, not without contradiction, the personal dimension of experience.

CREATION AS RADICAL PARTICULARITY: A "THEOLOGY OF *I*"

The attempt to get "from Being to *me*" and to discover creation en route at the heart of nature led Breuer, as it led Rosenzweig, to take issue with idealism. Breuer begins where nineteenth century German idealism began, in deep disquietude over the meaning and status of the *Ding an sich*. While a critique of scientific reason was the aim of *Die Welt als Schöpfung und Natur*, a critique of idealism is the target of *Elischa*. The search for the personal demands a "theology of *I*" that would explain why philosophers cannot understand the *I* in purely natural terms, that is, in a language that does not make reference to creation. It must be argued that individual, personal, unique existence discloses creation in the midst of nature, and that purely naturalistic methodologies, in this case the method of idealist epistemology, cannot help but lose the *I*. In *Elischa* and *Naḥaliel*, Breuer offers a number of meditations on the ontic situation of the *I*, each one exploring experiences of loss, love, pain, or joy. These experiences disclose, in Breuer's view, the created derivativenss of the *I* and give the lie to idealist theories of the subject as the source rather than the result of creation.

The title, *Elischa*, refers to the story of the prophet when he was abandoned by his master, Elijah (2 Kings, ch. 2). Elijah is lifted into heaven, and Elisha feels boundless confusion and grief. Only his possession of his master's mantle gives him the strength to go on and the authority and ability to continue his work. Breuer turned to this story during his personal bereavement following the death of his father in 1926. At a time when his own aloneness became painfully real, he read the story in such a way that it pointed toward a sublimation and redirection of grief into a life of discipleship. Breuer works out the meaning of individual life in terms of metaphysical childhood (*metaphysische Kindschaft*).[41] Childhood becomes an axiological vocation, which lifts individuated existence into the unitive realm of the Torah through consciousness of being a created being (*eine Geschöpflichkeit*).

Speaking of his own struggle to regain meaning after his father's death, Breuer argues that childhood is a metaphysical calling. By understanding parenthood from an ontological and not simply a biological perspective, one can grapple with one's own unique derivativeness and live out its consequences. Breuer tells us that he began to learn the true depth of parenthood in his youth while watching his father learn Torah.[42] He gained from his father the *Erlebnis* of Jewish history and was able, by learning Judaism at his side, to take the eternal life of the nation into himself. Only this experience of parenthood and childhood as a dialectical involvement in Torah enables parents and children to live out their biological roles as a metaphysical calling. The philosophers know nothing of this, and it is no accident that they scarcely mention in their systems crucial facts of personal existence such as our status as children.

> Is it not most odd and surprising that in the metaphysics of the philosophers hardly a modest little place for parenthood and childhood is to be found? That parenthood and childhood occur of necessity only in philosophical ethics, and there with a fleeting mention? For the philosophers, who do not know of the creation, parenthood and childhood constitute an essentially natural relationship.[43]

Rosenzweig began the *Star of Redemption* (1921) with a meditation on death in order to challenge the atemporal, amortal presumptions of idealism. Breuer's reflection on parenthood serves much the same function. Parents, like birth and death, are a scandal for philosophy. Philosophy treats man as a universal phenomenon whether under the aegis of a timeless epistemic subject or under that of a timeless moral subject. But man is not a Platonic Idea, nor is he Hermann Cohen's colorless, ethical-rational being (*sittliches Vernunftswesen*).[44] Man is the tiniest and most idiosyncratic particular piece of Being imaginable, yet the philosophers persist in the self-serving illusion that the *I* of man is a world *I* (*Welt-Ich*).[45] Consequently, they cannot understand parents on the level of metaphysics, but only as a topic in biology or ethics.

Breuer appeals to this inconsistency in the study of nature: if we are to understand man as he actually is, as a tiny, nuanced piece of Being (*die winzigster Bruchteil des Seins*). then we must understand him in the facticity of his derivativeness and individuality.

How does man derive metaphysically from his parents, and how does this relation confirm and reveal creation in the midst of nature? Breuer sees the creative activity of parents as a recapitulation of God's initial creation of the first human pair. God formed man from earth and spirit. Breuer interprets these two constitutent elements to signify 'is' (*Sein*) and 'ought' (*Sollen*). *Sein* and *Sollen*, however, are still universal, impersonal terms. A third element, 'will' (*Wollen*), is necessary to make a man an individuated, inflected being. Will affects a synthesis of a being who could have been nothing-but-being and of a being who could have been nothing-but-normative, into a being that is uniquely a composite of both. "Neither the 'ought' of the soul, nor the 'is' of nature produces the autarchic (*selbstherrlich*) *I*. The *I* is, in nature, will; conscious will."[46]

As we have seen, man discovers himself to be a dynamic will rather than a static natural or moral entity. In the process, he discovers that his will is what maintains him, but not, however, what created him. To discover oneself is to discover one's createdness. To be is to be a creature caused to be out of the world of nature and the world of creation, whose essence is to maintain itself but not to create itself. Breuer seems to follow Samson Raphael Hirsch's assertion that the world of Being is a world of the maintenance of created forms. Their origination, however, belongs to the world of divine creativity.

The awareness of metaphysical childhood is not only retrospective but prospective. Given creation, God was not yet satisfied. For creation, by definition, is not nature. It is not just something that is. Creation has a telos. The purpose of creation is revelation, Torah. Parents fulfill their mission by giving their creation a telos: they are not merely factors in the conditionality of *Sein*, but also in that of *Sollen*. Elisha inherits Elijah's mantle. Breuer receives his father's Talmud. Jewish parenthood gives the formal condition of all parenthood—imparting *Sollen*—a real content in a real context. Jewish childhood is the learning and living of the purposes of creation (*Lehrerkindschaft*).[47]

In *Der Neue Kusari*, Breuer further develops his views on the metaphysical nature of parenthood. Given his thesis that the will is that which has experience of the things-in-themselves, parents are the crucial factors in conditioning the way the will relates to the world. Parents determine that one experiences the thing-in-itself just so and not otherwise.

> Human parents belong not to the sphere of physics but to metaphysics. If the *I* experiences, by means of Mr. Weiler, the givenness of the world (*Gegebenheit der Welt*) as the irrevocable thusness (*Sosein*) of its will, so also does the *I* experience, by means of Mr. Weiler's parents, the derivativeness of this thusness. The world is not given to it for the first time, it is not pristine for the *I*; rather, the *I* takes over the givenness of the world by means of its already formed will, which was itself formed out of an archetypal, formative bonding with other *I*'s.[48]

The crux of his thesis is that the *I* perceives its world in a mediated fashion such that the mediation per se is not a mere instance of a universal, categorical schema (as it is for Kant) but a highly particularized, derivative schema. It is the *I* as will that experiences the deepest aspects of the world. Parents are those factors that determine the precise composure of the will. Parents are the transcendental condition for volitional experience. They are, therefore, a topic in metaphysics.

In *Elischa*, Breuer treats parenthood as what signifies the derivativeness, hence the createdness, of the *I*. Both parents and the Sabbath therefore have a similar function. They indicate createdness and mark a border between creation and nature. In a commentary to Leviticus 19:3, Breuer elaborates:

> "As 'personality' (*'ish*) should you revere your parents and guard My Sabbath." The word of God here presses parenthood and Sabbath into a single lapidary sentence, probably above all to establish forever their inner, essential likeness. The Sabbath is a memorial to the creation. The purposive creation of God remains in the extant world of the Creator's repose; the world as nature. It is the lot of man to complete, in

serving sovereignty, the 'ought' of the world as creation. Week after week, the Sabbath proclaims this.

The Jewish parents are also, like the Jewish Sabbath, a memorial of creation. While the Sabbath rips the veil off the world-as-nothing-but-nature and uncovers its creation origin, Jewish parenthood annihilates the delusion of the *I* as the subject of Being per se, as the bearer of norms per se. It annihilates every phantom of the sovereignty of the *I* and leads the *I*, as a created personality, before the throne of God-Creator. The Jewish Sabbath protects above all against divinizing nature; Jewish parenthood protects against self-divinization.[49]

If a Jew has abandoned father and mother, he can rediscover his vocation and purpose by finding his way back to them again. If father and mother have abandoned their child, as they do in death, there is no way back. The only salvation available lies beyond the particularity of the parents in the parenthood of God. Human parenthood is penultimate and symbolic; the ultimate home of the self-transcending *I* is God. The greater part of *Elischa* argues a case for the created derivativeness of man from God.

How does the *I* become conscious of its transcendental origin and essence? The *I* has no immediate intuition of this essence, nor does its essence become apparent to it in self-reflection. Breuer follows Kant in denying the *I* any intuition into itself qua substance. The *I* remains a logical condition that explains, in a transcendental way, why our experience is as it is. Although his metaphysical conclusions far exceed any of which Kant could approve, Breuer is careful, as a Kantian, to avoid reification of substances.[50]

Given creation, God was not yet pleased, for creation is by definition not a static condition but a purposive movement. The goal of creation is revelation. What existed prior to the process of creation and what is destined to become the content of revelation is unknowable; it is matter-in-itself (*Materie an sich*), that which is simply extant (*das Seiende schlechthin*).[51] In a mystery that remains his alone, God shaped and named the merely extant matter-in-itself. The report of creation in Scripture gives us the barest sense of this process. Matter-in-itself, Breuer infers, has two aspects: it is an undetermined something, yet to be formed, and it is something that is being formed and receiving form: "The matter in itself is that which assumes form but is now formless (*das gestaltlos Gestaltbare*). In its formlessness lies its namelessness. In its propensity toward formedness lies its ability to take on a name. It is the unrevealed object on which revelation becomes active."[52]

Breuer's depiction of potentiality within primeval matter strongly resembles Nachmanides' description of the creation process. In Nachmanides' thought, God created primeval matter (Breuer's matter-in-itself) out of absolute nothing. This matter is *tohu* (Gen.1:2). In the Talmud (T. B. Kiddushin 40b), the rabbis relate *tohu* to an expression for reflection or meditation, indicating that should one reflect on this matter, one could name it whatever one wishes. *Tohu* has no proper name (Breuer's *Namenslosigkeit*), for it has, as yet, no form. Nachmanides believes that *bohu* is the form (*tsurah*) with which *tohu* is "dressed" (*nilbeshet*) by God. Thus, in Nachmanides' view as in Breuer's, primeval matter passes from a stage of potentiality into actuality; from linguistic neutrality to linguistic positivity (*Namensfähigkeit*), before the creation of any actual entity.

Corresponding to the polarity of the raw material of creation Breuer posits a polarity within the Creator himself. God is an unrevealed, absolute Subject (*anokhi, Gott an sich*) who exists independently of matter. God is not the *I* of matter, but *I* alone.[53] But God is also the Creator who is engaged with matter. Creation is thus revelation, in the sense that creation reveals something of a God who has become active within it. Creation is no revelation, however, of God in himself.

Matter-in-itself does not become creation until it receives form. Breuer permits himself somewhat freer play here than he did in *Die Welt als Schöpfung und Natur* with respect to speculation about the creation process. Unlike the formulation there, the completion of creation is not so much a severence or truncation as it is a fulfillment. What takes place in the act of creation is that matter is given its "concept" by the Creator: "The completed creation is the unity of creation fact (*Schöpfungstatbestand*) and creation concept (*Schöpfungsbegriff*). It is a unity willed by God. The form of the completed creation is the form of the God who reveals himself and, at the same time, the form of the revealed creation; because only by virtue of this form do God and creation become revelatory."[54]

The dialectic between a partially revealed, effective God and a wholly hidden God outside of his creation recalls, of course, the kabbalistic conception of God as *ein sof* and as Sefirot. God is at once both remote from and radically engaged in creation. Breuer discusses this dialectical relation of God and creation in *Naḥaliel* as well. Breuer cites Isaiah 43:7, "All who are linked to My name, whom I have created, formed, and made for My glory (kavod)." In creating, God reveals his kavod. Kavod, Breuer notes, is a social term. It requires relationality, referring to a quality that emerges in social interaction between persons. Just as society is the place where man's kavod emerges, so too, creation is the place (makom kavodo) where God's glory emerges. Creation, however, is not God's glory as such, just as human society is not man's glory but the condition for its emergence. Both God's absolute I and the absolute inwardness of his creation are unrevealed. Only the relationality of God to His creation; the form-imparting and form-accepting intercourse of God and matter, are revealed. The inner reality of both poles of the relation remains a "creation secret."[55] Nonetheless, Breuer does venture a supposition about the inner reality of created things. Insofar as they have been called out of nothingness, nothingness continues to cling to them. Yet insofar as they continue to exist, they must oppose the embrace of nothingness moment by moment. Thus created things are the negations of nothingness: the will to exist and to be something pervades and defines them.

Creation as partial revelation of God's form-giving activity is not consummated until man appears: man is form-accepting matter, such that his form most fully expresses and renders intelligible the form-giving activity of the Creator. In both Elischa and Nahaliel, Breuer develops this view in the form of a commentary on Genesis 1:26, "Let us make man in our image." The question that must be answered is why God speaks in the plural. The plural "us" refers, according to Breuer, to both God and created matter. The two cooperate in the formation of man. "In our image" refers both to the image of the God who has clothed matter with form (tzelem ha-malbish tzelem) and to the image of form-accepting matter (tzelem ha-labush tzelem). In positing matter as one of the referents for "us," Breuer follows Nachmanides once again. For him, earth provides man's body, while God contributes man's spirit. Man resembles both the celestials and the terrestrials.[56]

As one who, like his Creator, imposes form upon matter, man names things. In a state of primal joy, he exults in the recognition that his concepts and the being of things correspond with each other. Names are the concepts that man, the lordly form-giving perceiver imparts to the created things that he perceives.[57] Man designates each thing as a "you" relative to his I. In an instant, however, the satisfying, epistemological mutuality of I and you, subject and object, is shattered. As we have seen, a wave of feeling, of will, wells up in man and storms over him, upsetting the peaceful correspondence of the perceptual relationship. Man becomes aware of himself as a being of will, who wills himself against the menacing nothingness of the world and who is willed by that world. Suddenly he is full of longing, he turns his back on the names he has uttered, and the first human tear drops to the earth. There is no *you* to which man in his totality corresponds; no *you* that truly answers his name-giving call. He has no "helpmeet for him."

With the creation of woman, the awful loneliness of the *I* is ended. With woman, man can at last experience unity that is not simultaneously separation. The love between man and woman, as that between parent and child, is thoroughly metaphysical. It is intimated, proleptically, by the cooperation of God and matter in the creation of man. While the world that man constructs out of intelligible things, phenomena, is real, the world that man constructs out of intelligible things, phenomena, is real, the world that God constructs for man—the relation of man and woman—is both real and eternal. Breuer quotes the language of the wedding service: God has formed for man an "eternal construction," the consummated dwelling in which is the first commandment of the Torah.

Were Breuer a sexually oriented mystic, the fulfillment of creation might occur here. But of course it does not. Creation is consummated not in man alone, nor in man and woman, but in the mitzvot; in the Torah. Man can impose form on the world-as-representation. He cannot will lawfulness onto the world-in-itself unless he wills Torah. In the example above, it is not sexuality per se that consummates creation, but the mitzvah of sexuality. The Torah creates accord between the unfulfilled, conflicting levels of reality. The Torah brings an ultimate, true Sabbath to the enduring, unresolved creation process.

CREATION AND THE "GIVENNESS" OF OBJECTS

Before exploring Breuer's doctrine of revelation, we must return to the analysis of those experiences that ground the *I's* sense of its own createdness. Breuer has argued in *Elischa* that we must affirm creation against idealism as a way of accounting for man's epistemic or experiential intuition that his *I* does not perceive the world as it is in itself, but only the world as it appears. There is a givenness to the world in which man the perceiver functions. Yet the world of appearances is in some way internal to man as well. Does idealism, with its denial of the extra-mental givenness of objects, best explain man's epistemic situation? Breuer cannot accept this. Creation, the givenness of things and subjects in their radical particularity within a divinely posited framework, is the antidote to all varieties of idealism. On the other hand, God lets man have a hand in creating that very framework. Man apprehends objects as moments in a *Vorstellungswelt* of his own construction. He apprehends them, that is, as features of himself. Thus: "The object of the perceiving *I* is not the creation as such. The creation as such is the created object of its Father, God. The object of the perceiving *I* is the formed *I* as child of the formed creation [*das geformte ich als Kind der gerformten Schöpfung*]."[58]

Man as *I* is both knower and known. In perceiving and knowing, man knows himself. Breuer has in mind here, I believe, Leibniz's doctrine of inherent ideas or Fichte's deduction of consciousness. In both, what the *I* is shaping into a world already exists within the *I* itself. In *Elischa*, Breuer accepts the notion that the data of consciousness are prepositioned in consciousness, but he argues that this can only be true because of creation.

Leibniz had argued that all the ideas the mind brings before itself are already inherent within it.[59] The mind is windowless and self-contained, storing the ideas God has placed there. God preserves our beings and affects us in such a way that we think the thoughts that we do. It does seem, of course, that things affect one another in the world and that this interaction is what generates the ideas. For Leibniz, however, God is our only immediate external object. The separate things or substances do not affect one another; they correspond to one another in mute, continent correlation. This correspondence is guaranteed by their Creator.

In Breuer's view, God's initial act of creation, whereby the structure of man is synthesized, takes the place of Leibniz's ongoing guarantee of correspondence. The philosophers have tried in vain to ground the givenness of objects without reference to creation. (Apparently, even Leibniz is guilty of this error.) Either they locate the givenness of objects wholly outside of the *I*, or they locate it within the *I*. If objects are located within the *I*, as is the case in idealism, what can serve to certify that these objects are not, without remainder, dreams of the subject? That is, what enables us to talk of objects at all? Would we not merely have to talk

of a self-contained, "absolute subject" as, indeed, Fichte does? If
they locate the givenness of objects outside of the subject, as Kant
does with the thing-in-itself, the *I* is still the decisive factor in cer-
tifying the existence of objects, insofar as it perceives the phenomenal form of objects and then, by transcendental deduction, infers
the things-in-themselves. In both cases, the givenness of objects is
entirely dependent upon the subject.

Breuer believes that he has solved the problem of how to establish the facticity of objects without reference to the perceiving
I. The *I* is a condition of the world as revealed creation; indeed the
I of man only arises in conjunction with creation as revealed creation. The *I* knows nothing of creation as it is in itself (*Schöpfung
an sich*). The representations of the *I*; the world of nature, are
nothing other than the "formed forms" of creation existing micro-
cosmically within the *I*. The true facticity of objects is located
without reference to the *I* in the creation-in-itself.

> The givenness of the objects of perception is nothing other
> than the givenness of creation. But it is not the case that the
> world as revealed perception is a copy of the creation in itself.
> The creation-in-itself; the absolute object of the Creator, does
> not enter into the perception of the perceiving *I*; it is not re-
> vealed to the perceiving *I*. The object of perception is merely
> the formed form of creation within the *I*, just as the subject
> of perception is only the forming form in the *I*. Outside of the
> forming form and the formed form in the *I* yawns, as far as
> the *I* is concerned—nothing [*das Nichts*].[60]

As in Leibniz, the *I* is something of a windowless monad
whose immediate environment is, if not the divine, an order of
greater divinity (perhaps the pleroma of the Sefirot?) than itself.
For Breuer, the *I* is located in the creation-in-itself, about which it
knows nothing. All the *I* knows is the creation-as-revelation; the
creation that discloses itself as intelligible within the internal,
epistemic process of man. "The formative element in the *I* is the
subject. That which has been formed in the *I* is the object. The
formative form perceives. The formed form is perceived. Only the
form is perceptible. Only it is in the percept."[61]

With idealism, Breuer affirms that our world arises out of the
structural relations of our own being. Like Fichte's world-
generating polarity of *I* and not-*I*, Breuer's 'forming form' and
'formed form' produce a world from within the subject. But unlike

idealism, this world is independently grounded in a divine reality without which, in Breuer's view, it cannot help but collapse into the *I*. Were it not for creation, the *I* would be alone with its world. Given creation, only God, in a sense, is truly alone. The absolute *I* of God, remote from creation in the inner recesses of its unrelatedness, is wholly alone and unrevealed.

To conclude this discussion, it can now be seen that Breuer has two main concepts of creation. In *Die Welt als Schöpfung und Natur* and *Der Neue Kusari*, creation is the inner aspect of the natural world against which perception forms and about which knowledge forms. In *Elischa*, creation is the setting of objective givenness in which the monadic subject generates its world. That subject is nonetheless aware of the limits and derivativeness of its world and itself through experiences of radical particularity. Finally, in *Nahaliel*, both trains of thought come together, and creation is presented as an unfulfilled dynamic within reality whose completion and pacification require the human practice of the mitzvot.

Common to all of these presentations is the conviction that creation solves a recurrent philosophical problem. Both idealist metaphysics and natural science, Breuer believes, stand in need of creation, indeed of Judaism, in order to account adequately for the way the world is. Philosophy and science require Judaism for their own ultimate intelligibility. It is Torah, with its story of creation, that establishes the context in which reason can even begin to give a phenomenologically adequate account of reality. We are now in a position to examine Breuer's doctrine of Torah revelation as such.

REVELATION AND THE CREATION OF CONSCIOUSNESS

Breuer's theory of revelation sets out from a methodological premise not unlike that underlying his views on creation. The necessity of revelation may be derived from the inadequacy of the concepts of both nature *and* creation to describe the lives that we are evidently capable of leading. In Breuer's terms, the insight that the *I* achieves into its derivativeness or createdness still does not bring it over the threshold of the life suitable for it. In a sense, Breuer uses the same polemic that Jewish medieval thinkers such as Saadiah employed: revelation is needed because unassisted reason cannot know the specific requirements of moral, human existence.[62] On this account, revelation supplements a kind of epistemological lacuna in the fabric of human experience. In Breuer, however, the prerevelatory consciousness does not merely lack a grasp of normative detail; it dwells in the outer darkness, unable to realize what it was created to accomplish. Breuer's systematic disprivileging of human reason enables him to posit a content and goal for revelation that are not reducible wholly to rational categories. Breuer therefore avoids a problem inherent in medieval rationalism: revelation is not per force an addendum to the project of secular reason. Revelation rather is the frame in which that project properly operates.

Revelation (*Offenbarung; hitgalut*) is conceptually necessitated by the fact that man as *I* cannot know what he ought to do. The makeup of man is such that, within the context of his created uniqueness, he is aware of a normative, and not purely actual, dimension of his being. He is aware not only of his *Sein* but of his *Sollen*. This awareness, however, is purely formalistic. Man knows that his *I* is partially 'ought' without experiencing a specific content for this insistent yet empty dimension of his being. To state the matter even more severely, man does not experience 'ought' as much as he experiences that he is not entirely 'is'. An external content for man's formal intuition of 'ought' is not a regrettable corruption of rational ethics (so-called heteronomy); it is essential for ethics. If divine revelation does not provide the content, then pernicious and dehumanizing moralities, generated by the State, sweep in to fill the void. The conflict between the ethics of Torah and the ethics of this world is the story of Jewish existence among the nations.

It should be apparent from this brief précis that revelation functions like creation. Creation completes the world as conceived by natural philosophy, while revelation completes the world as conceived (or misconceived) by moral philosophy. Creation, furthermore, is completed by revelation, which, as the reference to the existence of Israel among the nations suggests, is completed by redemption. The growth of the concept of revelation out of that of creation cannot help but remind us of Franz Rosenzweig's linkage of these two concepts in *The Star of Redemption*.

The linkage of creation and revelation long antedates both Breuer and Rosenzweig. The essential relation of these two concepts was already accomplished in rabbinic thought. The *Sifre* to Deuteronomy (Piska 37) interprets Proverbs 8:22, "The LORD possessed me as the beginning of His way" ("me" ostensibly refers to wisdom), to refer to Torah.[63] Torah becomes, on this interpretation, a preexistent reality. The rabbis believed that the Torah was God's first creation, preceding the creation of the world by hundreds of generations. In a famous midrash (*Bereshit Rabbah* I:1) we learn that just as a builder consults plans to construct a dwelling before he does the actual work, so God first drew up a blueprint (the Torah) then used it as the plan for the world. In rabbinic thought, the Torah given at Sinai is also the design chart for the cosmos.

This highly suggestive notion was greatly elaborated in the literature of the Kabbalah. Scholem points out that the kabbalists developed an ontological relationship between creation and revelation, not only as an inheritance from earlier rabbinic speculation but as a consequence of their own symbolic discourse. They operated with two distinct levels of discourse about the Torah. First, Torah was conceived in terms of divine emanations in the imagery of the Sefirot. This schema entails a description of the mysterious process of progressive creation, one stage of which is Torah revelation. The second image envisions torah as a collection of, or even as one great, divine name(s). In this symbol system, the emphasis is on language, the medium by which Torah becomes manifest in creation. Scholem argues that the existence of these two parallel symbolic frameworks for discourse about the Torah led to an analogy and eventually an identity between the processes of creation and revelation in Kabbalah.[64] The kabbalists took the classical rabbinic belief that God used the Torah to create the world and deepened it to mean that the harmonious and lawful structure of the world is nothing other than the harmonious and lawful structure of the Torah, because—as God's name—the Torah manifests God's Being and power, which is nothing other than what creates and sustains the world. To understand the Torah as a complex of divine names is to understand cosmology and physics.

These lines of thought transformed revelation from an historical event, and Torah from an essentially legal constitution, into a cosmogonic and ontological process, mysteriously interrelated to the hidden life of divinity. Furthermore, this transformation has pervasive theurgic implications. To perform mitzvot is to influence the inner life of divinity and the world, which is structured according to a pattern analogous to Torah. Breuer's elaborate philosophy of the commandments rests on such theurgic convictions. To will Torah is to act in an ontologically transformative way. At any rate, when Breuer writes of the divinity of the Torah (*Göttlichkeit der Thora*) it is this sort sefirotic-or logic-embodied divinity that he has in mind.

In Breuer's own generation, Franz Rosenzweig offered a powerful model of the close interaction of creation with revelation. For Rosenzweig (whom Breuer apparently took quite seriously) revelation is God's movement in love toward man and world. Creation holds the latent promise of this movement, standing to revelation as a prediction stands to a miracle. In creation, God is still concealed. God has not yet moved fully out of himself. Although more disclosed than the gods of myth, who exist in a self-enclosed configuration with respect to man and world, the God of creation could only be known by static attributes—such as the philosophers under their pagan mentors have attributed to him. The philosophers lack a living relationship with a living, revealed God. (Knowledge of God through such a living relationship is clearly the normative and typical kind of interaction for Jews and Christians, although not for Muslims in Rosenzweig's view.) Creation and revelation are interrelated phases in the complex interaction of God, man, and world with each other and with themselves. This mode of interrelationship is not temporal and successive as much as it is ontological, contemporary, and perspectival. Creation requires revelation because God, in his freedom, desires to love man and world. Had God not come forth from the lingering quasi concealment of creation, he could not have given himself fully to human beings in love. Revelation thus confirms the movement of God already initiated by creation.[65]

Like Rosenzweig, Breuer understands revelation to be already implicit in creation. He speaks of creation as an "act revelation" (*Tatoffenbarung*) that is later to be complemented by a "word revelation" (*Wortoffenbarung*).[66] Under this term, creation, as we have seen, is already a revelatory event. "God's revelation by means of matter and God's word revelation permit a far-reaching analogy."[67]

The logic of the creation/revelation continuum is that creation posits a beginning unlike nature, which is purposeless, perpetual becoming. Beginning implies end, direction, and goal. Creation therefore, unlike nature, points beyond itself into revelation, which is its telos, norm, and sense. The Torah is the thought that precedes the act. Following the rabbinic sages, Breuer recognizes in Torah both the goal and the means of creation. "Creation was formed with regard to the Torah and for the sake of the Torah. Torah precedes creation and creation form, just as the purposeful thought precedes the purposeful act."[68]

Breuer's view that something in the logic of creation calls for revelation resembles Rosenzweig's in one respect: revelation is a necessary development beyond, yet rooted in, creation. The nature of the necessity differs in the two thinkers, however. Unlike Rosenzweig, Breuer does not assert that God needs to reveal himself beyond the initial act-revelation of creation. That he does so responds to a need in his creation, not in himself. It is not that Breuer shrinks from speaking of the intradivine process. Clearly, his theurgic orientation toward the mitzvot commits him to such speculation. Rather, Breuer never entirely departs from a Kantian perspective: the angle from which he apprehends the creation/revelation process is the situation of the epistemic subject, not Rosenzweig's Hegelian triad of God, man, and world. Breuer does not write about revelation as a phase of interaction between the primal elements, although he does write about Jewish metahistory and the mitzvot in such a manner.

The difference in method and orientation between Rosenzweig and Breuer will become clearer through an analysis of Breuer's early theory of revelation found in *Die Welt als Schöpfung und Natur*. After developing his thesis on the twofold aspect of the world as creation and as nature, Breuer goes on to relate the world as creation to Torah: "The Torah is the revealed constitutional law of the divine kingdom of creation. It is older than nature. God undertook creation in order to realize the aims of the Torah. God enveloped creation in the dress of nature in order to realize the aims of the Torah through man."[69]

This passage immediately calls attention to the anthropological context of Breuer's thesis. Breuer does not neglect the fact that revelation is always revelation addressed to someone. It is not an undirected disclosure of divine Being, but a communication to man. The movement of creation into revelation is channeled through the self-consciousness of man. Man, not a juxtaposition of primal hypostases, is the decisive nexus between creation and revelation. Specifically, man's decision for or against Torah determines whether revelation and creation are in a proper relationship. "As long as the Torah does not rule upon the earth, creation is a torso and nature is sick."[70]

Echoing the theology of the Shema, Breuer maintains that the catastrophic dimension of nature arises from man's neglect of Torah. Insofar as revelation does not prevail over creation, creation is inadequately actualized over nature. Though not quite Rosenzweig's "chaos of the elements," prerevelatory creation is a state in which God appears as a *Katastrophen Gott* and nature threatens every human enterprise. "If man, who is called to be the organizer of the world as creation, lets anarchy tear into her, leaves God's creation commands unfulfilled and thereby arrests creation, can he then protest that the phenomenal form of the world as creation, that is, the world as nature, presents him with a similar picture [i.e. of anarchy]?"[71]

This "hemmed-in," nonactualized creation brought about by rebellion against Torah revelation resembles Rosenzweig's condition of the static God of attributes. Breuer writes: "The resting God remains the God of 'providence.' God provides for the correspondence of the world as nature and as creation. The individual phenomena of nature are of course bound to one another. But nature as a whole, the household of nature, has been severed from creation."[72]

When the world is limited to the world as nature, God can only be spoken of as a relatively passive God of providence. If man is not engaged in Torah existence, then creation and nature correspond—an effect of this divine providence—but are not identical. By "correspondence" Breuer means the fact that our experience is such that any representation indicates the existence of some thing-in-itself, that is, any perception in nature certifies the existence of a referent in creation. Once again, Breuer alludes to Leibniz, who equated the theological doctrine of providence with an epistemological event, namely the divinely preordained ordering of innate ideas within the mind. This God of providence (*Gott der Vorsehung*), like Rosenzweig's God of attributes, represents the truncated perception of divine reality available to the extrarevelational community. Whether they perceive God as a passive, providential guarantor of cosmic order or as an angry, catastrophe God of history, they cannot help but misappropriate nature and remain its prisoner rather than its redeemer.

The inherent tension between the world as creation and as nature necessitates an expansion and a more effective emplacement of creation over nature. The organon for this development is man.

Breuer understands the historical revelation of the Torah at Sinai to be an act of making explicit what is already implicit in creation but has been silenced by creation's retreat into nature.

Creation and Sinai are related and complementary processes that reflect two parallel orders of lawfulness: that of nature and that of man. Man's inability to attain his own idiosyncratic order of lawfulness solely on the basis of his encounter with the world as creation and as nature, which is to say, the world's inability to maintain its status as creation and not as nature, is what necessitates the moment of revelation. And yet, to maintain that nature is lawful, that the essence of nature is natural law, would seem to generate a contradiction. Why is a subsequent revelation of law necessary, if in fact the world presents itself to man not as chaos but as a system of laws?

To answer this question, we must understand more precisely what Breuer means by natural law. It is true that he equates natural law with the noetic operations of the understanding, but he also views natural law as an externalized, phenomenal form of God's original creation commands (*Schöpfungsbefehle*) on the basis of which the creation first came to be. The persistence of creation in nature, the secret life of creation under the Sabbath robes of phenomena, is nothing other than the endurance of the creation commands in the form of natural law. When God rested on the Sabbath, he evacuated creation and therefore instantiated nature, but traces of his creation commands remain in nature in precisely the form that is categorically appropriate to their phenomenal location, that is, the form of natural law.

> In things is not only the force of their relatedness but also the force of the continuously effective creation commands. Matter-in-itself, torn out of the nothingness, bears the tenfold articulated creation command, and owing to this command—this single yet enduring "be and it was so"—the things exist as a produced-yet-productive cosmos (*gewirkt-wirkender Kosmos*). In the repose of the Creator, the system of mutually conditioning natural interdependencies (*einander bedingender Naturabhängigkeiten*) simultaneously guarantees the continuity of the unconditioned creation-dependence (*Fortbestand der unbedingten Schöpfungsabhängigkeit*). That is to say, the world as nature is the organization of the world as creation. God-Creator, the absolute Lord of creation, by his own free will gave it a constitution (*Verfassung*) on the Sabbath. The laws of nature in their totality are the statute of organization of the creation that was called into being through the ten creation commands and brought by means of the Sabbath into an organic system.[73]

Nature does indeed bear the marks of creation, the creation commands, but the tragic flaw in nature's schema of organization is that these commands no longer compel. Nature is a status quo; a self-maintaining system. After God withdrew from his creation, the creative dynamic within nature became truncated. The result of this self-limitation of God (*Selbstbeschränkung Gottes*) is that phenomena simply exist; they do not exist toward a goal. "In the self-limiting of God, the creation commands and the creation goals part from one another."[74] While nature means permanence and persistence, creation means origin and destiny. The self-imposed quiescence of God silences the purposive dynamic of the creation commands but simultaneously occasions the conditions by means of which man can fulfill the goals of creation.

> The world as nature assimilates the creation commands only as forces for self-maintenance, for species maintenance. These forces became blind forces during God's self-limiting. Man takes them over as blind forces—he alone has sight. In the repose of the Creator he is supposed to be active. As a human creator, he is supposed to further lead the work of the six days, interrupted by the Sabbath, to its divine destination.[75]

This notion of the cosmos-maintaining, indeed cosmos-redemptive, function of man, over and against the self-imposed withdrawal of God, reflects the theurgic traditions of the Kabbalah. Certain kabbalists whom Breuer read, such as Recanati, had distinctly theurgic views concerning the supernal, intradivine consequences of performing (or neglecting) the commandments, but Breuer seems reluctant to move beyond a theurgy of world-maintenance and eschatological fulfillment. As we will see in the next chapter, Breuer believes that Israel can influence the direction of history. However, Breuer's general tendency away from hypostasis and mythic language severely restricts his theurgic discourse. He is not willing to speak like a kabbalist, for example, by suggesting that the neglect of the mitzvot may diminish God's supernal image. The neglect of the mitzvot may plunge history into catastrophe, but given the substantial or essential otherness of the world vis-a-vis God, chaos would not thereby be introduced into the divine.

Breuer would not be true to his method to locate the world-maintaining potency of the Torah solely within a cosmological context. Revelation and the necessity for revelation remain tied to the situation of the epistemic subject. Kant controls Breuer's forays into Kabbalah. Recalling Breuer's basic philosophical anthropology from chapter 2, the *I* is held to be tripartite. The *I* can be said to be merely existent; to exist under an order of norms; and to synthesize these aspects of its being through will. Breuer asserts that up until the Sabbath of creation, man was dimly aware of himself as merely existent. On the seventh day however, man became conscious of normativity, of himself as a norm-actualizing creature (*sollendes Geschöpf*). Man's soul (*Seele*) awakens precisely as nature's ought (*Sollen*); nature's intrinsic creation command, falls asleep.

Man recognizes in his soul that which is essentially unlike what he sees in his world. Breuer breaks with the rationalist tradition that distinguishes body from soul in terms of physical/metaphysical distinctions such as that between extended and nonextended substance. For Breuer, there is no continuity between nature and spirit in the sense of an underlying substance that might unify two ostensibly different sorts of entity. Breuer's fundamental ontological categories are 'is' and 'ought'. For him, *I* becomes conscious, that is, Being (*Sein*) becomes conscious Being (*Bewusstsein*) because of the fundamental opposition of is and ought. Consciousness of self, that is, knowledge of self-identity, does not arise from a *cogito ergo sum* or from Fichte's opposition of *I* and *not-I*, but from a dialectic of fundamentally disparate elements.

This attempt to derive consciousness from a confrontation of the existent and the normative aims to locate the normative in human origins as such. However, the drastic, dialectical limitedness of the normative necessitates revelation. Breuer evokes the need for revelation from an account of consciousness.

Breuer does not regard the dichotomy between *I* and not-*I* as an appropriate way to talk of the origination of human consciousness, lest such a dichotomy appear to exhaust all of Being. The language of 'ought' intrudes upon the idealistic fantasy of *I* as world *I* sharply delimiting the range of its being and placing the origins of consciousness into a nonnatural framework conditioned by divine imperatives. Thus man's *I* emerges from a confrontation between is and ought; between nature and creation. And yet Breuer avoids an identification of man's partite nature with these two orders, rejecting a straightforward reductionism or reification. It is not the case that the *I* in its normative dimension directly represents creation and the creation commands. "Not the elemental *I* of the creation, but the confected, derivative *I* of nature is the *I* of man."[76]

If it were the case that the soul, man's consciousness of himself as a being related to a normative order, to *Sollen*, were a pure expression of creation in the midst of nature, a fallen piece of divinity, then the soul would possess infallible normative intuition, affording man a gnostic avenue of transcendence. This false picture, which Breuer might say characterizes any anthropology that does not make room for revelation, is undialectical. It fails to take account of the veil of the Sabbath robes that hangs over all human reality. It fails to appreciate the dialectical relation of creation and nature: the former is not imprisoned whole and pure within the latter; rather, they are mutually interactive.

The soul of man does not represent creation *simpliciter*. It is a far more ambiguous affair. It discloses creation to a certain extent, but the fullness of creation, that is, revelation cannot be known to the soul from within, but only from Sinai. How then does the *I* arise?

> In the *I* of man there is both creation and nature. The *I* of man is neither merely under an ought nor under an is. The *I* of man is characterized by an is and an ought at once; it is an is-ought (*seiend-sollend*). Only because the already existent is the negation of the not-yet normative; because the not-yet normative is the negation of the already existent: only because the already existent in man apperceives the not-yet normative in man as a not-yet existent and the not-yet normative in man apperceives the already existent as a no-longer normative: only due to this structure of oppositions has the *I* of man arisen.[77]

In Breuer's view then, ought is the proper antithesis of is: it is that which is most truly not at all 'is'. Through this way of cutting the dichotomy, the antithesis of 'is' is not merely privative, that is, the nonexistent, but becomes something positive. Both *Sein* and its opposite, *Sollen*, are positive creations of God, are "very good."

The 'is' aspect of man first achieves self-awareness as it reflects upon what it is not, that is, upon its limitedness as 'is'. The result is that "by means of the 'ought' in the *I*, the being of the *I* becomes consciousness." Simultaneously, the normative dimension of man becomes aware of itself through reflection upon its opposite. "By means of the 'is' in the *I*, the 'ought' in the *I* becomes normative consciousness [*Bewusst-Sollen*].[78] These twin aspects of the formative self-consciousness are expressed by a biconditional: "I am if and only if I ought." "Whoever cannot say

'I am' can also not say 'I ought.' Whoever cannot say 'I ought' can also not say 'I am.' "[79] Breuer has taken the Kantian "ought implies can" and given it an ontological rendering.

In the second stage of the movement of consciousness, the conscious-existent being (*bewusst-seiende Sein*) that has emerged from the is-ought encounter opposes itself to merely existent being (*seiende Sein*) or not-yet-conscious being, which may properly be called "*not I*" (*Nicht-Ich*). Full consciousness of self arises subsequent to this encounter.

Given this account of the formation of consciousness out of the dialectic of ought and is, the question relevant to revelation still remains. Why is the *I*'s intuition into its constituent ought inadequate? Why is the *I*'s consciousness of its creation legacy radically insufficient to provide it with norms in the midst of its world of creation and nature? The answer rests on the unlikeness of the *I* and God:

> Man must be able to take a look into the laws of creation in order to perceive the laws of his "ought." But his soul does not grant him this insight. The soul is not volitional [*wollend*] but only normative [*sollend*]; that is, it is not the Creator, but only the creature. Man as a normative-conscious *I* becomes aware not of his creatorhood but of his creatureliness. Not in opposition to nature did the normative-conscious *I* awaken. It does not confront, as a sovereign *I*, the creation as its *not-I*. It does not know, by itself, what it ought to do, but knows only that it ought. It thus remains, despite its knowledge of [the fact of] its ought, entirely within the sphere of the creation.[80]

If man could occupy an Archimedean point outside of his world as creation and as nature, and thus be able to know the world strictly as creation, apprehending its creation laws, then he could actually ascribe a content to his ought. But this is not the case. Man exists, unlike God, within creation, which in turn exists within the Sabbath robes of nature. The *not-I* over and against which man's *I* comes to know itself is *Sein*, nature. God, of course, knows creation in its inner lawfulness because He has willed it to be so. God is the lawgiver of creation, man is only one who learns the law. As man intuits his own soul, analyzing the origination of his *I* and tracing it back to creation, he discovers only the fact that he is related to a normative order, not the laws of that order per se. Thus the *I* can never be a lawgiver, can never supplant God.

Breuer knows of course the rabbinic aggadah about the soul's knowledge of the whole Torah. The rabbis taught, *pace* the *Phaedo*, that before man is born the soul learns the entire Torah from the mouth of an angel. At birth, the person forgets everything. Earthly study of the Torah becomes *anamnesis*, knowledge as remembrance. Breuer takes this rabbinic teaching quite seriously, attempting to harmonize it with his own view. He suggests that knowledge of the content of the ought (*Was des Sollens*) might indeed be hidden away "as the most costly treasure" of the soul.[81] This speculation, however, does not affect his argument. He is simply content to leave open the possibility lest his own view be seen to conflict with the tradition.

Breuer has given the soul a formal, conceptual status and a role to play in consciousness without becoming committed to statements about its nature as a thing. Of the *I*, he held that we know that we exist as *I*, but that we are unable to isolate anything that is necessarily a content for the *I* without which the *I* would cease to be. In a similar manner, he has avoided reification of the soul. The soul is a dialectical moment of normative consciousness, involved in the synthesis of the *I* as well as its ongoing self-consciousness. The soul remains unknowable for the *I*, a limiting concept that makes—in a psychological sense—for restlessness and distress. Far from being any kind of salvific agent, this immanent but merely incipient normative consciousness disturbs and agitates man. He is unable to be simply an animal, yet not yet able to realize himself as fully human. Augustine's "Our hearts are restless until they come to rest in Thee" could apply quite precisely here, except that in place of the Thou would be the Torah. "The soul exhorts: 'Thou shalt! 'Thou shalt!' and the *I* replies, 'Soul, what shall I do?' but the soul gives no reply. Only God's revelation raises up the treasure of the soul. Only the Torah quiets the soul's 'Thou shalt!' "[82]

Breuer struggles in these difficult paragraphs to find a balance between a concept of metaphysical personhood that retains the biblical notion of an inherent divine image and one that is wholly natural. He seems to want to affirm the traditional Jewish view that "the soul that you have given me is pure," with all that it implies about conscience, right reason, and repentance, while at the same time downplaying such a sanguine anthropology in order, as we have seen, to sharply contrast natural reason to revealed Torah.

The *I* is hauntedly aware that something is required of it, that it is judged. But it cannot know what to do. It only knows that its motives and actions are not immediately natural. The law, in Paul's sense, has not taught it sin: its own generative consciousness fills it with a sense of anxious incompleteness. The creation commands are veiled by the seamless web of nature, which the *I* finds draped over its own essence and intuition as well. Yet it senses them and is ill at ease.

Breuer would seem to hold that values are entirely nonnatural. The intuition of normative consciousness, although real, is vacuous. Revelation is needed to realize moral truth. The world of phenomena is a world of facts, whereas values derive from the world as creation. Yet Breuer does not pursue his argument to this length. Instead, he asserts that natural man does indeed have a sense and repertoire of values. They are, however, failed values. They are not genuine consummations of the truncated creation process, but disvalues when viewed from the realized perspective of Torah revelation. They are values as viewed through the dark glass of natural existence.

In *Nahaliel*, for example, Breuer asserts that 'good' and 'evil' permit of a purely natural sense. Animals have "ideas" of good and evil in terms of what advances and what impedes their natural vitality. Breuer terms this natural drive, which human beings (qua *nefesh*) also possess, the "animal will" (*ratzon behami*). Human beings also appropriate good and evil in this purely self-referential manner.[83] Breuer relates such an animalistic, utilitarian notion of good to the generation of the flood in Genesis. But Noah's successors do no better. The natural concept of goodness as maximally unimpeded power of volition reaches its typical human expression in the war of all against all and, finally, in state against state. Social structures, arising in response to fundamental, natural dilemmas, are not able to break free of the animal will and its concept of the good.

Genuine values, which Breuer echoing Schopenhauer (echoing Plato) calls "Ideas" (*hazonot*), are nonnatural. Authentic goodness, freedom, justice, and holiness do not derive from the world as nature. Rather, they seek to penetrate the world and transform it. When man, under the tutelage of the Torah, is able to think the Ideas (indeed, to realize them through the mitzvot), he becomes a *neshamah*, a fully realized human being.

For Breuer, then, natural man is caught in the snare of the fact-value distinction. His internally divided consciousness and will are incompetent to discover the unifying act that will set him free from fact, necessity, causality, and self-alienation. Torah man, however, perceives values in the firmament of revelation. He knows their divine origin and wills them into actuality.

Such are the formal conditions pertaining to the creation of consciousness that have necessitated revelation. But what of revelation as such?

THE TRANSCENDENTAL TORAH

The substantial epistemological discussion in *Der Neue Kusari* began as an approach to the problem of the divinity of the Torah. The dialogue turned on the question of proof for the Torah's divine authorship and nature. The reply was an elaborate analysis of human perception and cognition that gradually marked off Torah revelation from the kinds of thing to which human understanding has access. Torah must be willed and acquiesced in, not rationally understood. In that discussion, the focus was on mind. Now we must concentrate on the Torah per se, to which mind must submit.

Breuer uses the term *divinity* to describe the Torah, ascribing both ultimate normative status and divine provenance to it. He also means to imply, however, that the divine being and power are in some sense embodied in Torah. He asserts an ontological relatedness between God and Torah, standing firmly on the hallowed ground of kabbalistic theosophy.

There are two general contexts in which this divinity is revealed. One is the context of the nation. God entered history, communicated with Moses, bound Israel to obedience of his law, and so on. In this context, the notion of divinity of the Torah refers primarily to divine authorship.[84] This sense of Torah as the divinely authored law of the nation of Israel is treated in the next chapter. The context that concerns us here is the normative one. Torah presents itself to individuals as that which claims absolute, divine authority and which the *I* must will with absolute fidelity. In both of these contexts, the ontological relatedness of Torah and God are recognizable.

The immediate problem in the relation of the *I* to revelation is that of the intelligibility of revelation. Why should Torah mean anything to anyone? How can Breuer have argued that our knowledge of ought is empty and formalistic;—that the ought cannot be experienced because it "is" not; and that Torah, like God, cannot be an object of experience because it is a commanding presence that addresses the person principally as will—and yet maintain that Torah is intelligible? If Torah is to provide a content to our thirst for normativity, then surely it must be, if not rational, at least meaningful. Breuer must account for the obvious fact that we do read, study, and understand Torah, while preserving its transrational, ontological character.

The problem of intelligibility is partly of Breuer's own making and partly an inheritance from the tradition. Kabbalists saw in Torah the great name of God. Torah's many words, sentences, narratives, and legal formulas give rise to the notion that Torah is something of a story and something of a law code. But in fact the Torah is a name, and in the name resides the power and presence of the Names. Such a mystical view must of necessity distinguish the Torah's mundane verbal appearance from its transcendental reality. The kabbalists accordingly distinguished increasingly esoteric levels of interpretation for the utterances of the Torah. They ascribed to Torah a mystical essence for which the textual corpus that lies at hand is merely the outermost shell. Breuer employs a similar approach, albeit from a Kantian perspective.

The dichotomization of the Torah into an intelligible, revealed communication and a mystical, recondite essence rests, in Breuer's account, on the familiar Kantian distinction between phenomena and noumena. The Torah, like the world, has a phenomenal aspect, its word signs (*Wortzeichen*), and an inner aspect, the Torah-in-itself.[85] This mode of existence parallels that of the world as nature and as creation. There is furthermore an essential relation between creation as world-in-itself and the Torah-in-itself. Torah-in-itself is the law of creation (*Schöpfungsgesetz*): the law of the world-in-itself. The question then becomes, How is our torah, the one that we learn, recite, obey, and presumably understand, related to this transcendental Torah? Breuer exercises no less ingenuity on this theme than he did on the relation of creation to nature. Just as in that discussion there was an ancillary polemical motive of affirming an account of creation against scientific and idealist cosmology, there is here to be found a defense of Torah against Bible criticism. Breuer argues that the traditional Jew, whose relation to Torah engages its ontological character, alone understands revelation.

The Torah has been revealed in words, and words are the principle vehicle of human understanding. Words are, Breuer says, a human device that can as little penetrate to the Torah-in-itself as to the world-in-itself. As we have seen in Breuer's account of naming, names are tags for phenomena. Words in general derive from the praxis of man within the world as nature. Words have no special power to disclose reality, other than the mere reality of phenomena. This is also true, at least prima facie, for the words of the Torah. Breuer has a nominalist theory of language. God's "speech" bears no relation to man's speech. The Torah was revealed solely in terms of man's speech. It may seem then that if an essential relation between God's pristine expression and this Torah of human words is denied, then the actual words of the Torah are arbitrary. One could change or critique them as Bible critics do. But this is not the case. The words of the Torah, like the events of nature, reflect a thus-and-not-otherwise character (*So-und-nicht-anders-sein*): a specific, immutable particularity and givenness that must be respected, precisely as the givenness of nature is respected by the scientist. Bible criticism makes as little sense as nature criticism. What is necessary is disciplined inquiry, not criticism. Breuer does not share the view of some kabbalists who followed the logic of a dichotomized Torah to the conclusion that the present division of words and letters of scripture is only one among thousands. Breuer would reject the practice of numerical translations of scriptural words (*gematria*) or other similar techniques for wresting esoteric meaning from the text. He takes his stand on the givenness (*Gegebenheit*) of the text, which is inviolable:

> If the Torah has entered into the form of our thought, that is, the form of words, in order to be grasped by us for the structuring of our lives, we are not permitted to derive, on the basis of the comprehensibility of the Torah formed of words, the right to attack it. We are not permitted to touch its singular givenness. Similarly, we know the world that is perceived by us without daring to negate or to correct that which appears to us puzzling, indeed, contradictory.[86]

Torah, as a revelation parallel to nature, deserves the same treatment as nature. Torah is word revelation (*Wortoffenbarung*), and nature is representation revelation (*Vorstellungsoffenbarung*). "Here, as there, the revelation exists in terms of givenness."[87]

The parallelism between Torah and nature as two orders of lawfulness, one for the world in general and the other for man in particular, also runs through Samson Raphael Hirsch's thought. Hirsch believed that the Torah is a fact in the same sense that nature is a fact: both are given realities, formed and ordered by God. One investigates these orders of fact with the methodology appropriate to each. In the case of nature, that methodology is science. In the case of Torah, it is the oral Law. Both are revelations, presenting their own orders of facticity.[88] The notion that nature and scripture are parallel orders of revelation is, of course, not new with Hirsch. It is found in Jewish medieval philosophy and perhaps goes back to the Stoic notion of Logos as the inherent rationality of both nature and culture. Hirsch does give the parallelism an important nuance, however, that reflects a Hegelian assumption. Hirsch asserts that each kind of revelation has its own scientific methodology. The nature of the totality (*All*) that the revelation is implies certain conditions for the nature of reason that is to be applied to the totality. System and methodology correspond with one another. Hirsch secures for Torah what Dilthey secured for the *Geisteswissenschaften*. Thus for Hirsch and Breuer the scientist commits a category mistake when he applies any scientific methodology to the Torah. Torah requires its own method, which the Jews possess in the hermeneutics of the oral Torah. Hirsch takes this methodological stricture a step farther in his own technique of etymological analysis based on sound similarities. It seems to him that the uniqueness of the Torah requires that it generate both its own facts and its own method. Hirsch's credo was "As Jews must we read it." Breuer's verion of this call to action is a radical fait accompli: there is no relation between the Torah of the Jewish people and the Torah of the Bible critics other than an empty name.[89]

Hirsch's concept of a double revelation in nature and scripture is given an epistemological construction in Breuer. For both, Bible criticism is fundamentally and categorically mistaken, but only Breuer attempts to argue this by recourse to an analysis of cognition and language. The result is a mystical conception of the divinity of Torah that Hirsch might well have found uncongenial.

As we have seen, Breuer understands science to operate on the order of sensory representations. Science is the analysis of the lawfulness of sense data. As a Kantian and an Orthodox Jew, Breuer feels compelled to remind the scientist of the limits of his activity by bringing the boundary principle of the thing-in-itself to his attention. This boundary marks off a world that is not organized according to the laws of man's own understanding but that is nonetheless transcendentally necessary in order to explain the world that is so organized. The same holds true for Torah. The Torah of the Bible critic is a text that follows the dictates of an understanding that seeks to master it. Israel, however, knows that there is a Torah-in-itself that conditions understanding without being conditioned by it. Israel knows the necessary existence of the unconditional, transcendental Torah, just as it knows the necessary existence of the creational world-in-itself. How does Israel know this? It knows it from its corporate act of will; from its willing of Torah.

The critic comes before the revelation in words and sees mere words. He misses the fact that the word signs exist as they do owing to a priori transcendental conditions. He assumes that their givenness is an historically conditioned givenness and proceeds, as understanding must, to apply the category of temporality to their origination. "The verbal givenness is not for the critic a revelation givenness [*Offenbarungsgebenheit*], but an historical givenness; not a revealed, but an evolved, givenness. The critic believes that he can go back into the evolutionary history of this development."[90] Thus the critic brings to bear on the Torah the methods of philology, higher and lower criticism, redaction criticism, and so on.

The critic, like the natural scientist, can only understand the relevant object in terms of what has arisen in time. The radical otherness of the creation, for example, is mistakenly brought by him under the category of temporality and made into a first moment of becoming. For Breuer, this is a pagan view. Creation, like God, is wholly other to nature and not its first cause. So too with Torah. The critic fails to grasp the transcendental conditions that enable the existence of words, that is, the reality of word revelation. In the name of philosophical enlightenment, he benightedly performs his various operations on the words, not noticing that their essence eludes him. The words have become empty husks. They have degenerated into objects of critical perception to which histories can be assigned.

> The understanding cannot cope with either revelation [that is, creation or Torah]. Instead of the deed revelation, instead of the one-time revealed act, the understanding sets the eter-

nal, beginningless, and endless act in perpetual concatenation. And instead of the eternally new, self-revealing word, the understanding sets the one-time, temporally originated, and spoken word. Because it is not able to grasp the act of the beginning, it takes the beginning away. And because it cannot grasp the beginningless word, it gives a beginning to it.[91]

Why does the critic dismiss word revelation and settle for word alone? It is because science, driven by understanding alone, compels him to do so. Critic and scientist are prisoners of their own minds, captives of naturalistic reason. They are constrained by an ontology that is phenomenologically inadequate given the transcendental reality of the Torah. As such, there is no bridge between what the biblical critic recognizes as the biblical literature and what the Jewish people accept as Torah. Only a name relates the two. In a vivid phrase, Breuer compares these two kinds of Torah to irreducibly plural ontological perspectives held by persons of different philosophical convictions. "Between the Bible critic and the Torah Jew there is as little agreement as there is between the solipsist who thinks that the world is his dream and the one who knows that there is an objective world. The Torah of the Bible critic has only a name in common with the Torah of the Jewish people."[92]

The analogy of the critic to the solipsist is apt because of the analogy of the Torah to the world as creation. Breuer coins terms to bring out the full force of this cosmological/ontological relation between Torah and world. Torah is God's speech act (*Sprachtat*), and the created world is His act of speech (*Tatsprache*). Torah is God's word creation (*Wortschöpfung*), while the world is His act creation (*Tatschöpfung*).[93]

What the world is with respect to our perceptual thinking (*anschauliches Denken*), that is what the Torah is with respect to our conceptual thinking (*begriffliches Denken*). As the world is not only our specially constituted perceptual thinking but, beyond that, a world-in-itself, so too is the Torah not only our specially constituted conceptual thinking at hand in certain verbal signs, but rather a Torah-in-itself, God's Torah.

The objective world and the objective Torah are only knowable because of the continuity of their transcendence.

Of course, to one for whom the Torah is a book among books, such a one cannot "know" the Torah, such a one recreates the Torah. One must climb to the primal ground in order to comprehend the epistemological essence of the Torah.[94]

We are now able to confront the question of the content of this impenetrably mysterious Torah-in-itself and of its relation to the intelligible Torah with which Israel is involved. Breuer has introduced the notion of the *Urgrund*, the "primal ground" of things in which the divine Torah-in-itself is embedded. The primal ground of things is equivalent to creation; to the world-in-itself. The Torah-in-itself that reposes there is incomprehensible to reason. The Torah of the primal ground is none other than *Torah she b'khtav*, the written Torah. The Torah of Israel, however, exists not in the primal ground, but in the Jewish people as such. This Torah dwells in the volitional, practical, and intellectual life of Israel. It is the *Torah she ba'al peh*, the oral Torah.

The distinction of the two Torot, originating in early Judaism, was used in Kabbalah, as in Breuer, to account for the simultaneously revealed and recondite nature of revelation. The oral Torah is the human meaning of the intrinsically mysterious written Torah. The Jewish people becomes the mystical body for the oral Torah, such that Israel itself becomes a metaphysical entity. Israel is thought of as a special creation in the midst of creation to serve, as Breuer puts it, as an "edifice of eternities," cradling the oral Torah. The other nations are merely a part of nature.

With this kabbalistic theory of Torah and Israel, Breuer takes a sharp turn away from Samson Raphael Hirsch. The Kantian differentiation of phenomena and noumena applied to the Torah allows Breuer to preserve a mysterious transcendence for Torah that Hirsch would not recognize. Breuer has reintroduced a mystical perspective at the very place where Hirsch labored to construct a thoroughly rational edifice. Hirsch is, at heart, a rationalist who—despite his agreement with Halevi that the investigation of Judaism must begin with the fact of revelation, not with natural theology—ultimately agrees with Maimonides that the Torah is a means to an end. He does not dwell on the intrinsic value, not to say mystery, of Torah as much as on its instrumental value. Torah educates man to perfection. The commandments are instruments for the achievement of spiritual and moral virtue. This is not to say that every commandment can be rationally explained; some will always defy our powers of understanding. It is to say, however, that a rationally discernible purpose informs the giving of the Torah. Breuer preserves to a much greater extent than Hirsch a sense of Torah as an ontological revelation rather than a moral instrumentality.

The realization of the commandments is an ontological activity. It is a cosmic-salvific praxis by means of which man redeems creation. Breuer affirms the ontologically redemptive function of mitzvot in the manner of theurgic Kabbalah, while Hirsch stresses the moral, human implications of the mitzvot. Gershom Scholem saw this return by Breuer to Kabbalah, which Hirsch rejected out of enthusiasm for contemporary German culture, as a desperate and incongruous attempt to breathe new life into an anachronistic Hirschian "assimilation theology."[95] Indeed, Breuer's selective appropriation of kabbalistic themes is incongruous when viewed against a Hirschian background. The main philosophical background against which Breuer must be viewed, however, is Kant and German idealism. Here Breuer found an opening for mystical speculation that is not in the least paradoxical. Nor is it as clear as Scholem thought that an institutional base in the Hirschian community precluded a mystical orientation. Hirsch's theology cannot be combined with Kabbalah, but Hirsch's radical dichotomization of organized Jewry does lend itself to a gnostic, dualistic interpretation. Breuer exploits this possibility to the utmost as he subtly rejects, qualifies, and renews other elements of Hirsch in the spirit of new orientation.

Before taking up the theme of redemption and the mystical meaning of Jewish existence, we must treat the concepts of the primal ground and the written and oral Torot in order to complete our discussion of the divine, transcendental Torah.

In kabbalistic literature, the written Torah and the oral Torah have often been ascribed to different Sefirot. The written Torah was identified with the third Sefirah, *tiferet*, and the oral Torah with the tenth, *malkhut*. Significantly, the tenth Sefirah was also identified with both the divine Shekhinah and with *knesset Israel*, the mystical Congregation of Israel.[96]

Speculations about the nature of the divinity of each Torah go back to the earliest work of Kabbalah, the *Sefer Bahir* (Book of Brilliance), which emanated from mystical circles in thirteenth-century Provence. In those circles, the view took hold that the written Torah is entirely submerged in the oral Torah. The written

Torah is wholly recondite and in a state of occultation. The oral Torah is the corporeal form of the written Torah, therefore it is the only medium accessible to the understanding. Moses alone was able to penetrate in unbroken mystical contemplation to the written Torah. The force of this teaching, according to Scholem, is that "strictly speaking, there is no written Torah here on earth. What we call the written Torah has itself passed through the medium of the oral Torah. Everything that we perceive in the fixed forms of the Torah, written in ink on parchment, consists, in the last analysis, of interpretations and definitions of what is hidden."[97]

Such a thesis applies well to Breuer. For him, the fact that the written Torah is comprehensible at all presupposes the intervention of the oral Torah. The written Torah is transcendental: it is the ultimate ground for the oral Torah, without which it would have no phenomenal form. Even the word signs of the written Torah are thus not words in any conventional sense. They are, in their precise givenness, seals and boundaries of our cognition:

> Not immediately the Torah-in-itself, but at present the oral Torah is the object of the activity of our understanding. Deriving from Sinai not less than the Torah-in-itself, it is, so to speak, the Sabbath dress of the Torah-in-itself, which envelopes the incomprehensible primal ground of the Creation and thereby makes the Torah-in-itself comprehensible. Not on the Torah-in-itself but on the enveloping wraps of the oral Torah do the divinely sanctioned sprouts flourish toward our understanding. The signs of the Torah of the written word are not verbal signs that our understanding is able to interpret out of its own resources. If that were the case, how could the Torah in itself, composed from such mere signs, be God's creation? Its signs are rather seals, which are only as decipherable by our understanding (which has been formed by the oral Torah) as God holds necessary for shaping the life of His nation. Beyond that, these signs are borders behind which a creation mystery lies.[98]

The written Torah then reposes in the primal ground of creation, its words serving to mark a boundary. The written Torah is not at the edges of languages, but over the edge. We know of it only what God reveals to us through the medium of the oral Torah. Like the first kabbalists, Breuer renders the Torah fully transcendent, without, however, invoking the language of the Sefirot. Breuer does use the term *primal ground*, though, which perhaps derives from the kabbalistic concept of *makor*, the "source."[99]

The sharp distinction between the oral Torah of Israel and the wholly occultated written Torah of creation was adumbrated by an influential Spanish kabbalist, R. Joseph ibn Gikatilla (1248–1325). Gikatilla writes of a primeval Torah (*Torah keduma*) that reposes in the first sefirah. The Torah that Israel possesses is a material revelation of this Torah.[100] The Torah of words is a revelation of the primeval Torah, but it is also its occultation: God, in giving Israel revelation, reveals that he is ultimately hidden.[101] Gikatilla develops this dialectical theology with the help of a distinction between God's names and his attributes. In transcendent reality, Torah is one great name of God. In this present state, Torah appears as a corpus of rather external descriptions of God, that is, as a collection of his attributes. Gikatilla calls these attributes "malbushim," garments or veils. Like the imagery of the veil, the suggestive dialectical theology of revelation as simultaneous occultation reemerges in Breuer's dichotomy of the Torah of the spoken and the written word.

In Gikatilla, the inaccessibility of the Torah of divine names, its tragic deterioration into a Torah of attributes, comes about because of Israel's exile and sin. The Congregation of Israel is the tenth sefirah. Due to Israel's sin, it has broken off from the other nine. Thus God himself is in exile from himself. The nations persecute Israel and worship the robes of God; that is, they mistakenly divinize his fragmentary attributes. Redemption is likened by Gikatilla to a union of love between God (in the nine upper sefirot) and the Congregation of Israel, the tenth sefirah.[102] Redemption is the consummation of the love affair between God and Israel, such that God becomes whole again and Israel is reunited with the transcendental Torah. Such themes of Gikatilla's Kabbalah may well have informed Breuer's expression of the ideal relationship of Israel to the Torah-in-itself:

By means of the oral Torah has our nation in centuries of endless offerings of love and trust executed a work of incomparably incisive and critical rational activity, unparalleled on earth, toward the Torah-in-itself. The Torah-in-itself has wedded itself in love to *knesset Israel*—the Jewish nation formed by the oral Torah—and entrusted God's secrets to it to a degree that is otherwise unreachable on earth.[103]

I turn now to a discussion of *knesset Israel*, the bearer of revelation and creation nation, whose task it is to bring creation and revelation together into redemption.

❖ 4

LAW, NATION, HISTORY, AND REDEMPTION

THE CONCEPT OF LAW

In our discussion of revelation, we concentrated on the relationship between creation and revelation, and then on the essence of revelation as such: the divinity of the Torah. The emphasis was on the cosmological character of revelation and the metaphysical form of its bearer, the Congregation of Israel (*knesset Israel*). Now the focus will shift to the social, legal, and political reality of the Torah and of *knesset Israel* in history. For Breuer, redemption implies the career of this transcendental creation people and of the creation law on the stage of history. Redemption is not an eschatological event as much as it is the politics of creation and Torah in the present. Redemption, on the human side, entails the organization of a society in terms of God's will; that is, in terms of transcendental legal norms such that the given society lifts itself out of the contradictions of the history of nations and lives in accordance with God's will for creation and history. Redemption is an end result of an immanent reality: a state organized on the basis of Torah. Redemption is the politics of Torah.

The subordination of creation to revelation as the principal topic of Judaism is now repeated in the subordination of revelation to the creation-revelation people and its history. This irreducibly different form of nationhood and history, Breuer terms "metahistory" (*Metageschichte*). In this chapter, we will explore the metahistorical character of the people Israel, its legal, social, and moral order, as well as its redemptive role in general history.

Here we focus on the Torah as law and move from an ontological analysis of Torah to a functional one. How, in Breuer's terms, does the cosmological creation-law become constitutional law (*Verfassungsrecht*) for the Jewish people? What is the relationship between Torah and the legal systems of other nations? What sort of social order and national history does Torah engender in contrast with other bodies of law? As in previous discussions, Breuer advances his own doctrine against a searching analysis of fundamental questions of philosophy as he sees them. The background of his discussion Torah as law is to be found in a profound analysis of legal and social reality.

Breuer was well qualified to conduct such an exploration. As a Doctor of Jurisprudence, he brought technical competence in legal theory to the task. His essay, *Der Rechtsbegriff auf Grundlage der Stammlerschen Sozialphilosophie* (The Concept of Law on the Basis of Stammler's Social Philosophy, 1912, hereafter cited as *Der Rechtsbegriff*), originally submitted although not accepted as his dissertation at the University of Strasbourg, is his major purely philosophical work.[1] Breuer does not discuss Jewish political or theological matters in this dissertation, owing to its academic audience. Nonetheless, as one reads between the lines, the essay is evidently rooted in all of his Jewish concerns. Breuer himself asserts that in order to understand his writings, it is essential to understand this piece.[2]

Der Rechtsbegriff lays out a constructive legal philosophy, building on—yet highly critical of—the Neo-Kantian social theory of Rudolf Stammler. As in the other branches of his thought, Breuer takes the Kantian tradition very seriously. With regard to that tradition, he struggles with Kant as an insider and then willingly takes his stand as an outsider, owing to the superior synthesis that he believes is available in Judaism. In *Der Rechtsbegriff*, however, Breuer does not yet step out of the philosophical tradition. He has not yet reached his mature repudiation of history, culture, and philosophy as frameworks of salvific value for humanity.

Der Rechtsbegriff is an argument for the essentially moral nature of empirical societies and their legal systems. The concept of a moral society articulated in the essay is in principle applicable to any human society. No sharp distinction is yet to be found between Judaism and humanity as such. This early effort is clearly at odds with the eventual turn of his thought into its hard distinctions between an eventually fallen, catastrophic humanity and an eventually saved, metahistorical Israel. Due to this hopeful, liberal attitude toward the possibility of a moral, free, social polity, Breuer was attracted to Stammler. Stammler sought to ground law in a moral ideal. In Kantian terms, he sought a transcendental deduction for positive law. Stammler's absolutizing of the grounds of law was meant to offset the threat of materialism, represented most formidably by Karl Marx. Law was to be given, not a material, political, or economic basis, but an a priori ground.

This sort of thinking must have been extremely congenial for an Orthodox Jew, raised on the notion of the extrahistorical provenance and validity of the Torah. Although building on Stammler's basic insights and Neo- Kantian method, Breuer's critique of Stammler is precisely that he does not go far enough in asserting the transcendental dimension of positive law. As with Kant, Stammler brings man to the threshold of insight but does not follow the logic of his argument into recognition of revelation, of Torah. Although Stammler attempted to draw practical conclusions from his postulate of an immanent moral essence to the law, Breuer did not consider his work a success. Nonetheless Stammler arrived, in a formal sense, at the methodological and theoretical requirements for a moral sociolegal order. It is this framework of analysis and plan of design that Breuer eventually carries over into his doctrine of Jewish law.[3] His Kantian version of proper political and social order becomes one of the main engines driving his practical quest for a Torah State. The realization of Stammler's vision shifts from history to metahistory.

The goal of legal philosophy, Breuer asserts in the opening pages of *Der Rechtsbegriff*, is the discovery of jurisprudential truth, which is both transcendental to actual social and legal experience and available to critical rationality. Such truth would, of course, be universally available. "We maintain that there is no less a jurisprudential truth than a logical or an aesthetic truth. This truth has claims to general validity [*Allgemeingültigkeit*] and necessity according to its form. Owing to this claim, it cannot merely be grounded through experience."[4]

The announcement of this task carries with it the implicit rejection of those philosophies that ground law solely in empirical reality. Stammler, like Hermann Cohen, a fellow Neo-Kantian, sought to regain an absolute quality for social knowledge in the face of the Marxist contention that social knowledge is reducible to ideology, which in turn is a dialectical projection of class interests. As such, law is susceptible to a purely positivistic analysis. The question of whether any given rule is "really right" is a categorically mistaken question on this view.

Stammler rejects such positivism. His guiding concept is that of 'right law' (*richtige Recht*).[5] Stammler's inquiry was directed to the development of a set of generally valid, a priori criteria by which any positive law could be evaluated. For Stammler, the question, Is this law right? is not only meaningful, but crucial. The answer to this leading question is not to be given in terms of power, authority, or procedure, but in terms of a moral teleology.

Breuer begins his study by taking sides in a contemporary academic controversy over methodology. The issue is what sort of science the study of social life is; indeed, whether it is a science at all. Like Wilhelm Dilthey, Breuer wants to develop the methodological ground rules of the "human sciences"—in this case, of jurisprudence. He denounces the influence of those thinkers who apply the framework of natural science and utilitarianism to legal philosophy. He asserts that law must necessarily be based on a nonnatural, atemporal, and absolute concept of justice.[6] Only Kant can lead us out of positivism and into a pure, formal analysis of experience and knowledge.

The Kantian approach also requires that legal theory reject the medieval approach of natural law, just as it rejects the modern approach of positivism. Stammler, whom Breuer follows on this point, mapped out a third way between legal positivism on the one side and natural law theory on the other. Law cannot appeal for its grounds to the nature of things, for that nature cannot be known by us. Right law is grounded in the nature of reasoning, not in the nature of things. Practical reason, with its postulate of freedom of the will, is the source of right law, not any alleged lawfulness inherent to nature. This methodological stricture is modified but not abandoned in Breuer's later work, where Torah is not a natural law but the creation law.

For Stammler, right law is essentially right jurisprudential reasoning. The rightness of law has to do with correct method in the posing and answering of legal questions. That is to say, given correct methodology, one who has a legal inquiry (for instance, a judge who must render a decision) can arrive at both a concept of law and an actual statute that would be right for all such inquiries. Rightness in law is analogous to rightness in ethics, where the will can be said to be a good will if it frames its maxim in accordance with the categorical imperative. Right law is rooted in right reason, issuing in right praxis, for Stammler. It is not rooted in any alleged ontological guarantee of coherence with the nature of things.

As a Kantian, Breuer joins Stammler in rejecting natural law theory as an appropriate analysis of legal reality. Breuer praises Stammler for breaking with the ancient tradition that sees in law some sort of counterpart (*Gegenstück*) to nature.[7] Law, unlike nature, has its basis in social life, and this requires that the science of law have a methodological determination different from that of the science of nature. The science of social life and the science of nature investigate two fundamentally different orders, the difference being that one order deals with necessity and causality and the other deals with freedom. The vocabulary of the science of nature is dominated by *cause* and *effect*. In social science, the discourse must be of *means* and *end*. Social science is an investigation of purposive behavior—one looks for reasons, not causes. Therefore, the methodological orientation of social science is toward teleology. Legal theory, for Stammler and for Breuer, is stamped by a teleological mode of reflection (*teleologische Betrachtungsweise*).[8]

Breuer's early view that nature and law are not parallel to one another is modified, of course, in his theological writings, where Torah revelation is held to be the law of creation. Nonetheless, Breuer really does not stray too far from the view articulated in *Der Rechtsbegriff*. He continues to reject the idea of natural law as an indwelling normative logos discernible in nature. The only sense of natural law that he accepts is nonnormative and deterministic. It is the law that governs the process of perception and cognition. The creation nomos, on the other hand, is teleological: an emergent law of freedom. It is, in a proleptic sense, part of the nature of things, that is, the things-in-themselves, but it needs revelation and redemption to achieve its full realization.

The study of society involves the discernment of those ends for which human beings have come together to form societies. Society is a purposive concept. According to Stammler, right law is to be derived from critical reflection about the purpose and telos of the legal order.[9] Right law is not a Platonic Idea outside of any given legal order, nor is it a body of allegedly transcendent natural laws, nor is it even an ideal criterion to be applied to a legal judgment from outside the legal system, such as the categorical imperative. Right law is that positive law that correctly applies as a relevant norm to a legal case on the basis of a valid deduction from the telos of the legal order. Right law is the precipitate, so to speak, of correct judgment about the most fundamental questions of social purposiveness. By understanding what law is *for*, one can ascertain which law is right.

Stammler believed that an analysis of any society, and therefore of any legal system, would reveal a single underlying purpose. He called this purpose the "social ideal."[10] The social ideal is the "community of free-willing men." By reference to this ideal, one can determine whether a law is just. A law that serves the ideal is just; a law that impedes it is unjust. Stammler synthesized the community and the individual in framing his concept of the social ideal. The perfection of the individual is not the goal of social life, nor is the perfection of the community (at the expense of the individual) the goal. The social ideal entails a balance. The freedom of each is to be compatible with the freedom of all.

The concept of a social ideal is not composed from sources other than law and society. It is an inherent norm, drawn from critical reflection on the nature of man within the social-legal order. Tied to an anthropology grounded in freedom, the social ideal acquires a universal dimension. Stammler's 'social ideal' owes much to Kant's doctrine of innate human rights. Kant held that one has at least one right by virtue of one's humanity alone. That right is the right to freedom, in the sense of independence from the arbitrary coercion of another.[11] Law, at least constitutional law, is for Kant that by means of which persons who have come together in a social contract secure their freedom while delimiting the possibility of arbitrary coercion. "Law is therefore the totality of the conditions under which the arbitrary preference of one may coexist with the arbitrary preference of another according to the general law of freedom."[12] In Kant's image of justice, legal agents act in a way such that they do not interfere with one another. Obstructing another's actions is unjust; removing an obstruction from another is just.

The basic Kantian concept of a legal order is of a set of morally grounded commands (commands derived from a will governed by the categorical imperative), governing the external behavior of persons who have come together in a social contract, such that the inviolable right of each person to freedom can achieve a maximal, communal realization. Stammler adopted this concept of law as a criterion for judging the rightness of law and for generating correct legal decisions.

As a criterion, this concept of law, or social ideal, is transempirical while being nothing other than law per se. This means for Stammler that the ideal (as not other than law) represents the law's own movement toward right law. All positive law has, according to Stammler, the internal dynamic of tending toward *richtige Recht*. We might compare Breuer's mature view, that the analysis of nature reveals mute but still insistent creation commands, to this Stammlerian position. Within the positive law of causality is a drive toward *richtige Recht*, which only revelation can effect.

Breuer's critique of Stammler is, in essence, that he does not develop this thesis of the internal dynamic of law far enough. Breuer criticizes Stammler for being, as it were, insufficiently Kantian. The problem arises because Stammler fails to secure a completely transcendental basis for law. The locus of the problem is in Stammler's discussion of the concept of a rule. Law is made up of rules, of course, and there is evidently a difference between legal rules and rules of custom (for example, those of etiquette). Breuer claims that Stammler fails to provide a transcendental criterion by which to distinguish among kinds of rules. Instead, he resorts to the notion that legal rules are simply rules backed up by force. Suddenly, the quite empirical notion of a sanction enters the supposedly a priori edifice of the law. Consequently Stammler's legal philosophy now lacks an object with an a priori character. For Breuer, that is a death blow to any would-be science. "Social life becomes an object of its own science as soon as evidence is furnished that social judgments possess a synthetic a priori nature."[13] That is to say, social and legal reality must be capable of derivation by transcendental deduction.

Stammler, Breuer argues, is not that different from an anarchist who claims that the founding of any social order—and therefore the founding of its system of laws—is essentially an arbitrary act (*Willkurtat*)[14] Stammler has not gone deep enough in his search for a transcendental or categorical basis for society as such. The inherent movement of law toward right law cannot take place against the background of an extramoral social order. For Stammler, moral purposes such as the preservation of freedom arise subsequent to the forming of society, but the facticity of society as such is premoral and prelegal. Thus society remains in the realm of the experiential, not of the a priori. Whether or not a being is social depends entirely on the presence of rules governing its behavior. The sociality of a human being is a question of fact lacking apriority.[15] Unless that apriority can be given to social life as such, Breuer believes, the claim to being in possession of a social science—and more importantly, of right law— must be given up.

For Stammler, the presence of rules was a necessary and sufficient condition for a common life. For Breuer, it is a necessary but not a sufficient condition. The sufficient condition must be the presence of an original moral act by which society came into existence.[16] If it is the case that rules derive from a social contract of free-willing men, then the rules themselves are insufficient to judge the morality of the act whereby the contract came into being. That is to say, 'right law' is only applicable as a criterion ex post facto. What is left? The categorical imperative is the only norm capable of application to the constitutive social act. For Breuer, it is the categorical imperative that rescues social reality from merely empirical status. That the very decision to found a society is subject to evaluation under the categorical imperative ensures for Breuer the transcendental aspect of society. Society per se can ground itself in the categorical imperative. Society per se has a synthetic a priori character. In this attempt to attribute fundamental moral purpose to the founding of society may be discerned, I suspect, an apologia for the *Religionsgesellschaft* founded by Breuer's grandfather and eleven other men. Breuer was concerned to give his community a radical, archetypal ground, often referring to it as a "mother community" (*Muttergemeinde*) in Israel. His community, although founded in freedom, is the original, ancient Jewish community of Frankfurt restored to its pristine holiness. It is not difficult to intuit the mythic presence of that community in Breuer's abstract philosophical doctrine.

The assertion that the founding of society is, formally speaking, a moral, not an anomian, act leads to the judgment that social science is akin to moral philosophy. Both deal with man qua free man.[17] Yet this conclusion raises an immediate problem. Insofar as ethics deals with the autonomy and purity of the will, how can social science and the order of extrinsic rules that it investigates and that is the content of its knowledge come under the category of ethics? Breuer follows the Kantian distinction between ethics and law as that of two orders of rules; the former governs the internal disposition of the will, the latter that of external behavior. If law deals with external behavior, and if social science, jurisprudence in this case, has law as its content, then what relation can such science have to ethics? Of course, the problem here is more important than that of the nature and order of the sciences. The root problem is, how can man follow an external command and yet be free? If Breuer wants to locate ethics at the heart of society and law, then he has to reconcile the apparent logical discrepancy between the autonomy and the heteronomy of the will traditionally coordinated with each framework.

This is an issue of surpassing importance for Breuer. Although he does not mention it in this work it is a fundamental issue for modern Jewish philosophy. Samson Raphael Hirsch had maintained that only by following the commandments of the Torah could the *Mensch-Yisroel* be free. Breuer also believes that true freedom of the will is only found in accepting the "yoke of the commandments." There is a serious contradiction between Kant's concept of freedom as self-legislation and Hirsch's and Breuer's concept of freedom as submission to an emphatically Other-originated legislation. Breuer argues in *Der Neue Kusari* and other works that what seems to be heteronomy is actually autonomy because the will and the Torah become one. The will wills Torah, and the will is willed by Torah. A complete identification of the individual will with the will of the Congregation of Israel, which is a will acting in accordance with God's will, obliterates the distinction between heteronomy and autonomy. On the other hand, Kant's concept of autonomy actually reduces to heteronomy. The will that seeks freedom and postulates itself as free is actually enslaved by the very desire for freedom. So-called autonomy of the will is a fantasy conjured up in bad faith by a will that knows itself to be subordinated to its own thirst to be free. Freedom is found not in that thirst but in Torah.[18]

In *Der Rechtsbegriff*, Breuer's answer to the discrepancy between law and ethics still operates within a conventional Kantian framework. The discrepancy is overcome by the inherently moral nature of society. Underlying social law is the categorical imperative. Underlying empirical society is the kingdom of ends (*Reich der Zwecke*). The situation of man acting under the laws generated by a structurally moral social order is not fundamentally different from that of individuals acting in accordance with the categorical imperative. How can moral judgments about individual *N* be made? The moral philosopher performs a thought experiment, Breuer maintains.[19] He asks of his own will whether it would act as *N* acted under circumstances *Y*. If the moral philosopher could act with a free will as *N* did under *Y*, then *N* can be judged to have acted freely. The actual social, public nature of moral action and judgment implies that the will is not private. "My own act, originating out of pure will, is a generally valid measure for me of the acts of another."[20]

Now the lawgiver, Brewer suggests, can perform the same sort of thought experiment with respect to *N's* action under a rule. Is such an act (*Rechthandlung*) good in the same sense that a will is good? The matter is no more mysterious now than it was before. The legislator's duty is to determine whether *N's* action under rule *R* could be a moral action, that is, whether it could be the product of a free will. Breuer is saying that the procedure for moral judgment is the same in ethics and in law. It is possible to ask the question (and to receive an answer to it) whether the will is free with respect to a moral or a legal act. The difference is that in the former evaluation, circumstances *Y* are merely given. In the case of the legislator, the circumstances (here, rule *R*) are not givens but variables. The lawgiver must design *R* in such a way that every *N* can act freely under it.

The behavior of man under law and under the direction of his own conscience is open to evaluation by means of the same procedure. This goes some way toward closing the gap between autonomous and heteronomous willing. Breuer also asserts that man himself is of such a nature as to marginalize the danger of heteronomy. Man has a moral nature (*sittliches Wesen*) that is, at the same time, a social nature.[21] Breuer wants now to say that man is of a moral nature if and only if he is of a social nature. The moral law (*Sittengesetz*) cannot be thought of as governing the practical reason of isolated individuals. The moral law, rather, creates a world where moral willing and behavior are possible. Ethics requires a social context. Man is not a moral being outside of the kingdom of ends. Moral law and legal rules are, precisely, constitutive of this kingdom.

The moral law is therefore not a criterion for judging *N's* will alone; it renders possible social judgment (*soziales Urteil*). We judge the acts of another in society on the same basis as we judge the will in isolation. Such judgment would not be possible unless social agents were understood to act in accordance with principles reflective of the categorical imperative. That is to say, those legal rules in terms of which social agents act and in terms of which they are judged must have an a priori, binding nature. Furthermore, acting freely under social-legal rules, as in the case of free action under moral maxims, is possible if and only if one can be both the subject and the legislator of those rules. If rules have an a priori, binding character, then one is in fact both their subject and their author when one is a member of the kingdom of ends. Insofar as one is a moral being, one is a member of the kingdom of ends. On Breuer's analysis, social-legal rules are shown to possess the same universal, formal validity as the moral law. They are creations of moral beings who are both subject to the rules and authors of the rules. The aim of the rules is to order the external behavior of moral agents with respect to the kingdom of ends in a manner parallel to the way moral maxims order internal states of the will. "There are thus social rules with formal general validity and necessity. In this conception, I unite individuals insofar as they are all supposed to stand under rules of external behavior."[22]

Breuer bases the concept of society on constitutive social-legal rules with an a priori, binding nature. Rules, if they are properly understood as possessing an a priori character, are now necessary and sufficient conditions for society. Stammler understood that the concept of society entails the concept of a rule, but he contented himself with a social science that studies the syntax of rules, so to speak, rather than their transcendental etymologies. Breuer clearly agrees with Stammler that rules have central importance for the concept of society. Breuer holds this view, with Stammler, against the view of another contemporary, Georg Simmel, and his student, Martin Buber. Simmel and Buber held that rules are epiphonomenal to social reality rather than essential (der Kern und Wesen).[23] It is not difficult to see why rules should be seen as a sine qua non of social reality by an orthodox Jew such as Breuer and reduced to marginal status by a Jewish antinomian like Buber. Breuer's philosophy emphasizes the legal nature of the revelation of God's will, whereas Buber makes it clear that revelation is a personalistic, not a legalistic, event. But these concerns are of course not stated in Breuer's critique of Simmel and his school.

Against Simmel, Breuer insists that rules are primary, constitutive structures of social reality. Rules are the data by which the object of social science becomes known: rules are the content of the knowledge of society. Critical method asks, Through which property does society become an object of its own, appropriate science?[24] The answer is that the content of social knowledge is a set of rules that possess a necessary, universal character.

The very same moral law that philosophers thought of primarily in relation to individuals is in fact an inherently social concept. The kernal of individual ethics is social ethics. Man qua moral being is necessarily man qua social being. "As an ethical being, man is necessarily made social. The form of this social existence is necessarily law, which directs itself to man with authority."[25] The legal order that confronts man with binding authority is an empirical fact, which can be deduced transcendentally from the concept of man as a moral being. Because man is both moral and social he requires rules as a consequence of his very being. To be self-conscious as a moral being is to be cognizant of duties owed to others and of duties that others owe to oneself. The system of rules, the legal order, gives expression to that framework of duties.

Breuer, while rejecting natural law theory, does affirm a parallelism between the role of law in nature and the role of law in human social life. The kingdom of ends is coordinate to the kingdom of nature.[26] By belonging to the kingdom of ends, however, man becomes free of the rule of nature, that is, of the law of causality that governs the kingdom of nature. Man enters the causality of freedom (*Kausalität der Freiheit*).[27] The rules of the kingdom of ends differ from those of natural law in that they are reasons for, not causes of, action. Because these rules are reasons that are chosen by free agents, rather than implicit, autonomous causative factors, the kingdom of ends is not a presently existent state of affairs in the way that the kingdom of nature is. The kingdom is a social ideal, a telos of law and of moral praxis.

The implication of the futurity that characterizes the kingdom of ends is that social life per se is an obligation. The founding of society, far from the arbitrariness given to it by Stammler, is a moral act, indeed, a moral duty. As a consequence of this, every social whole stands under inherently moral rules, whether the members of that whole are conscious of those rules or not. (An implication of this view for Breuer's later thought is that the Jewish society where the members are conscious of the rules and accept them as their society-forming, constitutional concept realizes the social ideal in the most exemplary fashion.)

The universal, a priori aspect of social rules does not depend upon the historical discovery of the rules by the philosopher. Men stood under the judgment of the categorical imperative long before

Kant gave expression to it.[28] Similarly, the laws of the natural world do not depend for their efficacy on our scientific perception of them. For these reasons, the kingdom of ends, the true normative character of social reality, is both future and present, both ought and is. The kingdom is the telos of social order as well as its immanent, sufficient reason. This sense of the futurity as well as the immanence of the normative kingdom carries over directly into Breuer's theology. Redemption has precisely this dual aspect of present and future norm.

Two other consequences of this normative theory of society carry over to his theology. The first is that, owing to its transcendental, a priori character, human law, like natural law, is not invented by man but discovered by him. The second is that law is always valid and authoritative despite the individual—or the society's—failure to recognize the law as law. Authority and subjective assent are unrelated. Both of these principles echo traditional Jewish notions of the legal character of Torah and find a broad resonance in Breuer's later works.

The notion that law is not invented by man but discovered by him is a very old one. The ancient Israelites shared with Mesopotamian peoples the belief in the heavenly descent of law. The rabbinic sages believed in "Torah from Heaven," the descent of the preexistent law into the midst of the nation. What later generations of sages discover has already been intuited by previous generations. Medieval thinkers outside of the Jewish tradition held to this view both in the philosophical theory of natural law and in the first-order operation of common-law traditions. In Germanic society, for example, ascertaining the law for any given case meant finding the appropriate rule from the wisdom of custom and inherited tradition. Law was always found, not made. A Teutonic chieftain might give expression to the law in a statute or assize, but he did so in the name of all of the tribe, past and present, whose property the law was. He recognized that the law was timeless, archetypal, and independent of the expression he had given to it. Law was both an atemporal norm and the property of a group.[29]

This ancient universal notion resurfaces in Breuer's theory of law. The body of positive laws that govern our external relations with one another is traceable to the moral law, which is not made but found. In every human circumstance to which a law could apply, the question could be asked, What ought so and so to do? These oughts Breuer suggests, are the sentences of law that the legislator must find. The ought is a formal constant behind any

positive law. The content of the ought is the empirically appropriate variable. The legislator discovers this content when applying
the formal norm to the actual case. This mix of formal- constant
and empirical-variable elements in law leads Breuer to another
comparison of positive and natural law. "The law is the 'natural
law' of the kingdom of ends."[30] Just as the sentences of natural law
change as science changes, so too in jurisprudence. The sentences
of law change to meet new empirical circumstances, but the underlying legality in both realms remains the same. Our expression
and comprehension of the law in both realms are historically conditioned. An unchanging verbal expression of the law would only
be possible for one not entrapped under the veil of Maya.[31]

In the Jewish theology that Breuer subsequently builds upon
this legal philosophy, the unchanging, eternal law is the Torah-in-
itself. It assumes the role of the natural law of the kingdom of
ends, that partially real, partially ideal, unstable dynamic that
Breuer identifies as creation. The historically conditioned discovery of that inherent law is the oral Torah, the statutes of which are
the unique and constitutive possession of the Congregation of
Israel.

The other concept derived from the transcendental authority
of the law that plays a role in Breuer's Jewish thought is that of the
binding nature of law irrespective of human apperception or attitude. It does not matter what a man thinks of rule R: rule R commands his obedience despite his indifference to its authority. This
is not to say that Breuer believes that all rules are just and command obedience. Like any serious legal philosopher he must develop a set of principles to determine what rules are right law.
Breuer follows Stammler in this regard. Just laws are those that
bind sovereign and subject to an equal extent and that can be derived from the social ideal. Those laws that meet these criteria are
authentic law and command without respect to private subjectivity. "The law [*Recht*] is a coercive rule, binding upon external behavior, that has been derived immediately from the moral law."[32]
This pervasive ethicizing of law has rendered positive law strictly
deontological. Law is understood as duty; as a demand of the conscience. The moral law still commands despite the individual's
indifference to his conscience. Similarly, the Prussian law still
commands despite individual's feelings about or even disbelief in
the existence of the Kaiser.

In Breuer's Jewish thought, this line of reasoning, coupled
with his epistemological assault on individuation and subjectivity,

serves to secure for those who are faithful to the law in its objectivity, and to them alone, title to the Jewish inheritance. Jews are distinguished from the remainder of humanity by their well-formed consciousness of the will of the Creator. Those Jews who fully and consciously execute that will fully realize the promise of their Jewishness. As in legal theory, empirical-historical description of how a legal system functions is irrelevant from the point of view of one subject to the law. What counts is the transcendental moral logic of the system. In describing law or in analyzing the condition of the Jews, it is not a matter of is but of ought. Consequently, although Breuer is merciless in describing the actual condition of the Orthodox (let alone of the non-Orthodox), his descriptions of Jewish law per se are highly idealized. Breuer idealizes positive law as incarnate moral law. Consequently, he presents an idealized halakhah as the incarnation of creation law.[33]

Breuer has attempted to ground empirical, positive law in a transcendental moral norm. In the process, he attributed radical moral value to human sociality as such and to empirical society, at least to those societies that exemplify the social ideal. He envisions law and society as sanctified instruments for the pursuit of a secular version of the millenium, the kingdom of ends. Written before the First World War, in the midst of a happy world that he himself described as a "paradise," Breuer's theory is awash with optimism. It reflects a faith in social perfection, in moral freedom under just law enacted on the social stage.

Why should Breuer have rejected these views of law and society? Or more precisely, why should he have restricted them to an ideal Jewish polity? Undoubtedly, the bitter and disillusioning experiences of the First World War shook whatever remained of his liberal faith. Epitomized by characters like Falk Neft in his novel, *Falk Neft's Heimkehr* (1923), Breuer's post-war disillusionment profoundly altered his view of history, of which the theory of society and law forms a part. As I have suggested, Breuer holds onto the theory he worked out in *Der Rechtsbegriff* but limits its applicability to Jewish law and nationhood. These become concrete expressions of ideal, transcendental norms. The law, nationhood, and history of the Gentiles slip away into the "kingdom of nature," where merciless necessity and need rule. Nonetheless, and somewhat paradoxically, Breuer continued to preserve a high regard for all law, and for the human desire to ascertain right law (*Rechtssinn*). He retains the view that man does make legal progress and that there is messianic potential in that purely human fact.[34]

As mentioned above, for Breuer society is a purposive concept, and a social science, unlike a natural science, must be marked by a teleological outlook. The Stammlerian social ideal entails a constructive, future-oriented human purposiveness. Society and law are uniquely related, defining one another in a dialectical fashion. At this point, the exposition of Breuer's legal theory can be supplemented with a presentation of his social theory. The latter is not as highly developed as the former, but it is its necessary complement. To contrast kinds of law (Jewish and German, for example), one must contrast kinds of society, kinds of social ideal.

LAW AND SOCIETY

Just as Breuer located his epistemology in a philosophical anthropology, he came to situate his legal theory in a social theory, which in turn he subordinated to a philosophy of history. Breuer reiterates, qualifies, and refines the understanding of society expressed in *Der Rechtsbegriff* in the last work published during his lifetime, *Moriah*. The purpose of this work is to establish the character of world history, such that the unique historic career of Israel can emerge as light does out of darkness. *Moriah* contains a concise exposition of Breuer's basic theory of social reality.

Man is created as a social being. Man is needy. Without parents and a broad network for mutual assistance, human beings cannot develop. Sociality is therefore, in a sense, grounded in need.[35] This need, however, is spiritual as well as physical. Man cannot develop into a being who uses moral and other evaluative concepts without society. The solitary man—who exists only in the imagination—could not love or hate. He could not be a man. Culture, the world of shared meaning, is to man as space is to objects. Culture is a necessary existence condition for inherently social man. Yet if natural need were the only ground for society, then society would be strictly naturalistic in character. Breuer must ground society in transcendental elements, in the manner of *Der Rechtsbegriff*, to lift it out of the realm of natural phenomena alone. Thus Breuer distinguishes between human society and animal society. Animal societies, for example those of ants and bees, are entirely natural and instinctive. They are "analytic," that is, they are nothing more than the sum of their individual parts. Although human sociality is also natural, the fact that we are self-conscious beings immediately distances our forms of sociality from all others. For we recognize value in phenomena. Even though society is natural for us, that is, it is part of the realm of cause and effect, the perception of value in the effect lifts the effect out of the causal nexus and places it on another level.

But it is not simply the human perception of value in human social life that distinguishes the latter from animal sociality. For 'value' could mean utility, and this sort of ascription (X is good because it promotes my life) is virtually animalistic. What definitely distinguishes the human from the animal is human consciousness of the order of society. Only by means of their perception of order do human beings recognize themselves to be social beings.[36] Here Breuer's methodological labors on the question of the criteria for the social sciences are reiterated. The perception of order, of rules, secures knowledge of human sociality for the human agent.

The order (seder) of society is not fixed by nature. Natural order, the result of the repose of God and the transformation of creation into nature, represents the end product of God's creation commands. God said, "Let there be!" and it came to be. Nature is the "it came to be" of God's word. But God did not answer his "Let there be" with a consummated "and it came to be" when he created man. He gave man freedom, depriving him of the instinctual, determinitive drives of the animals. He let man call forth in freedom his own "and it came to be."

Thus man proceeds to construct social order intentionally, not instinctually. The family, the first stage of social order, is governed by rules and principles that serve to complete the passage between God's unfulfilled "Let there be" and the human response of "and it came to be." Breuer distinguishes 'order' from 'organization' (irgun). It is not the natural components (father, mother, etc.) that, in the requisite organization, constitute the family, but the conscious, intentional purpose to which this organization is put. Order is a teleological concept, organization is a static one.[37]

Breuer now distinguishes two fundamental kinds of order enacted in human social life. The first is purely consensual society, represented philosophically by anarchism. The other is coercive society. The former kind, like the society of ants, is analytic: nothing remains of it once its individuals are subtracted. The latter however is synthetic. Individuals give up something (namely their individual sovereignty) in order to create it. Something more than an organization of private sovereigns has arisen: an order in which one may be coerced against one's will. Although private consent was a factor at the time of grounding the social contract, it subsequently acquires the status of a dependent variable. The constitutive, synthetic dimension to this kind of social order is law. Law is what binds the members of society, whether they consent or not, into a formal union that has, as it were, a life of its own.[38]

Of course, 'law' in this sense is a strictly formal concept. Of just and unjust law nothing has yet been said. In order to move from the formal characteristics of social order and law to an evaluative analysis, Breuer moves down a path familiar from *Der Rechtsbegriff*. Nonnatural properties—in that work, the categorical imperative,—and in *Moriah*, Ideas (*ḥazonot*)—determine whether a particular order and its law are just or unjust, good or evil. Ideas such as 'justice', 'goodness', 'beauty', and 'holiness' are not products of the natural framework of cause and effect. To ask of an action, Is it just? is not to ask, What caused it? The Ideas are appropriated by man in freedom. Mere concepts (*musagim*), on the other hand, are natural. They occur within the matrix of perception and cognition and are shared, to a certain extent, with the animals. As we have seen, Breuer inherits this Platonic doctrine of Ideas from Schopenhauer. Breuer, unlike Schopenhauer, ascribes the source of the Ideas to God, however, by means of the Ideas, man is able to mold his reality rather than be molded by it.[39] The Ideas are a gift of God.

To derive the Ideas from God is not to render them obscure or inaccessible. Breuer believes that the Idea of justice is universally human, as Kant has shown. All human beings long for it; all sense that power and oppression are not the final word. And yet the Ideas, particularly that of justice (the Idea of Ideas, *ḥazon he–ḥazonot*), remain without effect or realization on the plane of history. The historical and political experiences of actual societies everywhere subvert the Idea of justice. Thus the comparative study of societies, on Breuer's view, is a study of the extent to which their rules (their 'orders') exemplify the Ideas, particularly the Idea of justice. His claim for Jewish sociolegal order is that it realizes this Idea to a greater extent than any other form of order. Furthermore, to depart from the Torah's specific, Ideal form of order is to impede the redemptive realization of the Idea.[40]

An early study of Breuer's presents such a comparative analysis of two conflicting visions of sociolegal reality, the Jewish and the German. Here, without the grand historiosophical structure that characterizes his later work, Breuer presents a decisive contrast between revealed law and its social order and the forms of order chosen by humanity at large.

Die Rechtsphilosophischen Grundlagen des Jüdischen und des Modernen Rechts (The Legal-Philosophical Fundamentals of Jewish and Modern Law, 1910, hereafter cited as Die Grundlagen) develops a deep structural comparison between Jewish and modern law through an analysis of the relation between law, ethics, and society in each system.[41] Breuer tries to isolate the inherent social ideal incarnated by each system of law.

Die Grundlagen begins with a commentary on a sensational incident in the contemporary press. A German judge in a ruling concerning the divorce of two Jews who were Russian nationals determined that Jewish law was inadmissible in a German court because it ran counter to "good morals." While the German civil code provided for a mutual right of divorce, Jewish law provides only for the husband's right to divorce his wife. The German judge, in the case brought before him by the Jewish wife (who sought the divorce), ruled that the husband could not appeal to the principles of Jewish law to frustrate her because Jewish law entails unequal treatment of the sexes. This ruling, although later rescinded by the judge, touched off a wave of uneasiness in the Jewish community. An official declaration to the effect that Jewish law ran counter to good German morals sent tremors through both liberal and Orthodox Jewry.

Breuer found an opening in this sensation for a systematic study of the differences between Jewish and modern German law. Unlike many of his contemporaries, he was not daunted by the possibility that Jewish and modern law may very well embody disjunctive moralities. Breuer is at his most characteristic in this essay. He eschews any facile, apologetic harmonization between the two systems, welcoming the possibility of discrepancy between them. In exploring this discrepancy, Breuer begins to apply some general legal-philosophical concepts to an analysis of Torah.

Breuer points out that there are indeed areas in which Jewish law diverges very considerably from modern law. Modern law is grounded in the proposition that all persons are, respecting their legal status, equal. Although positive law falls short of this norm, equality before the law is nonetheless a key normative principle, an ideal of modern law. Jewish law, on the other hand, enshrines certain fundamental inequalities. In addition to the relevant disabilities for women, the slave and the Gentile are not equal to Jewish males under Jewish law. Breuer categorically rejects an historicist explanation for these inequalities. He affirms, on the contrary, that the whole Torah is contemporary, valid law. Torah is not a museum piece invalidated in some way by history. The legal matter of the Torah is timeless or, at least not time-bound. The assertion leads Breuer to make the bold claim that although the practice of slavery has vanished from the world, the principle of slavery must still be valid! Any jurisprudential analysis of the underlying principles of Jewish law can do no less than treat the law under the assumption of atemporal validity. Appeal to historical influences is reductionistic and methodologically intolerable.

But why must one come to Torah with a methodology that takes seriously Torah's transcendental claim? Although Breuer is not explicit, we can assume that his view of the transcendental, normative nature of law as such is at work here. It is not just a matter of his Orthodoxy. It is a matter of his Kantianism as well. History and historical development, in an Hegelian sense, for example, are largely irrelevant to the phenomenology of law. Breuer insists that the phenomenologist or philosopher of law take an "internal point of view."[42] Explicitly, Breuer asserts that the student of law must bring to his subject the perspective of those who are themselves subject to the law. To appeal to history is to apply an extrinsic standard of rationality to the phenomenon. One must understand Torah from the hermeneutic perspective of the obedient insider: the law in its entirety is binding and valid. Derived no doubt from Hirsch ("As Jews must we read it") and philosophical sources, Breuer's orientation enjoys broad acceptance today among phenomenologists.

In his description of modern law, Breuer enunciates the same basic points he expresses in *Der Rechtsbegriff*. The essence of modern law consists in the balance of individual interests against each other in order to secure a society of free and equal individuals. This is how law appears from an external point of view.[43] From the internal point of view, this arrangement of balanced interests appears as an arrangement of powers granted to those who make and enforce legal rules. The sentences of the law, as we have seen in Stammler, aim to maximize the freedom of activity of individuals in some relevant circumstance (for instance, entering into a contract) while preserving the order and freedom of the community. Modern law is throughout a law that is conscious of and responsible toward the social ideal. It is not lopsided in favor of the sovereign, nor does it elevate the collectivity over the individual. It tries to balance claims and rights in such a way that the good of every individual and of the group per se is served.

The law is not only social, but—as we have seen—moral. The sentences of law, while addressing concrete problems in an expedient manner, need to be justified by something higher than expedience. Modern law justifies itself by an appeal to universal, human moral norms. Breuer grants modern law considerable moral dignity, by basing it on human dignity. Human dignity is the criterion by which the law is judged and justified. On the basis of the dignity of human persons whom the law posits as free and rational, the law derives the equality of all human beings as legal agents. Modern law will not tolerate the notion of fundamental inequality. Equality must govern law as it already governs ethics.

The discovery of equality before the law has been wrested from centuries of social struggle. All human beings can be conceived as equals because all belong to the human community. Modern law is based on a universalistic vision of humanity as a single community. Accordingly, the law rejects any remnants of legal tribalism and moves inexorably in the direction of international law. True law is no respecter of borders. For this reason, the German judge would not admit the applicability of Jewish law in the case of the Russian nationals who were married under it. The good morals of German law are universal morals, respecting no geographical or legal frontiers. Jewish law appears, in comparison with modern, universalistic law both immoral and tribal.[44] Precisely the overcoming of tribal law, which denigrates the status of foreigners, and the achievement of an internationally oriented law constitute the greatest progress in legal history.

Breuer provides a fair characterization of the system of modern law he aims to critique. He does not set up a straw man that could easily be knocked down. The ideal, universalizing dynamic that Breuer finds characteristic of modern law and ethics has come under siege in recent debates. In his own way, as we shall now see, Breuer puts the questions, "Whose justice? Which rationality?" to a self-confident, universalistic legal theory. He advocates neither an antimodern return to tribalism nor a postmodern abandonment of all universalisms.

Breuer now turns to an analysis of the presuppositions of Jewish law. It might seem from the foregoing as if the discovery of the unity of the human community were the achievement of modern law alone. Jewish law, however, is the very place where that unity was first made known! The biblical declaration that man is made in the image of God immediately secures the concept of human community, exceeding all of the universalistic strivings of pagan antiquity. Judaism's concept of the unity of humanity is the hopeful message that Christianity borrowed and spread. Judaism does not originate, as does modern law, in the notion of community and the correlative notion of equality; rather, Judaism *presupposes* those notions.

Why then does Jewish law seem to propound some fundamental inequalities, as if to repudiate its own presupposition? The answer is found in the fact that the Jewish concepts of the unity of the human community, of human equality, and of dignity are indeed constitutive of modern law but only presuppositional for Jewish law. Modern law is a purely human undertaking. Naturally, it can envisage no norm higher than dignity and equality. Jewish law however is a divinely revealed system: it entails a purpose higher than the achievement of a social order commensurate with human values. For Jewish law, holiness, not dignity, doing God's will, not individuality, is the norm-setting principle. While human law aims at securing an appropriate human order, Jewish law aims at the realization of a divine redemptive purpose.

This is not to say that an appropriate human order and the divine redemptive purpose are exclusive of one another. To the contrary, the latter includes the former. Modern law sets as its purpose the preservation of the freedom of individual agents and of group life. Jewish law presupposes such autonomy and balance. It begins with freedom and then moves to another purpose. That purpose is the perfection of obedience to the divine will by means of the execution of duties that God has assigned to humanity. The Jew is to receive the divinely ordained duties and to execute them against the background of a society of balanced interests with a will that wills freedom.

It could still be argued, however, that this apparent formal complementarity between the two systems of law begs the question. Does the fact that Jewish law presupposes human equality matter if human equality drops out of sight in the dispensation of human duties? Breuer replies, as we might have suspected, by moving beyond the notion of a putative complementarity. In fact, he argues, the alleged cohesion between ethics and modern law is more apparent than real: only in Jewish law are dignity and equality actually achieved. Here we begin to see the outlines of his conviction that humanity is fulfilled in Judaism. Human law aims at what Jewish law has implicitly achieved.

Breuer claims that in modern law statute and norm, law and ethics are alienated from one another. This is so because ethics deals with internal states of the will, with whether the will wills autonomously or heteronomously. Ethics is not concerned, as is law, with general classes of action, but with the internal, practical reasoning of the agent. Ethics addresses the individual act; law addresses the typical action. The very attempt, culminating in Kant, to secure a universal, transcendental authority for ethics severed ethics from empirical circumstances, partitioning ethics and law. Because the law must speak to typical classes of action, which are correlated with concrete circumstances, law could no longer look to ethics for immediate guidance. The business of law—balancing interests in society—was increasingly left to nonmoral, utilitarian considerations. Any modern attempt, such as Stammler's (or Breuer's own, for that matter), to reintegrate ethics into law, whatever its theoretical pretensions, tends to amount, in practical terms, to applying ethics as a control for legal power. That is, ethics is reintegrated as a boundary concept. Moral considerations such as mutual freedom, are set up as criteria to evaluate how the legal system is working. Ethics becomes a theory of legal boundaries rather than the heart and soul of the law. Even for the best theories of modern law, ethics and law diverge into separate categories.

I suspect that Breuer's critique of modern law is also a critique of Kant. In expressing his discontent with the idea of ethics as a boundary concept, Breuer, like the German idealists, seeks a positive content for those concepts to which Kant assigned not a content but a role. Breuer's critique of modernity, which is so often a *Kantkritik*, expresses a dissatisfaction from within the Kantian orbit. It is true that Breuer interprets and applies Kant in quite unorthodox ways, but the same might be said for the idealists a generation or two after Kant's death. Of all that has been written with Kant in mind, Breuer's work is not the strangest.

Given the separation between law and ethics, modern law is not inherently moral. It relies on ethics to correct its inherent abuses. Law aims at ethics; ethics strives to direct law. The law, however, does not achieve a positive moral worth because ethics is not inherent to it. Ethics functions only as a check: legislate such that rule R does not infringe upon the freedom of agent N. Alienated from law, ethics is unable to invest law with positive, categorical worth. In this "categorical vacuum," law is abandoned to hypothetical considerations. Ethics functions only on the level of the legislator's or judge's conscience. Consequently, the idea of a unified human community of free moral agents, that is, the moral postulate derived from the concept of human dignity, is—so to speak—the conscience but not the essence of modern law.[45]

The claim Breuer now makes for Jewish law is that in it, ethics and legal statutes become one. Jewish law need not aim at freedom; it presupposes it, reflects it, and supersedes it in its pursuit of holiness. Ethics is not a formal regulative principle but inherent to every statute of Jewish law. Ethics does not merely judge an intention; it prescribes an action.[46] Ethics so permeates Jewish law that the balance of social interests that law in general affects is replaced by a distribution of duties. The balance of interests and the delegation of power to social agents, both of which pertain to legal systems in general, do not pertain to Jewish law. Delegation of power is replaced by distribution of duties. The task of balancing social interests is preempted by the distribution of duties as well. Non-Jewish law must guard human freedom and dignity by balancing interests and delegating power; in Jewish law, freedom and dignity depend on the degree to which duties are fulfilled.[47]

There is therefore a fundamental and crucial distinction about what law and ethics are for humanity at large and for Judaism. For the former, ethics is independent of law; the relation between them constitutes a challenge. For the latter, insofar as law falls entirely under the concept of duty, law and ethics are coterminous. Of course, this equation of law and duty would not suffice to render such duties moral were it not for the fact that the duties of Jewish law are duties delegated by God. The Creator of ethics is also the Creator of law in Judaism.[48] In Judaism, therefore, what is meant by law is not a structure that balances the interests of diverse agents in society by means of coercive rules, but a structure that prescribes spheres of obligations to diverse classes of social agents. The total system of these spheres of obligations produces a harmonious, balanced society.

If it were the case that Jewish law were a purely human affair, then grievous imbalances of interests and of power, as, for example, between man and woman, master and slave, native and alien, would indeed be offensive to ethics, whose norm is the unity of the human community. But since that law is divinely ordained and its norm is the fulfillment of differentially prescribed duties, there is no offense to ethics. The master and the slave have different roles to play: ethics concerns itself not with a comparison of the status attaching to these roles, but with the degree to which the roles are fulfilled. Ethics in Judaism begins with the assumption of a fundamental differentiation of roles, which philosophical ethics cannot help but misunderstand. The differentiated sets of duties specified by the Torah are *ex hypothesi* inherently moral.

In purely human legal systems, the abuses that arise are criticized by the moral conscience. But how is that conscience to become legally effective? It must become effective through the same legal mechanisms of coercive rules that are themselves in need of correction. New rules must be formed to reform old ones. But again the autonomy of ethics results in the heteronomy of law. The law that must protect "good morals" itself fails to be moral, for it is backed by the threat of sanctions.[49] Whenever the law seeks to regulate relationships that cannot, in society, be left to conscience alone, the potential of legal sanctions, which are feared, bases compliance with the law on the heteronomy of the will and thus robs that compliance of moral value. Breuer seems to say that when one takes action under a profane law, that is, under a law that has been separated from ethics, one loses one's freedom. One might conclude, although Breuer does not do so explicitly, that the German judge who thought himself to be an upholder of ethics failed to be moral in a fundamental way.

In *Der Rechtsbegriff*, it was precisely the nonseparation of law and ethics in any legal system for which Breuer argued. That view is discarded here in favor of the exclusive claim of Jewish law to inherent morality. This means, of course, that only under Torah can humanity truly enjoy its dignity and freedom, a central theme in Breuer's work. Owing to the freedom one enjoys under Torah, the Jewish people are the true nation of humanity. (*Menschheitsnation*), whose communal existence is a light, if not an eschatological vanguard, to the nations.

The task of preserving the genuine social ideal of the free human community falls to the Jews who continue to live under Jewish law. Only there can one pursue duty in freedom and autonomy, rather than under the cloud of heteronomous compulsion. Within the system of duties prescribed by this uniquely ethical law, the legal subject is perfectly free to fulfill or not to fulfill the commands encumbent upon him. (Breuer evidently does not believe in religious coercion. Although he insists on Jewish society being objectively constituted by "Torah institutions," he seems to leave room, surprisingly, for fundamental disaffection with the religious system.) The ideal of human community is handed over to free subjects to protect and to realize, not to coercive legal mechanisms. Consequently, institutions such as polygamy and slavery, which crippled societies in need of moral correctives for these ostensible imbalances of interest and power, led to no diminution of national vigor in Israel. The Jews were able to sustain the presuppositions of dignity, equality, and community within these institutions precisely because they understood them as a distribution of heaven-sent duties. This is not to say that some Jews did not abuse these institutions and profane them; they did. The Second Jewish Commonwealth was destroyed precisely because the idea of human community was abused by those given freedom by God to protect it.[50] Nevertheless, the proof that the ostensibly immoral institutions of Jewish law bear no relation to parallel institutions in Gentile law, and that, consequently, those Jewish institutions are not contrary to good morals, is that Israel survives. The inconsistency of ruling out an appeal to history at the beginning of his essay and concluding with one was apparently lost on Breuer.

The nations, with their struggle to relate ethics to law, make desperate progress and then fail. Israel, given its divine moral law, often fails to fulfill it but, unlike the nations, has already—at least in principle—"arrived." The possibility of redemption for the nations is fully eschatological: law and ethics must be reconciled, only then can history be redeemed. (It is pertinent to note that Breuer saw in the Balfour Declaration a redemptive dynamic, on the side of the Gentiles, whereby law and ethics came at last into correlation.) The redemption of Israel, on the other hand, is in a sense immanent, for law and ethics are already reconciled. Justice already prevails within the Congregation of Israel, although it does not yet fully prevail in empirical Israel. For that the Torah community must achieve its full historical stature. To this dynamic I now turn.

FROM HISTORY TO METAHISTORY

Breuer has built his philosophical system on a series of oppositions: willing will versus willed will, creation versus nature, and so on. Underlying the whole structure is the opposition: Israel versus the nations. The opposition that crowns the whole construction is the dialectic of history versus metahistory. As in the opposition of creation and nature, the two terms represent internally related realities. *Metahistory* refers both to a perspective, a view that a subject has of history, and to a unique history per se. Breuer presents the metahistory of the Jewish people as both a hermeneutic and an ontological category.

This ambiguity stems from what Nathan Rotenstreich has termed the "classical tradition" in the philosophy of history, represented by Hegel, Marx, Comte, and others. History refers to both the course of events and the understanding of the course. The disposition of the subject is a key factor in the conditionality of the object.[51] Thus much of Breuer's historiography is devoted to critical analysis of the typical situations of those who make claims about the nature of Jewish history. Breuer's metahistory is directed against secularist-nationalist and historicist readings of Jewish history. *Metahistory* refers to the perspectival stance one must assume in order to grasp Jewish reality correctly. *A parte objecti,* 'metahistory' refers to a particular, irreducible reality: the order of a human society under God's law articulated over time. God is actually present in this temporally extended order. The continuum of divine presence, often intuited by the metahistorical agents as divine absence, means that Jewish metahistory is messianic or providential history, unlike history per se. Messianism represents both a hermeneutic perspective on events and an ontological characteristic of the events within metahistory. Thus an early discussion of the unique character of Jewish history immediately involves the concept, indeed the praxis, of messianism.

The essential opposition between Jewish and world history is inadequately recognized by contemporary Jews. In *Messiasspuren* Breuer begins to develop his philosophy of history by attending to the epistemic subject who cognizes history. The great danger to modern Jewish existence, represented paradigmatically by Zionism, is its secularization. Secularized concepts of law, society, and nationhood lay the Jewish reality on a Procrustean bed of alien interpretations. To understand Jewish history, one must stand loyally within that history by accepting the sociolegal reality of Torah, which alone enables there to be a Jewish nation fit to act in history. Law constitutes society. Consciousness of the order of the Jewish sociolegal reality is a necessary precondition for cognizing Jewish history.

The immediate object of analysis in *Messiasspuren* is messianism, for Jews cannot understand either their own history or world history apart from its telos. Reappropriating Jewish messianism is the way for Jews to become truly historical. But messianism, Breuer asserts, has been abandoned by modern Jews for the false ideology of nationalism and its versions of political redemption.[52] The Jews must regain their own authentic, that is, messianic response to history. To reappropriate messianism is to regain an appropriate self-perception (*Selbsterkenntnis*) and to repudiate the fractured vision of himself that the Jew encounters in the splintered European looking glass.

The concept of messianism that Breuer articulates is emphatically this-worldly. Messianism implies an immanent eschatology of political praxis. Traces of the messianic possibility are discernible in the present. Messianism is the possibility of this-worldly perpetual peace between nations, the realization of which depends upon Israel living in a distinct, political way under the rule of Torah. The exile of Israel indicates the exile of all nations in history (*Golusgeschichte der Menschheit*).

Gershom Scholem has shown that Jewish messianism has always had both active and passive dimensions. There are classical formulations that emphasize the discontinuity of present history with the messianic kingdom. Such apocalyptic formulations imply the futility of human effort and foster an attitude of passive expectation.[53] There are also messianic formulations in which human activity has a role in precipitating the consummation of history. These views opened up the possibility of radical and often disastrous messianic movements, such as that of Sabbetai Zevi in the seventeenth century. The essentially conservative rabbinic tradition preferred the disjunctive, passival concept of messianism.

Medieval Jewish rationalism protected the passive rabbinic tradition that delegitimated messianic praxis, and yet this rationalism produced an unforeseen result. For Maimonides, the end time is entirely deferred to divine grace and initiative. However, its posthistorical, disjunctive features reacquire—owing to Maimonides' rationalism—purely historical characteristics. Rationalism, while agreeing with apocalypticism on the issue of God's initiation of the messianic period, neutralizes the apocalyptic, disjunctive features of the messianic scenario. The end time becomes very much like the present time. Indeed, for some contemporary messianists, Gush Emunim, for example, the end time *is* the present time.

The rationalistic domestication of the end time had the ironic effect of stimulating messianic praxis anew. If the end time is not wholly unlike the present time, then the notion that some activity in the present could conduce toward the consummation of history is tacitly readmitted. Although this development is not found in Maimonides, it is found in the way both medieval kabbalists and modern Jews have interpreted him. In the modern period, the rationalistic, anti-apocalyptic version of messianism provided by Maimonides was translated into a program of moral progress by Reform Judaism on the one hand and into a program of restorative-utopian activism by Zionism on the other.

Liberal proponents of Judaism as a "religion of reason" read Maimonides to imply that the pursuit of a moral social order could bring about a secular millenium. Hermann Cohen, for example, taught that the messianic era comes about as the product of Israel's moral-missionary activity in the diaspora. Israel per se is the messiah who converts the nations to the knowledge of the one true God. This conversion founds a moral, international order that is not supernatural in the sense of being apocalyptically disjunctive with the present order. (It is in Cohen's terms "supersensible" (*übersinnlich*) in the sense that it is within the range of human possibility but has not yet achieved realization.[54] Maimonides, one imagines, would not have agreed with Cohen's deciphering of his intentions.

Breuer's messianism is in the rationalist, Maimonidean tradition, modified by elements of Kabbalah. While the end time is a nonapocalyptic, supersensible possibility, it is reachable through religious praxis and historical movement. The concept of the messiah does not refer to an opposition between this world and a disjunctive world to come, but rather to the opposition between this tragic world and the world into which it could be transformed. "*Messiah* does not mean the opposition between 'this worldly' and 'other worldly.' Eden is on earth. *Messiah* means the opposition between present and future; *messiah* means historical self-liberation."[55]

Although their strategies for historical consummation differ, Breuer and Cohen agree that Israel's self-conscious praxis in the diaspora is a necessary condition for the messianic fulfillment of history. Additionally, the diaspora, at least initially, receives a positive evaluation for both thinkers.

For Cohen, the diaspora is necessary for Israel to fulfill its conversionary mission. Not only the destruction of the Jewish State but the elimination of all traces of Jewish nationalism and particularism is essential to this mission. It is the suffering of the Jews in the defenselessness of the Diaspora that gives them the right to convert the nations.[56] Yet despite *Leidensgeschichte* and

Diaspora—or perhaps because of them—the Jews continue to enjoy a remarkable kind of unity. This unity is nothing other than a symbol for the eventual unity of mankind. Indeed, the concept of messianism for Cohen expresses nothing other than the ideal unity of the longed-for moral community of humanity. Messianic Israel, in the present time, is a sign and a symbol of the universal community to come.[57]

Breuer's conception of the messianic nationhood of Israel bears many similarities to Cohen's, but there are also important differences. Although he does not discuss the notion of a Jewish mission in *Messiasspuren*, he takes up this term and firmly rejects it in *Weltwende*. Breuer rejects Cohen's notion of a Jewish mission: it is not the business of Israel either to convert anyone or to spread any kind of salvific knowledge.[58] Individuals may have a mission, but nations cannot. *Mission* implies a complete dedication of one's energies and substance to a task. The missionary exhausts himself in pursuit of his selfless goal. Nations cannot do this, for their task is self-related: they must maintain themselves. Israel has an assignment (*Sendung*), but not a mission. Israel has indeed been formed and sent by God to execute a redemptive purpose in history, but that purpose is achieved by Israel's self-maintenance under the Torah.[59] Israel, as in Cohen, is indeed called to be a salvific, messianic force in history, but Israel executes its messianic service to humanity by living its own distinctive life. That life perfectly synthesizes national consciousness and ethics, *Gesetz* and *Lehre*, in a way that is impossible for the nations. Israel is a model, in the midst of the nations, of the national-historical existence they require to transcend the tragedy of their histories.

Thus Israel is the "nation of humanity," called out of the other peoples and providentially placed in their midst for their own sakes. While Breuer rejects Cohen's mission theory and all that it represents in terms of an apologetic defense of Israel's distinctive way of life, he does not entirely dispense with it. In fact, his dependence on the notion of Israel as a "suffering servant" for the sake of the nations is just as pronounced as in Cohen.

The messianic suffering of Israel becomes intelligible against the etiology of nationhood.[60] In the garden, man rebelled against God and sought to establish himself as the object of his own worship. This archetypal human tendency toward *amor sui* is played out on the level of history in the phenomenon of nationhood. The nations, although created by God to serve him, turned in to themselves as objects of intrinsic value. They alienated themselves from the transcendental unity of humanity—represented by Israel, the creation-nation—and pursue their own self-oriented aims rather than the aims of humanity per se.[61]

Nationhood is not evil, for it has been created by God. Rather, the nations' construction of their ontological status (nationhood is a function of the individuation of reality in nature, of existence qua existence in the *principium individuationis*) as an axiological status is evil. Nations are the legitimate, if rebellious, children of humanity, and humanity searches for them in order to reunite them under its transcendental banner.[62] The ontological status of nationhood, although not fully worked out in *Messiasspuren*, ought to be seen against the background of the ancient Jewish notion that God created seventy nations. Rabbinic (and nonrabbinic) exegesis of Deuteronomy 32:8 ("When the Most High gave nations their homes and set the divisions of man, He fixed the boundaries of peoples in relation to Israel's numbers.") saw in this verse a divinely ordained status for the gentile nations. In rabbinic speculation, there are seventy nations that correspond to Jacob's seventy descendants (Exodus 1:5), each having its own angelic intercessor.[63] In *Moriah*, Breuer refers to the tradition regarding the angelic princes of the nations to indicate not only the archetypal, but also the synthetic, character of nationhood. The personification of nationhood indicates that a nation is something more than the sum of its human individuals. The angel represents a new sort of entity, which has its own unique synthetic character on the stage of history.[64]

Breuer's view of the ontological character of nationhood is as much informed by his Jewish traditionalism as by his Kantianism. For Kant, nations ought to stand in a moral order not unlike the moral order that must prevail between persons. Nations acquire, analogically, personal characteristics. Kant envisioned a system of world government under international law, wherein international relations would embody the interpersonal norms of the kingdom of ends.[65] The humanity of the national 'other' would be apparent to the moral nation-states. Nations would treat one another as ends, not as means for their own self-aggrandizement. The community of man would be the norm-setting principle of international relations.

Breuer argues that the Kantian vision of perpetual peace is already an indwelling reality for Israel, the *Menschheitsnation*. Israel's history is different from the histories of the nations. The pattern of radical differentiation is already to be found in Abraham. Neither the founder of a religion, a prince, nor a sage, Abraham was the initiator of a new kind of humanity. He rediscovered humanity in the midst of the nations in their alienation from humanity.[66] Abraham creates a new nation that can be a true *Menschheitsnation* because it is God's nation *(Gottesnation)*. Abraham achieves consciousness of the unity of humanity because he rediscovered the fatherhood of God and, consequently, the role of all human beings as servants of God *(Gottesdienerschaft)*. By accepting anew the sovereignty of God, his nation was able to free itself from the false perception that sovereignty of God, his nation was able to free itself from the false perception that sovereignty belongs to the nation as such.[67] The *Gottesnation* is free to be a nation in the service of humanity because it does not suffer from the transcendental illusion that it is an end in itself. It has vanquished, in its own collective consciousness, the individuation of reality through grasping its created derivation from God. Consequently, after Abraham history is fully dualistic: there is the history of Israel, in which the ideal and the reality of the unity of humanity endures, and there is the history of the humanity-alienated *(Menschheitsentfremdete)* nations. Hermann Cohen's view that monotheism implies the uniqueness of one people, Israel, in which the future unity of humankind is adumbrated is thus fully reiterated in Breuer's early work.

In *Messiasspuren*, Breuer tempers the dichotomy of Israel and the nations with a vein of Kantian optimism. The nations have a veiled messianic purpose, while Israel has an explicit, self-conscious one. The dichotomy between Judaism and humanity already in place has not yet hardened into the almost gnostic dualism that characterizes Breuer's later work. The grave pessimism apparent in *Der Neue Kusari*, for example, has not reached maturity.

Israel is distinguished from the nations in part because Israel is conscious of the historical situation and is able to do deliberately what the nations can only do inadvertently. Both sets of nations are in exile; Israel recognizes its exile, the nations do not. The history of the nations is the history of the exile of humanity. The history of Israel is also an exilic history: the exile of God from his creation *(Golusgeschichte Gottes)*. The nations are driven by God through catastrophe in order to be turned toward humanity. Israel is driven through catastrophe in order to bring a new consciousness of the claims of humanity upon the nations. Israel is aware of its exile and responds with the intention of raising its national existence into a messianic vehicle for historical redemption by submitting that existence to Torah. The nations, however, blunder through their histories of catastrophe scarcely aware of their meaning. The nations' response to history is not messianism—submission to the will of God owing to the lessons of history—but politics. The eyes of political man, unlike those of Abraham, are covered by the veil of Maya. But ultimately the inadvertent progress of the nations through politics and law, and the deliberate progress of Israel through Torah, point toward the same end: the termination of the exile of God and humanity from one another. "The history of the Jewish nation and the history of the political nations strive for the same end. How could it be otherwise? The exile of humanity does not cease one moment earlier than does God's exile."[68]

Thus in *Messiasspuren* the dichotomy between Israel and the nations is not entirely complete. Breuer still entertains a Kantian vision, tempered by idealism's romantic nationalism and Cohen's messianic internationalism, of a future of perpetual peace won by distinct nations that can yet remain true to their own genius and identity. This presupposes that the national spirit of each human community is, at heart, a spirit in the service of humanity. Israel, more conscious of its genius than the other nations, has as its special fate and duty (*Schicksalslast*) the task of bringing the nations to self-awareness, that is, bringing them to realize that nations exist under the fatherhood and kingship of God. Israel in its dispersion thinks the thoughts of the nations' thinkers; enters into the inner life and genius of the nations; indeed, follows Jeremiah's call to work for the peace of the land.[69]

This more or less complementary vision of Jewish-gentile messianism disappears in *Die Welt als Schöpfung und Natur*. No longer does Breuer analyse the dichotomy of history in terms of the concept of nationhood. Instead the concept of the State comes to dominate his writing. History is dichotomized into the history of the Torah State and the history of the power State (*Machtstaat*) that appears to be the necessary embodiment of gentile collective existence.

Breuer's critique of the social conditions in Europe that led to the First World War displays the same negative judgment on bourgeois, "philistine" life that formed the substance of the intra-Jewish critique of the *Neuorientierung*. The common man has learned nothing from the war, because he is trapped in a privatized, ahistorical form of consciousness. The war must be understood as a revelation, a messianic *Erlebnis* that should completely reorient the lives of the nations. Instead, it is understood by the philistine, for whom the *summum bonum* is a *still und ruhig Leben*, as a grave, but passing misfortune. The philistine is unable to realize that history is the language through which God speaks to the nations. Philistine religiosity knows only of private, subjective revelations, of private, subjective history. It cannot conceive of world history or of the fate of nations, for its religious language is that of private faith.[70]

Breuer's critique of philistinism is also a critique of Christianity. Like many German Jewish critics, he considered Christianity to be a private, subjectivistic religion of personal salvation. In *Moriah*, for example, he characterizes the very source of Christianity as the despair of history. Christianity attended to the Father and neglected the King. It substituted one son of man for Judaism's many gentile and Jewish sons of God. In its despair of history and its certainty that history was virtually consummated, it rendered to Caesar what was Caesar's. This was the decisive break with Judaism. For Judaism cannot abandon the world to the secular. When history did not end and Christianity became a church, Christianity's message was well-suited to individuals but lacked a language in which to speak to the principal actors in history, states. States do not have faith, neither can they love. States require just laws and institutions, but by rejecting Judaism's Torah, Christianity deprived itself, offering the State to Caesar.

Nor was Christianity's version of social order sufficient to subjugate and transform the political structures that arose during the Middle Ages. Although the heathen conquerors of Rome were "civilized" by Christianity, they eventually overthrew it. Modern nationalism fills the void left by the steady attenuation of Christendom. Christendom's heathen counter-history has now fully reasserted itself. Modernity, with its "freedom of conscience" and "separation of Church and State" was already adumbrated by earliest Christianity. Whenever the language of religion emphasizes faith, conscience, and individuals over social and historically transformative law, privatization of the religious sphere is inevitable.

Breuer shows a keen understanding of the dialectical consequences of values such as freedom of conscience. While not assaulting such values in a reactionary manner, he does not shrink from pairing them with the growth of pernicious ideologies and structures.[71]

Christianity and its secularized successor, philistinism, came about through an overemphasis on individuality, which in turn came about through the disproportionate acquisition of power by the State. Individualism, represented by French revolutionary doctrine and British liberalism, ought to be understood not as the opposite of the *Machtstaat*, as Breuer sees it, but as its complement. Rather than construe these two as opposites, Breuer synthesizes them into one dialectical expression of social pathology.

The Romans, Breuer believed, created individuality by giving legal expression to a radical distinction between the State and the home. Philistinism is the social and conceptual precipitate of private law.[72] Rome created individual privacy, restraining the power of the State from entering the door of the home, in order to give man a sense of freedom, while arrogating the power of public life to itself. The personal freedom of Roman private law is thus an elementary form of bad faith. The State now erects itself into a juristic person (a *persona ficta*), ontologically and morally free of actual persons. actual persons are no longer agents in history: states become the sole *personae* on the world-historical stage.[73] As the State wins the freedom of historical movement, ethics is banished to the realm of interpersonal relationships, such that states can no longer be governed by ethics because ethics seem no longer to apply to these fictitious persons. Law becomes dichotomized into private and public legality. Private law tenders a little piece of the world to the philistine and regulates what he does with his property in his illusion of freedom. Public law, which the State claims to create and which can appeal to no higher authority than the State, is dominated by concerns of utility and power that serve only the State. The result is that both order of law lose their connection with ethics. Law isolates man and the State from the normative human community postulated by ethics rather than relating them authoritatively to it. The State's claim to create law destroys the law. History becomes a lawless "slaughter bench" of fictitious persons and states to whom no law applies.[74]

Much of this analysis of the threefold rupture of law, ethics, and society was adumbrated in *Die Grundlagen*, but the connections with the State and with history are new. Breuer's conception of the State as a self-divinizing collectivity owes something to Hegel. Indeed, Breuer concurs with Hegel's conception of what the State *is*, only to reject his conclusion that that is a satisfactory state of affairs. Like Hegel, Breuer rejects the premise of pure contractarianism: the State is more than a composition of its individual members. The State has a reality and an Idea all its own.[75] The State is the highest synthesis of reality. Not a means but an end in itself, it is a sort of incarnate divinity that exists in order to will itself. Hegel believed that "the State is divine will as present Spirit which unfolds itself into the actual form and organization of a world."[76]

The individual is "sublated" in the State. Henceforth, his worth and dignity, indeed, the meaning of his individuality, are tied to the State, in which he finds fulfilled, if subordinated, existence. Breuer accepts this view of the ontological, historical ultimacy of the State without accepting its axiological implication. He remains attached to Kantian views, which Hegel rejected, about the relation of moral norms to international behavior. Yet Breuer also shares Hegel's critique of individualism. or him, individualism is as objectionable as the power State, which is not, in fact, individualism's antithesis but its parent. For this reason, Breuer was unable to have a positive appreciation of liberal democracy. The concept of individual rights, of negative liberty, on which liberal democracy is based remained objectionable to him. He did not find either natural right or constitutional separation of powers to be sufficient barriers to the totalizing, inherent dynamic of the State. In terms of his dichotomy, if the law did not come from God, it had *pro tanto* to come from the State and could not, in any effective sense, serve to restrain the State.[77]

In Breuer's condemnation of the ahistorical bourgeois ideal of private life, a cutting criticism of his own Frankfurt community is to be discerned. Its philosophical origins, in addition to those discussed in chapter 1, may be traced to his rejection of the presuppositions of Roman law. The influence of the jurisprudential thinker Otto von Gierke (1841–1921) is apparent here. Gierke belonged to a legal school that exercised a considerable attraction for law students of Breuer's generation. Gierke was a Germanist; he sought to free German law from Roman influence and rediscover authentic German legal concepts. Although this particular task might not have concerned Breuer, the methodological point—gaining authentic knowledge of one's own tradition and shaping one's consciousness and institutions in the light of that rediscovery—would have been apt.[78]

For Gierke, German law, unlike Roman law, reflected a federalistic orientation. Roman law vested ultimate power in the State, which then might grant legitimacy to subsidiary groups. German law, however, recognized a pluralistic presence of free associations out of which some overarching entity could develop. German law, in Gierke's phrase, was a *Genossenschaftsrecht*, a law of associations. The State reflected the common interests of the associations of persons that made up the many layers of *Genossenschaften*. But the State does not create either the groups or their law, as the Roman theory would have it. The State declares their preexistent social and legal reality.

This is the path Breuer follows. It is the Torah that creates the Jewish State. The polity is a product of its law and not the other way around. The Torah State represents an ordering of law and political actualization that is precisely the opposite of that of the experience of the nations.

As desirable as Gierke's model of law-state relations is, it is Hegel who understands agency in history. After the rise of the State, the nations are unable to relate to God. The interposition of the self-divinizing State between the nations and God cuts the nations off from God in such a way that they lose the knowledge of creation. Adam's offspring rebelled against God as individuals, while Noah's descendants (at Babel) rebelled as a group. In the latter rebellion, humanity fled from its inherent normative dimension (the *sollende Seele*) with which man was endowed at creation. Man fled into the universal State, seeking to augment his weak, mortal *I* by sublating it in the super-individual *I* of the State.[79] The turn toward the State represents a primeval flight from freedom. Human history could have been a history of God's free creation, a history for the sake of creation. While creation changed into unfree nature, human history was intended by God to preserve creation's original freedom. Man alone could hear the creation commands still struggling to speak through his soul. Man could have carried them out in the world of nature, but the decision to subjugate himself to the State imposed a new form of naturalistic, deterministic existence upon him. The State negates his freedom and thus denies creation. It animalizes its members and imprisons them anew within the world of nature.

> Human history is the history of free creation, just as natural history is the history of unfree creation. Only the knowledge of the God of creation leads to the knowledge of the God of history. Denial of the God of history entails denial of the God of creation. The power state, which annexes a portion both of

the free and of the unfree creation, immediately, elevates itself, above all, against the God of creation.[80]

Against this background of human failure and flight from
freedom, God brings forth a second creation, Israel, whose essence
is the knowledge of the first creation and its unconsummated creation commands. Israel in its self-consciousness is the witness to
creation in history. Israel's history is creation history, the history
of the divinely- intended, purposive cosmos moving toward redemption through the fulfillment of the creation law. The history
of states, on the other hand, is a history of pure catastrophe. The
experience of God, outside of Israel and mediated through history,
is thus an experience of God as *Katastrophen Gott.* Breuer has
turned the tables on the Christian theological dichotomy of law
and love. God, as experienced by the nations in their histories, is
far from loving.

Insofar as Israel, the second creation, continues to express the
freedom and purpose of the first creation, and the nations do not,
history can be said to be divided into two separate orders: creation
history (or metahistory) and general history. In one, the goals of
creation remain active and effective; in the other, they slumber as
in the state of nature. But creation does not remain active in Israel
automatically. As we have seen, Israel must act upon its revelation, through which it knows the goals of creation. Because creation was wrapped in Sabbath robes, revelation of the Creator's
will was required. Sinai had to follow creation in order to give the
implicit creation goals an articulated content. After Sinai, history
has the possibility of being redeemed.

The chronicle of metahistory is set forth in *Moriah.* Breuer
relates Jewish metahistory from a single point of view: the Jewish
story is the temporally extended quest to live under God's creation
law. Yet if metahistory were only this human story of struggle, it
might not, after all, merit a special category. In Breuer's view,
therefore, God enters Jewish metahistory at decisive junctures.
Metahistory, like creation, remains the realm of God's freedom as
well as humanity's.

God's presence is sometimes intuited through his absence. In
Breuer's treatment of the fall of the Second Commonwealth, for
example, Israel did not merit divine assistance as they had in the
time of the Maccabees. They could not win the battle against
Rome because they were fighting for Herod's state rather than the

Torah State.[81] Yet, by virtue of the continuity of divine presence within metahistory, Johanan ben Zakkai, representing the aspiration of a Torah State, appeared before Vespasian to ask for "Yavneh and her sages." God was both present and absent for Israel.

Throughout his account of Jewish metahistory, Breuer's conception of events resembles that of the author of the Scroll of Esther. The events appear to be ordinary, in the sense that God's presence is not obvious to the observer. Yet on reflection the whole process appears divinely ordered. Metahistory is thus history in the hands of active Providence. Breuer takes the Scroll of Esther, in fact, to be a potent illustration of the endurance of metahistory in the midst of exile and the departure (siluk) of the Shekhinah.[82] God uses general history to save his metahistorical people. He is the Creator of time and stands, veiled, behind it. Human beings will their decisions into the fabric of time— the decisions are theirs—but the consequences of their acts are not theirs. The act belongs to time, which belongs to God. Breuer takes the use of the lot mentioned in Esther to be indicative of human action in history: whatever intentionality we invest in the act seems irrelevant to its outcome. Another force determines the result. Repeatedly, Breuer describes events in Jewish history, such as the writing of the Shulkhan Arukh, as providentially ordered acts that facilitated the survival of Israel in periods of hardship.[83]

There is a certain ambiguity, and perhaps an ambivalence, about specifying the manner of divine intrusion into the historical/metahistorical process. Breuer is eloquent about the nature of Jewish action in history, but he is reserved about describing God's participation. Often he indicates a mysterious cooperation between God and His Jewish partners. Both, for example, are to destroy the memory of Amalek (Exodus 18:14). Both are Amalek's victims. Both are to set history aright.[84] Yet Israel is unable to fault God when he fails to be discernibly active, when metahistory seems to dissolve into the tragedy and chaos of history.

In his treatment of Purim, Breuer breaks into a wrenching lament about the Jews of Europe who are being slaughtered as he writes. (Nahaliel was written during the Holocaust.) Why is there no Purim-like miracle? Why? he asks repeatedly. But Breuer offers no elaborate theodicy. He turns the question back to the questioner, back to himself. Whom do you ask? One asks the Father of Mercies. Are we more merciful than he? The Jew asks, What have I done? What has humanity done? such that the Father of Mercies had to act in such a way toward his people.[85] Here there can be no ambiguity. God's justice is beyond question. The rightness of his action in metahistory is above reproach.

Breuer is equally emphatic in giving a univocal interpretation to another event: the Balfour Declaration. Either the Balfour Declaration was the work of God or it was the work of Satan. There is no merely historical, that is, ambiguous way of looking at it. The Balfour Declaration is God's work. It is a powerful sign that, in our period, history and metahistory are coming together. The nations are stirring to consider a way of justice toward the Jews. There is messianic potential in the moment.

The only organization fit to respond in a metahistorical, messianic way to Balfour and the Mandate, Agudat Israel, had utterly failed to do so. While individuals responded to this revelatory event, the organized Torah people did not. They failed to grasp the significance of Balfour because they failed to understand the historicity, or metahistoricity, of Jewish existence. Orthodox leadership failed to recognize the radical character of the era. In the new, they saw only danger. Instead of living in metahistory and reckoning with its revelatory character, they remained bound, in a way, to mere history: to the *stetl* culture of the previous centuries. Agudat Israel, instead of becoming the embodiment of the Congregation of Israel, the eschatological avant garde for the imminent messianic epoch, contented itself with being a *shtadlan*.[86]

Breuer's many discussions of metahistory are informed by both a deep sense of tragedy about human history in general and a genuine messianic enthusiasm. He evidently believed that some sort of messianic consummation was possible, if not probable. History and metahistory were converging, and Israel had the means, but apparently not the will, to unite them. Building up the land of Israel in preparation for a Torah State is the final, crucial phase of the messianic process.

From the preceding discussion, it is clear that Breuer fought against the dominance of a secular paradigm of Jewish nationhood such as Zionism or *Wissenschaft des Judentums* represented. Philosophically, the thrust of his attack was directed against historicism. Breuer was particularly open to the threat of historical reductionism in so far as he privileged the category of history in his phenomenology of Judaism. He did not need to establish that Jews have a history or that Jews can live in history. Rather, he needed to distinguish the mode of Jewish history from history in general in order to escape, not only from history in general, but from a historicist hermeneutic.[87]

In this, Breuer resembles contemporary Protestant theology's grappling with the problem of historicism. Ernst Troeltsch, for example, struggled with whether Christian experience in history had a coherence apart from the accumulations of social forms recognized as Christian expressions. Was there an essence of Christianity? Was there a Christianity not independent of, but not entirely subsumed under, the flux of history, such that by living such a Christianity one could have freedom and control over history?[88] A Jewish parallel to this is that early twentieth century search for authentic Jewish existence in history that has been characterized as a search for counter-history.[89] Both Martin Buber and Gershom Scholem, for example, can be spoken of an engaged in the task of mining Jewish counter-history out of previous Jewish historiosophy, in order to live a Jewish existence freed from the fetters of its apologetic rationalism. With relevant qualifications, Breuer can be seen, I believe, as engaged in the same task. Breuer's life-long effort to raise the metahistorical awareness of his Orthodox colleagues, particularly with respect to the messianic meaning of the First (and Second) World War and the Balfour Declaration, is an attempt to promote a particularly radical view of the essence of Jewish history, past and present. He too believed in a stream of subterranean meaning and power that the philistine consciousness is incapable of grasping. Breuer's close identification with highly conservative institutions has, no doubt, obscured the counter-historical radicalism of his thought.

Unlike Franz Rosenzweig, Breuer does not locate the eternity of the Jewish people in categorical otherness to history. Breuer agrees with Rosenzweig that the Jews are fundamentally distinct from the nations, but he disagrees over the relation of this distinct people to the history of the nations. For Rosenzweig, the eternity of Jewish law and of the Hebrew language raises the Jew above the transcience of historicity. Judaism knows this transcendence as a vertical in-breaking of eternity into time. The nations live in time and try to control time by continually adapting their laws and customs. This process of shaping and reshaping is supposed to secure a structure for the future.[90] The eternal people, on the contrary, occupies a changeless, eternal present. Their law, custom, and language do not change. They cannot be adapted to fit historical exigencies: they can simply be affirmed or denied. A consequence of eternity is exile. Eternity means being rooted in no soil other than self, not in land, language, or history. The Jews contain the *All* within themselves. They are "with the Father," unlike the nations, who are always "on the way."[91] The Jews have reached the goal toward which the nations are moving: the inner unity of faith and life.[92]

For Breuer, metahistory is not an eternal depth discovered by the Jew in every present moment, nor is it the omnipresent stasis of his law and custom. Metahistory is a horizontal dimension: it is Jewish national life as correct history. The eternity of *knesset Israel* does not ensure eternity for the empirical people of Israel; on the contrary, metahistory is the task of the people, a continual struggle for eternity and redemption. Furthermore, *Torah im derekh eretz* as a peoplehood-shaping principle (*Volkstum gestaltendes Prinzip*) implies that the customs of Israel are just the opposite of eternal. Indeed, the entire metahistorical vocation of Israel is to transform nature and history into metahistorical redemption. Breuer is reported to have said "We are the most earthbound of peoples."[93] In this respect, the Jews are not above the flux of history: they are at the heart of history. It is there that transcendence is possible and Providence breaks through.

While Rosenzweig could not see beyond the Exile until a gracious intervention of God (this is also true for Hirsch), Breuer believed that building the National Home in the land of Israel heralded the messianic age. The Balfour Declaration indicated divine intervention in history on the order of the miraculous. The time had arrived for all Torah-loyal Jews to go up and prepare the land for ultimate redemption. For Rosenzweig, redemption will come about as the world is configured into the kingdom by discrete acts of human love and, in collective terms, by the prayer of the community. Soul and world must be brought into conjunction through the love of neighbor. The prayer for the kingdom offered by the community actually affects the transfiguration of the world into the kingdom. The possibility of the redemptive kingdom therefore depends upon the work of man as an individual and in community.[94] The context of this work, however, is not history, at least not history as Breuer conceives of it. The context is the eternal present in which the Jews live. Rosenzweig's view of redemption, while sharing certain pragmatic elements with Breuer's, departs significantly from his over the question of context.

For Breuer, the work of redemption is not so much liturgical as political: it is the struggle to remake history in the image of Torah, to apply the mute, yet revelationally articulated, creation commands to the natural-historical world. This is accomplished by submission to Torah, on the part of persons; by bringing Torah to the institutional structures of Jewish life; by rising to the meta-historical moment and returning to the Land. The world must be brought to freedom, to the *Kosmonomie der Thora*. This is not to say that Israel must wage the battle for Torah in the minds and institutional sphere of the Gentiles. Israel need only remake itself to complete the work of redemption.

For Rosenzweig, the Jews are already with the Father. For Breuer, this was true in a particularly radical way. But it is also not yet true. Israel is not identical with *knesset Israel*, the transcendental Congregation of Israel. The eternity that Rosenzweig attributes to the empirical people, Breuer preserves for the transcendental Congregation. The great danger for the people is precisely that it will confuse its own empirical condition with the ontological status of its cosmic archetype. Were this to occur, messianism would degenerate into nationalism and merely historical politics. Eternity is to be found in *knesset Israel*, the entrance to which is gained by the collective assumption of the yoke of heaven.

Rosenzweig envisioned that the work of redemption is gradually completed, although in different ways, by both Judaism and Christianity. The Christianization of the nations is a part of the process of redemption. In this respect, the nations have a crucial role to play in the ultimate drama. This assignation, of course, is utterly lacking in Breuer. Although Christianity, in his view, has brought the nations to glimpse the comforting Fatherhood of God, it cannot bring them to the kingship of God. Christianity and the history of the Christian nations have nothing to do with bringing the kingdom. That task devolves wholly on Israel.

METAHISTORY AND THE MITZVOT:
THE POLITICS OF REDEMPTION

To live as the nations do in history is to be subject to an inevitable process of growth and decay, rise and fall. History is a record of transient states and changing bodies of law. Metahistory, however, is a protest against this chaotic flux. The nations realize the transience of their social and legal institutions and try to achieve permanence by mortgaging those institutions to the power State. The result of this "transcendental illusion" is pervasive oppression. History becomes a struggle between self-divinized states fighting to maintain themselves against the inevitability of their decay. Israel, however, orders its being in term of a law that is beyond change. The creation law embodied by the Torah does not require the institutions of state power to buttress its eternity. Jewish law and the Jewish nation it has formed have survived the destruction of the Jewish State and the expulsion from the Jewish land. Yet Jewish law survives as the constitutional law of a Torah State, while Israel survives in its dispersion as a *Staatsvolk*, a political people.[95]

The individual Jew is a citizen of a state, the outward form of which has disappeared. To live in metahistory is to live *as if* the empirical state still existed. It is to live, in this epoch, in intense and activist anticipation of its reconstitution. Breuer agrees with Spinoza, as it were, that the Torah must be understood in national-constitutional terms. He disagrees that the destruction of the ancient Jewish commonwealth entailed the abrogation of its law. Both law and state continue to exist in the as-if (*als ob*) context of metahistory:

> If the kingdom of God, that is, the sovereign authority of the Torah, also persists in the continuing Exile, then it follows that we, whenever and wherever we are not hindered by the Exile, are obligated to actualize the kingdom of God, the sovereign authority of the Torah as members of the polity of the Torah State. Only those Jews belong to the polity of the Torah State (*Staatsvolk des Thorastaats*) for whom the kingdom of God, the sovereign authority of the Torah, is effectively actualized; for whom, even after the downfall of the Torah State, the land and law of the Torah State survive. It is the indestructible essential characteristic of the Jewish land to be the political home of the Torah State. If there were to be a suspension of these characteristics, the metahistory inaugurated by God would immediately come to an end. If the Jews were to cease to be the political people of the Torah State, God would have to choose a new people and a new land, and metahistory would have to begin all over again.[96]

The endurance of the Torah State is not a matter of disembodied, Platonic Ideas or of mystical speculation. The Torah State continues to exist in communities that are actually governed by the Torah. To the extent that such communities exist (for example, in Frankfurt am Main), God's kingdom becomes actual in a preliminary way in history. The kingdom of God is nothing other than the sovereign power of God at work upon an actual social order. For Breuer, the kingdom of God can have an empirical address.

The empirical address of the metahistorical kingdom will be the community that understands itself as a Torah State, thus anticipating the universal submission of history to the cosmic rule of the Torah. The members of such a community live under the rule of Torah not in terms of subjective affirmation of religious conviction but as citizens vis-a-vis the law of a state. All of the internal institutions of their community as well as their external affairs are regulated by Torah. In a sweeping survey of the constitutional foundations of contemporary Jewish communities, Breuer confirms that the only ones that fit these strict criteria are those of German separatist Orthodoxy. What is the constitutional principle that ensures that a community be a Torah community (Thoragemeinschaft)? It is the Frankfurt Principle of noncooperation. Only Samson Raphael Hirsch's community has not denigrated the status of Torah from constitutional law to religious principle. Only that community is true to the inherent constitutional claims of Torah and hence to the metahistorical character of Jewish existence.

Yet shortly before these words came to print, Breuer had visited Israel for a second time (1933) and had come to the conclusion that German Jewry could develop no further.[97] Although Frankfurt had an objectively valid community, an incipient Torah State, it lacked precisely what Tel Aviv had: Jewish men and women engaged in a fundamental form of Jewish activism. Frankfurt had a community without Jews; Tel Aviv had Jews without a community. As we have seen, Breuer made the decision to leave Frankfurt, with its abstract, correct political structure, in order to go to Jerusalem, which lacked structure, in order to begin to build, if only intellectually, the rudiments of a Torah society, if not a Torah State.

The philosophical claim that social order needs to be derived from revelation and is, furthermore, a condition of redemption is corollary to Breuer's doctrine of natural and revealed law as parallel processes. Natural law describes the state of things, the organization of phenomena; revealed law describes the perfected state of consummated creation. This state is the social order of revelation, the Torah State. The dwellers in this perfect state, which—like creation and revelation—is already partly actualized, are, in part, the empirical Jewish people and, in full, the Congregation of Israel. *Knesset Israel* is the nexus where creation and revelation, metahistory and the Jewish people, meet.

> *Knesset Israel* is the Jewish people qua metahistorical creation. Just as the metaphysical creation arose through a tenfold process of becoming, the phenomenal form of which is nature, so too through a tenfold process of becoming metahistorical *knesset Israel* arose, the phenomenal form of which is the Jewish people. And just as the metaphysical creation only endures on account of the continuously effective creation commands, so too does the metahistorical *knesset Israel* endure only because of the continuously validating Torah (*der immerfort geltende Thora*).[98]

Israel as a people is an eternal people if and only if there is no separation between *knesset Israel* and the oral Torah, hence Breuer's utter rejection of any movement that diminishes the sovereignty of the law over Israel. Such a movement is national, if not cosmological, suicide. In metahistory, Israel qua *knesset Israel*, the oral Torah, and the kingdom of God are, if not ontologically identical, eschatologically coterminous. The task of the Jewish people is to identify itself with *knesset Israel* and thus to incarnate Torah and the kingdom in history. Then metahistory, and with it redemption, become fully alive in history. Historical redemption is the identification of the empirical Jewish people with the Congregation of Israel, such that the Congregation of Israel emerges from the realm of creation, where it reposes behind the Sabbath veils, into the order of phenomena. This identification or transformation of people into Congregation occurs wherever Jews live together in a correct sociolegal order.[99]

Thus *knesset Israel* has both an actual and a potential dimension, like creation and revelation, of which it is both part and fulfillment. Its actuality, like the other two elements, is partly dependent on the Jew's will and partly autarchic. That is, *knesset Israel* does not only await the Jew's affirmation. The Jew is free to associate himself with the transcendental Congregation, to accept his destiny and become a conscious member of the Congregation; to not do so, however, only gives offense to *knesset Israel* and Torah and impedes the redemptive process.[100] *Knesset Israel* is a normative concept; its being is intrinsically moral. For the Jew to reject his status as a member of *knesset Israel* is not a neutral act. Breuer carries the vision of an archetypal moral community living under right law over into the framework of his theology. The kingdom of ends, the social ideal, has become the kingdom of God and the metahistorical Torah State of the people Israel.

Breuer believes that whether a Jew enters into the congregation of Israel determines whether the Congregation enjoys God's love and favor. If the Jew performs the mitzvot, then harmony reigns between the Congregation and God. The Congregation can pass that love on to the people, who in turn can disseminate it into history. If the Jew repudiates *knesset Israel*, he distances it from God and dooms the Jewish people to an "eclipse of God." This has been the arch temptation and classic sin of the Jewish people in all ages. *Knesset Israel* conducts fullness or privation to the Jewish people and all of its parts. *Knesset Israel* determines the fate of the Jewish people in the sensible world, while the Jewish people determines the fate of *knesset Israel* in the world-in-itself.[101]

Such a doctrine brings us once again fully into the realm of Kabbalah. In the *Sefer Bahir*, for example, there is an identity between the tenth sefirah, *malkhut* (kingdom), God's immanent presence, Shekhinah, and *knesset Israel*. This identification is developed by Joseph ibn Gikatilla. For him, redemption will consist of the unification of the tenth sefirah, qua *knesset Israel*, with the upper sefirot. Redemption is the reunification of the inner and outer life of God. The fate of the people Israel, which is the outermost aspect of God's life, depends upon the actions of the people Israel: the historical agency of Israel is a factor in cosmic and intradivine redemption. If Israel could live without sin, that is, if Israel could entirely identify with *knesset Israel*, then it could be ruled directly by God. Insofar as Israel does sin, the connection (*tsinor*, literally "pipe" or "tube") between God and *knesset Israel* is ruptured, and Israel experiences the distance of God.[102] For Gikatilla, this means that the power of the gentile nations waxes in history; idolatry increases, and Israel knows only the robes (*malbushim*) and attributes *(kinuiyim)* of God, rather than his presence and name. Furthermore, to the extent that evil now rules history in the idolatry and cruelty of the nations with respect to Israel, discord prevails among the sefirot, that is, within the life of God himself. Evil, the so-called *sitra ahara* (other side) has invaded *malkhut*. God is so extended into the world, that is, at the point of

Israel, that he is vulnerable to harm given the actions of Israel in the world.[103]

Although he has not employed the apparatus of sefirot, typical of Kabbalah, Breuer has come very close to this kabbalistic view of history. Breuer's notion of the transcendental status of *knesset Israel* is more than a reflex of his Kantian dualism; it is a full- fledged adoption of a kabbalistic theme. *Knesset Israel* functions for Breuer as an intermediary between God and Israel and completes creation and revelation.[104] *Knesset Israel* occupies center stage as the chief actor in the metahistorical drama of redemption. Following Gikatilla, Israel, not God, is the primary agent of redemption. Israel's theurgic practice of the mitzvot effects redemptive change within the divine order. For Breuer, the fate of creation and history depends upon Israel's collective action. The plan for that action has been submitted in the Torah and prompted by the events of history.

In the posthumously published *Naḥaliel*, Breuer lays down a systematic program of messianic, metahistorical praxis. He offers not only a metaphysical-metahistorical commentary on the mitzvot, but a political vision of the Torah State. This vision provides a positive constitutional content for what had been a largely negative formulation of constitutional doctrine (i.e., the Frankfurt Principle). In his detailed interpretation of the mitzvot, Breuer quotes large sections of Maimonides' *Mishneh Torah*. He deals, like Maimonides, with bodies of civil, criminal, and institutional law that give form to his concept of a Torah State. The extensive reliance on Maimonides enhances the political cast of Breuer's work. Breuer sees in the *Mishneh Torah* a comprehensive presentation of Torah as constitutional law.

Naḥaliel is tightly bound to Breuer's German works but innovates a slightly different symbolic vocabulary for basic concepts. As in *Die Welt als Schöpfung und Natur*, the Torah is the creation law through which creation continues to speak after the onset of the Sabbath. Breuer makes the claim that the mitzvot circumcize the world-in-itself. The mitzvot order the will-entrapping, depth dimension of reality and impose Sabbath upon it. The Torah, through Israel's practice of mitzvot, redeems the tragedy of man, world, and history by giving each its requisite form of pacification and fulfillment. Creation is at last stabilized by revelation, lived out as redemption.

Insofar as the purpose of the mitzvot is to provide for the circumcision (*milah*) of creation, Israel, as the creation and revelation people, is restrained in crucial ways from the rebellious, self-aggrandizing sovereignty that characterizes the nations. While other nations, for example, exercise normal sovereignty over their lands, Israel cannot. Other nations become bound to their land in an unfree, animalistic way. They cannot survive qua nation apart from their land. Israel on the contrary survives apart from its land, while being the most bound to a land of any people. But its boundedness is ideal, not natural. That is, Israel relates to its land, enjoys sovereignty over its land, in terms of the relevant Idea of justice revealed by the Torah. Through the Torah, Israel knows that its land is God's and that it has no real sovereignty over its land. Its peculiar sovereignty is to acknowledge genuine, divine sovereignty. Hence Israel exercises its sovereignty over the land by giving back to God what is his. By so doing, Israel achieves the only legitimate ("circumcized") sovereignty that human beings can attain.[105] Breuer develops the extensive halakhot of tithes from this point of view.

The circumcision, by means of mitzvot, that Israel enacts upon itself and its world also applies to the Jewish practice of statecraft. The Torah State is radically different in kind from other states, including ecclesiastical states or theocracies. This difference is so fundamental that the term state (medinah) really should not be used in reference to the Torah polity. Kingdom of priests and holy nation would be a preferable designation.[106]

It is not the case that the radical distinction between the Torah State and others derives simply from the quality of its laws and institutions. Breuer is willing to grant an occasional similarity between "Bibel" and "Babel." That gentile law sometimes resembles Jewish law was already noted by the sages in their discussion of Samaritan law.[107] It is not the content of the mitzvot or of a conciliar institution such as the Sanhedrin that is decisive, however, but the origin and the teleology of these phenomena. While the division of political institutions in the Torah State (Sanhedrin/kingship/priesthood) bears a superficial resemblance to the modern principle of separation of powers, the telos is entirely different. The modern state, through its institutional arrangements, balances interests and powers in order to allocate rights on the basis of utility. Its interest is not the sanctification of the animalistic aspects of human existence, but their management. The modern state, at its best, achieves Pax but not shalom; organization, but not the Sabbath of the political. Thus the mitzvot that relate to civil and criminal matters show points of resemblance to other legal systems; but their aim is to sanctify social relations and thus to bring metahistory into an effective relationship with history.[108] Not civil peace but corporate holiness is the thrust of the Torah.

The dialectical interrelatedness of history and metahistory surfaces in Breuer's account of the Sanhedrin. Relying on Maimonides, he views the effectiveness of the institution primarily in terms of the virtues of its members. While the Sanhedrin as a whole possesses some crucial institutional powers (appointment of kings, declaration of war, etc.), Breuer tends to reduce its political dimension to a moral one. What is crucial is the wisdom and virtue of judges rather than the political role of the institution in the governmental system. The political dissipates as metahistory fully overtakes history. When a properly virtuous Sanhedrin is at last constituted, it is joined by the Shekhinah.[109]

Accordingly, although Breuer spends considerable time describing political institutions and relations in the Torah State, his ultimate vision is postpolitical. *Nahaliel*, unlike the *Mishneh Torah*, culminates with an interpretation of sacrifice and the Temple, rather than with the Sanhedrin and kingship. Although the Sanhedrin begins to restore the Shekhinah to Israel, the Temple is to be the central institution of the State, the link between metahistory and history.

While the Torah is fulfilled in the Torah State, the Torah State is not an end in itself. Its purpose is ultimately redemptive. The Torah State returns the Shekhinah to the midst of all humanity, to creation as such. All humanity yearns for the sublation of history into metahistory. Yet they have neither a clear vision of the process nor a distinct remembrance of the Edenic condition that preceded the universal exile. Israel however does.[110] The Temple, in the midst of Torah State and Torah Land, is the laboratory in which Israel fuses its metahistory to history and returns the Shekhinah to the now-circumcized reality of man, world, and history. In the Temple, the eternal Torah reposes in *knesset Israel*, its ark. Israel continuously sacrifices the animal and rational dimensions of its will, synthesizing them in the sacrifice into a Sabbath-will, a "will of Ideas." The synthesis of the human personality into its final, ideal, completed order occurs at the altar. In sacrifice, the animal *I*, is offered to God. There is no redemption of humanity without Israel's practice of sacrifice. In the sacrifice, the primeval and perenniel rebellion of man against God finds its universal atonement.[111]

In the Temple, Israel achieves wholeness and freedom and affects the ontological repair of creation for the sake of the nations. Israel not only can but must bring about this restoration. If Israel does not restore the Shekhinah to history, Israel will lose her own metahistorical being.[112] On Yom Kippur, through Israel's agency, God and not-God meet in the Holy of Holies and are reconciled. The day on which "all is Sabbath," when history is given back to the messiah who steps out of metahistory, is a real, if not imminent possibility. Indeed, that day coexists now in the metahistorical-historical correlation. Its full disclosure is in God's hands, however. Until then, Israel must equip itself ever more deliberately to practice the metahistorical messianism of the mitzvot in the Land.

Without the Temple, prayer can still effect the anthropological synthesis-santification and the universal atonement metahistory requires. The *I*, at any rate, returns to the One who gave it its hidden essence, where it lives in splendor in the world to come, from whence it came.

Breuer's shift from a pragmatic program of messianic politics to an increasingly kabbalistic, theurgic vision of the mitzvot finally culminates in a redemptive vision of prayer, not unlike Rosenzweig's. Quite possibly, this shift reflects his awareness, at the end of his life, that a political State of Israel was coming that would not be a Torah State in any way. Breuer shifted his focus from the political to the social, from the pragmatic to the moral and spiritual. The conclusion of *Naḥaliel*, with its emphasis on sacrifice, Yom Kippur, and prayer confirms, in a sense, the intuition of his first published work, *Jerusalem*. Prayer more than historical activism is the supreme response to history. In this final turn, Breuer seems to have made his private peace with the obduracy of the Jewish reality, signifying in the process, I suspect, his wish to resolve the tension between Kant and Kabbalah in favor of the latter.

❖ 5

Toward a Critical Appreciation of Isaac Breuer

In the preceding exposition, I have sought to present the key philosophical elements and themes in Isaac Breuer's thought. I have attempted to convey both the depth at which he engaged his topics and the complexity of the argumentation and apparatus he employed. I have also sought to evoke the philosophical and religious sources from which he drew his ideas, as well as the cultural milieu that provided him with particular concerns.

The question remains whether Isaac Breuer represents a living source for Jewish philosophy or an "episode."[1] In a sense, this book has been a wager that elements of his thought and method do command the attention of the Jewish thinker and not only of the historian of Judaism. I would now like to argue that premise.

Isaac Breuer provides, in my view, two sets of powerful arguments relevant to the renewal of Jewish thought in our time. He argues for the primacy of Jewish Being, expressed as participation in and loyalty to normative Jewish community, over culturally conditioned projects of theoretical, theological reason. As such, he offers a postmodern, in the sense of postsynthetic, standpoint for the philosophical and ideological critique of Jewish and general modernity. Second, he argues for a renewal of Jewish peoplehood, based on a reappropriation of sacral and sacramental aspects of that peoplehood. He offers a version of a resacralized peoplehood that avoids, at least in principle, the dangerous pitfall of romantic nationalism.

Having said this, I must also say that aspects of his thought are deeply flawed. I will attend to a critique of certain problems with his views before I develop the positive elements.

While I believe that Breuer has much to say about the culturally and historically conditioned character of reason, such that he enables a fundamental Jewish critique of reason and its contemporary canons, I do not think that his particular attempt to critique scientific reason, for example, is a success. Breuer will not provide, at least on his own terms, a neutralization of the power of scientific worldviews and of their disintegrative effects on traditional cosmogonies. Whether he preserves a compatibility between a scientific appreciation of natural causality and divine, providential agency in history is another matter.

Breuer's philosophical devotion to Kant, and particularly to Schopenhauer—perhaps more than his Jewish orthodoxy—causes him to truncate and misconstrue science. He stresses the primacy of Being, expressed as will, over reason and so delimits reason's grasp of Being. This move relegates science to the sphere of phenomena. Science is understood to be descriptive: it describes the order and connectedness of phenomena essentially through conscious articulation and repetition of the laws of thought. Science is the discourse of the dwellers of Plato's cave. Judaism is the discourse of those beyond its walls.

Here I believe Breuer's idealism has brought him to a dead end. Breuer is forced to construe science as similar in kind to common sense. He cannot really grapple with particular scientific world-pictures because he has already decided that *all* knowledge is knowledge of phenomena and such knowledge is essentially commonsensical. The tissue of the common sense, *mutatis mutandis*, scientific world-picture is causality of a highly mechanistic kind. What would Breuer do with scientific world-pictures that, to be fair, are not in any way commensensical?

Could his model of scientific reason phenomenologically account for acausal relations in the subatomic sphere or for reverse causation in evolutionary theory? His understanding of causality is too rigid and universalized to do justice to domains of science in which commonsense causality does not apply.

In a famous debate between Frederick Copleston and Bertrand Russell, Copleston tried to argue, in a manner similar to Breuer, for the dependence of scientific explanation on causality, while Russell argued for radical discontinuities in the world and hence for the merely partial dependence of science on causal explanation. Russell was not convinced that either all events or the universe as such have a cause and claimed that physics supports such a view.[2] Such a philosophy of science is incompatible with Breuer's. While Breuer would agree, I think, that causality begins with "the seventh day" and so the universe has no cause, properly speaking, this new compatibility of science and Torah would actually undermine his position. For science has come to this radical insight on its own. Further, science would no longer have to have the sort of explanatory structure Breuer claims it *must* have.

His conceptualization of science therefore is inadequate. Nonetheless, this does not mean it has to remain inadequate. There are sufficient resources in Kant to broaden the base of modes of scientific explanation beyond causality. Breuer's neglect of other categories may have been due to Schopenhauer's simplification of Kant's doctrine of the categories. Breuer's inadequacy does mean that he will not directly deliver a model of scientific-religious compatibility for the contemporary Orthodox thinker.

But it is not at all clear that such a model is necessary. Yeshayahu Leibowitz is the outstanding example of an Orthodox thinker who has given up—on principle—on any intellectual synthesis of science and religion. From the postmodern, post foundational point of view, real discontinuities in discourse—genuine cognitive pluralism—are preferable to a totalizing rationality. I believe that Breuer's insistence on standing in a community of discourse as a condition of intelligibility implies irreducible cognitive pluralism. Thus Breuer indirectly delivers a model of scientific-religious compatibility. Although he has, en route, dismissed the original problem of incompatibility as a serious problem. This dismissal is his real contribution to Jewish thought.

Another area in which he is open to critique is his concept of the will. Here, as with his concept of science, his overall system is rich enough to salvage his error. Will is a fundamental concept in

Breuer's system. It functions to establish the primacy of Being over reason and to enable the individual to enter into the sacral, meta-historical continuum of *knesset Israel* through sacramental action. But Breuer, like Schopenhauer, gets to will through argument. He has to establish the ontological, extrarational ground of will. In *Der Neue Kusari*, as we have seen in chapter 2, he argues episte-mologically that will precedes perception. Hence, willing is more fundamental than perceiving, cognizing, knowing, and so on. This was a key argument because it enabled Breuer to claim that, owing to the ontological priority of willing, will is more a fundamental mode of relating to the world than thinking. The Torah, as the inherent law of the world (as creation), must thus be approached through will, not reason.

Breuer's argument is flawed, even on its own terms. He uses *will* in two disparate senses and then confuses them, rendering his argument incoherent. He wants will to mean, first, an automatic movement of self-assertion by the *I* against the flux of phenom-ena. In this sense, the will is preconscious and nondeliberate. Breuer tends to use his neologism *Erwollnis* for this sense, but un-fortunately he does not do so in a consistent fashion.

The second sense of will is the conventional sense. Here, will is the conscious, deliberate assertion of self against world as well as the choice and affirmation of some object or course of action, for example, Torah. In short, the latter sense of will is the sense used in ordinary language, whereas the former sense is philosoph-ical, ontological.

When he asserts in *Der Neue Kusari* that willing precedes perception, he claims to have refuted the conventional wisdom that first one perceives and then one wants—wills—what one has perceived. The supposed conclusion, that first one wills and only then can one perceive , and so forth, is important because it estab-lishes for Breuer the primacy of will. Hence, willing can be held to be more fundamental than reasoning. Torah can be willed prior to its being understood or accepted by reason.

But in fact, Breuer has not refuted the conventional wisdom; he has begged the question, by using the unusual, nondeliberate sense of will when the questioner called for the conventional sense. Having established, Breuer thinks, the primacy of the will (in the nondeliberate sense) in the interaction with phenomena, Breuer asserts that the will (in the deliberate sense) must also pre-vail over noumena, by willing, that is, choosing, Torah. This kind of willing is supposed to enable the *I* to control the things-in-themselves as it controls the things of perception.

Breuer has not taken sufficient care to keep these senses straight and to avoid *petitio principii*. It is not at all clear what the preconscious, nondeliberate reaction of the will against the world of perception has in common with ordinary volition. Therefore, it is not at all clear why this nondeliberate sense constitutes a sense of will at all. Breuer has not provided any general, overarching definition of will of which these two senses could exemplify different aspects.

I think that Breuer has been led into this confusion, once again, because of his reliance upon Schopenhauer. For Schopenhauer, the universe per se is will, hence, all transactions within and between the worlds of self and things are significations of changes in a single substance. Being *is* volition. An overarching definition is available in Schopenhauer that accommodates many different exemplifications. Breuer seems to assume that he has taken over enough of Schopenhauer's metaphysics to assimilate his doctrine of will without incoherence. But this is not the case, for Breuer is not a monist. He does not say, as Schopenhauer does, that the things-in-themselves are will. He only says that they are reached by will. The thing-in-itself qua substance is a mystery for Breuer. It is a givenness lodged in the creation that serves as a guarantee against the equation of all of Being with the phenomenal—or natural—order. There is no single substance acting and being acted upon in Breuer's universe. There is rather an infinity of concrete, unique things and of unique selves, and a unique God. The metaphysical schema is fundamentally different from Schopenhauer's, but some of Breuer's assumptions about will have been taken over without the requisite modifications.

Breuer's reliance on Schopenhauer's tragic view of existence came about in conjunction with his effort to establish the soteriological necessity of Torah and of the metahistorical bearer of Torah. *Knesset Israel* must will the Torah to transcend the oppositions that characterize reality. Given this overriding concern, the epistemological critique is meant to motivate the Jew to commit himself to Torah in an unequivocal way. Indeed, in terms of particular reason, if I may put it in this way, "willing Torah" appears to mean nothing other than the *rational* choice of complete obedience to the *Shulchan Aruch*, and complete identification with a social order of a certain kind. If indeed the addressee of Breuer's argument, the will, requires reasons, such as are provided by these arguments, then what implications does that have for Breuer's own metarational epistemology and anthropology? Here the failure to probe the consequences of the implicit distinction between nondeliberate and deliberate will returns to haunt him.

If in fact deliberate will must be motivated by reasons to make its choice—an inherent implication of Breuer's whole procedure—then there is certainly no connection between such ordinary willing and the special kind of willing to which Breuer appeals. The alleged movement of the will against the world-as-perception, being nondeliberate, becomes a matter of causes, not of reasons, while the deliberate movement of will that wills Torah is a matter of reasons not causes. There is no essential connection between the two "kinds" of will.

Breuer tacitly admitted, in two ways, that his argument had deep flaws. In *Der Neue Kusari*, he tried to speak of the idiosyncratic, philosophical sense of will in terms of a dialectic of willed will (*gewollte Wille*) and willing will (*wollende Wille*). In this manner, he tried to show that this will of primal self-assertion that finds itself entrapped by world has both deliberate (that is, conventional-language) and nondeliberate (that is, philosophical) characteristics. But he was unable to sustain this terminology. The solution of *Naḥaliel* is even more offensive to the principle of parsimony. He simply distinguishes three kinds of will: the animal, rational, and ideational, and requires that the former two be sublated into the final one. The two halves of will in the nondeliberate sense are now passed into the animal (which becomes the willed will) and the rational (the willing will). The third effects the synthesis between them. Will finally becomes, if not rational, then directed by Ideas. Thus, willing the Torah becomes a highly deliberate act, at the farthest remove from the sort of primal self-positing through volition with which Breuer began his argument.

I do not think that any of this is fatal, for the problem is not in his metaphysics but in his terminology. He needs to restrict *will* to its conventional-language senses and call the nondeliberate, self-positing force of the subject by some other name. After all, in Breuer's scheme, the *I*'s mode of maintaining itself against the world is a different operation from the *I*'s willing Torah upon the world. To clearly distinguish between these operations terminologically would not destroy the metaphysical background against which the operations take place. What is lost is Breuer's claim to have demonstrated the priority of willing over perception. He would still, however, have demonstrated the priority of whatever this self-positing is to be called over perception, and could then claim that willing Torah, or ideational willing, is what introduces ontic stability into the dialectic of self-positing. Thus the primal self-positing and willing would still be positively interrelated.

I turn now to the criticism of a set of ideas that cannot be reworked, for they express Breuer's most basic convictions. I refer to his political utopianism, his dismissal of the concept of rights, and his general negation of liberal democracy.

Breuer reflects a deep pessimism about political life outside of the Torah State. He seems convinced that both romantic nationalism and totalitarianism are the natural inherent dynamics of any polity. If the law of the State is not God-given, then it is manmade. But since the law must claim authority for itself, the State must function as God. No political mechanism is sufficient to restrain the State from taking this role seriously, that is, to an extreme. Breuer held that the concept of natural right, on which liberal democracy is based, was part of the problem, not part of the solution. States, not individuals, are the agents or subjects of history. A system that protects the rights of individuals, whatever internal merit it might have, still leaves the external sphere of interstate relations lawless. Furthermore, precisely because of the negative boundaries against state interference the rights-based system erects, a vacuum of meaning arises. A state devoted to privacy cannot articulate, much less pursue, a public good. Breuer cannot imagine—other than the Torah State—a form of polity that is not either privatistic to the point of anarchy or collectivistic to the point of totalitarian terror. One is tempted to say, for a thinker who came of age in the period of the First World War and lived through the tragic chaos of Weimar and the Third Reich, this loss of faith in a rational politics is not incomprehensible.

As we have seen, Breuer reoriented his highly idealized political vision from history to metahistory. Eventually, it seems, he dissolved politics entirely into ethics and worship. Thus, he did not discard Stammler's social ideal, rendering politics simply pragmatic, utilitarian, or profane. He retained a political utopianism and an ideal content for law, but restricted the context for their realization. The dichotomization of history is Breuer's, but the political utopianism must be credited to Kant.

Isaiah Berlin offered a penetrating critique of Kantian, and by extension, Breuer's political thought.[3] Like Kant, Breuer must be seen as a proponent of positive rather than negative liberty. Breuer, as we have seen is utterly dismissive of the notion of individual rights. Against his metaphysical critique of individualization, he views freedom as freedom to transcend the *principium individuationis*. Freedom from interference, such that agents can pursue their own goods regardless of the wisdom of their choices, is a retrograde idea from his point of view. Indeed, real freedom can only be found through the transformation of individuality into a project of corporate holiness.

For Berlin, as soon as Kant distinguished between the empirical self and the rational self and made the freedom of the latter the point of politics, he turned his back on the modest politics of rights for the sake of a grandiose politics of transcendence. Rights relate to the mere empirical self. Freedom is the noble quest of the rational, true self. A necessary support of this politics is an idealized concept of law. True law is that which enables the rational self to realize its freedom. In Berlin's view, once an elite knows what such true freedom is and has the epistemological and anthropological theories to prove that human persons really require it, the door is open to coercive, utopian politics. The banner for this politics is (positive) liberty: the freedom of the group to achieve a certain vision of man at the expense of the individual. The individual's freedom to be left alone by the philosophically energized group, to simply pursue his own aims, vanishes.

Breuer's heavy emphasis on freedom as the ground and effect of law is of the positive type, as indeed any metaphysical concept of freedom must be. The empirical self, which becomes animal-like in Breuer, is trapped in the web of desire and causality. Its own concept of the good and of freedom (negative liberty) is worthless. Only a true law, the creation law, can extricate this self (which must become the Kantian rational self—Breuer's ideational—self) from heteronomy with its illusory freedom. The representatives of *knesset Israel*, who are fully active in metahistory, become the elite who alone are fit to rule. This already might say more than the evidence allows. Other than the description, taken from Maimonides, of the qualifications for membership in the Sanhedrin, Breuer does not specify the characteristics of the putative ruling elite. Nor does he detail a program for building a Torah State. Precisely what may be accomplished before the messiah comes remains unclear.

What is clear is that his portrayal of how the Torah State would function leaves no room, on principle, for a doctrine of individual rights. (This is not to say that dissent, for instance, would not be tolerated. I believe that it would. Toleration, however, is a sorry substitute for democratic liberty.) Rights are replaced by duties. Spheres of activity in which one is "free" are arranged in terms of the discharge of duty. Thus, women lacking certain duties that men have in Judaism would not be allowed entrance into the relevant spheres of activity granted to men. The law, being an ideal, metaphysical law, could not allow basic reform of this disparity, nor could it allow a grievance procedure. Without concepts of individual rights and equality before the law, gender-based disparities in the distribution of duties do not even appear as injustices. Breuer is not unaware, of course, of the logic of naming what is just and unjust. His intricate discussion of Jewish and modern law examines exactly this point. But he rejects the logic of equality and thus the imputation of injustice to Jewish law in the name of both its divine origin and its inner logic of freedom. Breuer would simply not admit the validity of the premises required to argue a rights-based case against his version of freedom.

Breuer has offered an unintended contribution, I think, in framing the contrast between Jewish and modern law so starkly. His theocratic politics displays in a transparent form the inner logic of a traditional religious case against liberal democracy. It seems to me that all who take Jewish law to aim at being the law of a state must hold presuppositions similar to his and must be equally uncomfortable with democracy. At some early point in his argument, the Jewish theocrat must repudiate the classical liberal notion of the individual as sovereign within his own political domain. Moses Mendelssohn's exemplary liberal theory in *Jerusalem* owes little, as his contemporaries recognized, to earlier Jewish political thought. For the individual is not sovereign within his own sphere of action or of thought in Judaism; he is God's steward, and God is his master. His body, for example, is not his own. He has no absolute rights over it. He has duties toward it, which the law details.

Breuer's position forces the traditional Jewish thinker to confront the tension between the social concepts of the democratic tradition and those that both ground and emerge from the covenantal nomism of the halakhah. His own radical insistence on the normative ideal of the Torah State serves to discourage overly facile attempts to reconcile religion and state in the traditional Jewish context. Breuer is at his most eloquent when he refuses to let Judaism be construed as a matter of conscience or private preference. He is explicit about the course of intellectual and social history that made for the subjectivization and political marginalization of religion. In his rejection of the typical modern solution to the problem of religion and state, he most offends against the Enlightenment, in both its moderate and its extreme versions. Breuer's theocratic theory is wholly irreconcilable with democratic thought. What is not expressed in his theory is the turn toward pragmatic accommodation that he took in actual practice. His life demonstrated a greater disposition toward moderate and realistic political policy than his system does. *Ars longa, vita brevis.*

Were Breuer's political vision (either of Frankfurt or of Jerusalem) his chief legacy, then it would be true that his thought is denied the possibility of further development. Baruch Kurzweil, while granting Breuer's writings a broad and honored place in the history of modern Jewish thought, believed that it would be tragic, in fact, dangerous to pursue their political *tendenz*.[4] Breuer requires interpretation and commentary, not expansion.

Yet, it must be possible to learn from Breuer and to follow his lead when his view is sound. Kurzweil detected a profound tension in Breuer between his anti-individualism and his own striking individuality. The man who taught the wisdom of personal assimilation into the archetypal mold of the "Talmud Jude" was himself quite unassimilable. Misunderstanding was the only common basis for his "followers."[5] His true companions, Kurzweil claimed, were not the Agudists who followed his casket, but all "aristocrats of the spirit."

In this articulate tension of struggle with modernity, particularly with modern rationality in its relation to Judaism, Breuer leaves a fertile legacy. Like Rosenzweig, Breuer experienced disillusionment with academic canons of reason. Rosenzweig believed that German idealism had brought philosophy to the point of its own negation, while historicism had fully relativized meaning in history. Rosenzweig came to revelation as an objective standpoint by means of which God, man, and world could be newly and more truly thought. Breuer also understood that reason is a captive of its own history. From the standpoint of its captivity, it cannot even understand itself let alone set itself to work practically on the world. Breuer constructs reason, as we have seen, as a castaway on the sea of creation. On its little island of phenomena—which reason deludes itself into imagining is the whole of Being—law prevails. But this law is discomfitted and undermined by the scandalous particularity of Being, the irrefragable, idiosyncratic givenness of oneself. It is undermined by the unruly passion that desires what thought thinks and by the most unruly passion of all: the passion to be free of passion.

In his relentless critiques of the pretensions of reason, even of chastised Kantian reason, Breuer speaks not as a naif, but as one who has been disillusioned. A man who thanked God for giving Immanuel Kant of his wisdom and who retained membership in the *Kant Gesellschaft* until he fled Nazi Germany was himself a prisoner of the hope for a rational design for moral, social, and political life. His undermining of reason is a repudiation of the reasonableness of such a hope in the name of a hope beyond disillusionment. Yet at no point does Breuer advocate a blind, fundamentalist turning from the contemporary canons of reason. He advocates no irrational leap into Jewish experience. Both lawyer and Talmudist, he argues his way from reason to *knesset Israel*. If some of these arguments are unsound or unpersuasive, this does not mean that his procedure and example are unsound or unpersuasive.

Breuer holds culture in a truly dialectical tension with Torah. He seeks neither rejection nor synthesis, but continued tension. Reason is required both for itself and for its limits. Breuer refined this tension across a range of concerns: philosophy, law, and politics were all dialectical moments for him. Modern Jewish philosophers, Orthodox and non-Orthodox alike, can find a model in this reluctance to dissipate essential, indeed existential, tensions.

Thus Breuer's conception of philosophy coincides oddly with that of another contemporary, Wittgenstein. Breuer does epistemology in order not to have to do epistemology. (Wittgenstein does philosophy as a therapy in order to cure the confusions that have led him to do philosophy.) Epistemology is to prove nothing other than the pathos of the epistemic subject. Epistemology is an essay in the tragic *conditio humana*, not a ground for self-sufficient reason or for a predictable, domesticated revelation. Belonging to the Congregation of Israel—a shared way, rather than a solitary path of thought—is the ground against which both the figure of reason and true experience of revelation emerge.

Though phrased in the language of *Erlebnisphilosophie*, Breuer's stress on standing in the Congregation of Israel is compatible with current notions of revelation as the master narrative of a community. Breuer would argue that Torah revelation is unintelligible outside of Judaism, that a correct phenomenological account of the life of mitzvot requires the experience of willing mitzvot.

Israel and the oral law, furthermore, are locked in an ontological embrace. They mutually condition one another's being. Thus, while Torah is uniquely Israel's story, Israel is Torah's unique actualization. Breuer's ontologizing language, however, introduces a kind of descriptive proposition unwelcome in theology after its "linguistic turn.".

Does Breuer really intend to reify *knesset Israel*, the Torah-in-itself, and other such putative entities? Said another way, How much of a kabbalistic ontology does Breuer really wish to appropriate? For a thinker who is judiciously reluctant to reify the concept of self, it is difficult to believe that he has the extensive ontological commitments apparently implied by his discourse. The fact that Breuer, for all of his thematization of kabbalistic concepts, never appropriates the symbolic apparatus of the Sefirot adds credence to this view. Breuer wanted to speak, I believe, about the way the world is from a certain standpoint. More precisely, he wanted to speak about how the world ought to be and will be when the requisite action is taken. 'Creation' and 'metahistory' are not hypostases, but explanatory categories that cannot be reduced. They are also performative utterances: they effect action as they are spoken. They situate their speaker and make him effective in the performance of his Jewish task. They are *kavannot*, intentions to focus the mind prior to the deed. But undoubtedly Breuer also wanted to say more. He wanted to hint at a structure the world and Jewish Being have that conventional language, commonsense reason, is at a loss to describe. He used the language of Kabbalah, with its theosophy and theurgy, to articulate such structures. Yet Breuer always remained circumspect about burdening himself with too many ontological commitments. The lack of clarity in his thought about the relationship between human action and Providence reflects an uncertainty about how to describe God's action without reification. Talk of divine action is meant, it seems to me, to situate human action.

This situating of Jewish action in metahistory, with its assertion of the sacral dimension of Jewish peoplehood, is another fertile legacy. Breuer manages to construct metahistory as both a proleptic eschatological reality and an active historical process. His Jewish people is not ahistorical or confined to love and prayer in a present invaded by eternity, as is Rosenzweig's. Breuer can write a metahistory of Israel, *Moriah*, that is related to the course of world history. Most importantly, the social action of Israel in the history/metahistory interplay counts for the out-working of redemption. Historical change requires metahistorical response. Breuer's keen sense of the metahistorical need to return to Zion, exemplified in his own biography, seems to me more fruitful than Rosenzweig's eschatological quietism. Of course, Rosenzweig was heroically active in the nurturance of community, but he abandoned history to Siegfried and the Church. History needed the Jews, but only as an aloof artifact of revealed eternity. Breuer, on the other hand, took an activist stance toward history. He wanted his movement to seize a historical moment through which Israel could join its metahistorical destiny to its ancient land. He tried to speak for millenia of Jewish religious striving and to discern "signs of the times."

Ironically, Breuer's thematization of the categories of history and metahistory represents a more typically modern impulse than does Rosenzweig's putative traditionalism.[6] While Rosenzweig imputed an ahistorical posture to the Jewish people, Breuer threw them back along the axis of history, albeit on a metalevel. Breuer's Kabbalah-informed theurgy is directed toward a historical and metahistorical effect, while the effect of action in Rosenzweig's schema is more theosophical. Breuer's forthright reliance on Kabbalah might have led him to a more atemporal ontological-theosophical orientation in which the locus of effect is the inner world of the Godhead or the configuration of divine and other elements. But his gaze remained fixed on history. He endowed it with a contrapuntal trajectory of catastrophe and redemption. History as locus of action indicates a modern sensibility, but it also signals a return to a biblical mode. Breuer is committed to history as the locus of God's effective presence (and absence). He links Kabbalah with a more ancient tradition of historical consciousness, thus producing a complex hybrid. I would suggest that Breuer's frequent use of prophetic citations is not a mere scriptural adornment to an alien metaphysical structure, but a genuine attempt to return to a biblical sense of history.

Theocracy stands at the margins of Jewish philosophical possibility, but what of sacral peoplehood? Is this metaphysical concept of Israel just another romantic nationalism, filled with awful dangers for Jews and others? Breuer saw Zionism as precisely that kind of romantic nationalism. Although its historical inclination was sound, its conceptualization and program was poisoned by nationalistic self-absorption, in his view. He intended his entire project of Torah peoplehood to be a correction of modern nationalistic politics. The key corrective element was Torah as law. Implementation of a Torah constitutionalism would hold the people responsible to the revealed will of God and not to their own general will. God's will would become the general will, indeed, the will of all. Breuer bypassed constitutional safeguards for checking political will, relying—as we have seen—on a classical conception of private virtue. His structure does not allow for either modern checks and balances or biblical prophetic critique. The ideal justice of the law, in the hands of qualified interpreters, seems to ensure that the nation ultimately will not err. It is difficult to see how this political construction does not amount, from an external, functional point of view, to the very romantic nationalism Breuer deplored. Government by *tzaddikim*, in the name of corporate holiness, may be the nineteenth century's most extravagant political legacy.

Yet Breuer's attempt to shore up Israel's old mystical sense of self against self-secularization and moralistic apologetics is instinct with philosophical possibility. Gershom Scholem, questioning the very success of the secularization of Jewish nationhood, wrote that "questions about the Eternal life of the Eternal People before the Eternal God are not of the sort that can be forgotten."[7] When they are forgotten, they emerge again as a return of the repressed. Breuer represents a complex attempt to think through the relation of the Eternal People to its law in a philosophical and kabbalistic key. He highlights in an acute way the conceptual tension between an Israel, so conceived, and modern constructions of society and nationhood. He displays, albeit inadvertently, the dangers of sacral nationhood. He also displays the orienting and self-critical force it provides. We can learn, I think, from both his disciplined reflection and from its problematic implications.

Breuer is a high and powerful expression of a cultural synthesis that is no more. But voices older than those of German Jewry speak through him. They and their German accents speak, I believe, to the ages.

NOTES

CHAPTER 1

1. Gershom Scholem, *On Jews and Judaism in Crisis*, ed. Werner J. Dannhauser (New York: Schocken Books, 1976), p. 62.

2. Ibid.

3. Frederic V. Grunfeld, *Prophets Without Honor* (New York: Holt, Rinehart and Winston, 1979), (Philadelphia: Jewish Publication Society of America, 1979), p.31.

4. Jacob Katz, "German Culture and the Jews," *Commentary* 77 (February 1984): 54.

5. There is some controversy as to whether Hirsch was actually successful as a rabbi in Nikolsburg. Professor Mordechai Breuer, in a review essay, argues persuasively for Hirsch's popularity and success. In the same essay, Breuer points out that an objective (nonhagiographic) study of Hirsch's work needs to be written. See Mordechai Breuer, review of *Tradition in an Age of Reform*, by Noah H. Rosenbloom, *Tradition* 16 (Summer 1977): 142–43. On general reasons for the relative scholarly neglect of German Orthodoxy, cf. Y. Wolfsberg, "Popular Orthodoxy," *Leo Baeck Institute Yearbook* I (1956): 237–54.

6. Cf. Isaac Breuer, *Der Neue Kusari: Ein Weg zum Judentum* (Frankfurt am Main: Rabbiner Hirsch Gesellschaft, 1934), p. 139.

7. Isaac Breuer, *Mein Weg* (Jerusalem/Zürich: Morascho Verlag, [1946] 1988), p. 9.

8. For a thorough discussion of the educational philosophy of the IRG, see Mordechai Breuer, *Jüdische Orthodoxie im Deutschen Reich 1871–1918* (Frankfurt am Main: Jüdischer Verlag bei Athenaeum, 1986), ch. 3.

9. Breuer, *Mein Weg*, p. 37.

10. Ibid., p. 35.

11. Ibid.

12. Ibid., p. 94.

13. Ibid., p. 95.

14. Ibid., p. 26.

15. Ibid., p. 81.

16. Cf. ibid., p. 88. Baruch Kurzweil believes that Breuer's polemical sharpness was the mark of unresolved inner tensions. Cf. Baruch Kurzweil, *Lenokhaḥ Ha-Mevuchah Ha-Ruḥanit Shel Doreinu (Facing the Spiritual Perplexity of Our Time)* (Ramat Gan:Bar Ilan University Press, 1976). p. 118.

17. Ibid.

18. Cf. M. Breuer, *Jüdische Orthodoxie*, p. 317

19. For a description of the mood of the period, cf. Paul R. Mendes-Flohr, "Rosenzweig and the Crisis of Historicism," in *The Philosophy of Franz Rosenzweig* (Hanover: Brandeis University Press, 1988).

20. Isaac Breuer, "Neuorientierung," in *Programm Oder Testament* (Frankfurt am Main: Kaufmann Verlag, 1929). Cf. Mordechai Breuer, *Jüdische Orthodoxie*, ch. 7.

21. M. Breuer, *Jüdische Orthodoxie*, p. 323. Rivka Horwitz, "Voices of Opposition to the First World War among Jewish Thinkers," *Leo Baeck Institute Yearbook* XXXIII (1988): 247.

22. Mendes-Flohr, *Franz Rosenzweig*, p. 8.

23. Breuer, *Mein Weg*, pp. 43ff.

24. Ibid., p. 45. M. Breuer, *Jüdische Orthodoxie*, p. 339.

25. Breuer, *Mein Weg*, p. 42.

26. Ibid., pp. 48–49.

27. Ibid., p. 54. Jews learned from Kant to ground ethics in epistemology. Breuer's privileging of epistemological discourse betrays his thoroughgoing Kantianism. Cf. Friedrich Niewöhner, " 'Primat der Ethik' oder 'Erkenntnistheoretische Begründung der Ethik'? Thesen zur Kant-Rezeption in der Jüdischen Philosophie," *Judentum im Zeitalter der Aufk-*

lärung, Wolfenbütteler Studien zur Aufklärung, Vol. 4 (Wolfenbüttel: Jacobi Verlag, 1977), p. 136.

28. Breuer, *Mein Weg,* p. 55.

29. Ibid., p. 58.

30. Friedrich Niewöhner notes instances where Breuer approves of Cohen. Cf. Niewöhner, "Isaac Breuer und Kant," *Neue Zeitschrift für systematische Theologie und Religionsphilosophie* 17 (1975): 142–50. Cf. also Rivka Horwitz, "Voices of Opposition," pp. 241–42. Because Breuer's retrospective statements in *Mein Weg* need to be evaluated against available contemporary sources, one runs the risk of assuming Breuer's own bias in reconstructing his life from his autobiography.

31. Breuer, *Mein Weg,* p. 65.

32. Ibid., pp. 66–70.

33. Ibid., p. 75.

34. M. Breuer, *Jüdische Orthodoxie,* pp. 331–37.

35. Breuer, *Mein Weg,* p. 96.

36. Ibid., p. 99.

37. Cf. George L. Mosse, *The Nationalization of the Masses* (New York: New American Library, 1975), pp. 133–34.

38. M. Breuer, *Jüdische Orthodoxie,* p. 333.

39. Breuer, *Mein Weg,* p. 100.

40. A near complete bibliography of Breuer's works is found in Isaac Breuer, *Concepts of Judaism,* ed. Jacob S. Levinger, (Jerusalem: Israel Universities Press, 1974), pp. 339–43. My bibliography is more selective.

41. Breuer, *Mein Weg,* pp. 96, 100.

42. Cf. ibid., p. 104.

43. Horwitz, "Voices of Opposition," p. 243.

44. Ibid., pp. 241–42. Breuer lived to see an atomic bomb dropped on Hiroshima. At the end of his life, although reposing his hope in a liberal democracy in Palestine, he retained a disenchanted neutral attitude toward the U.S.-Soviet rivalry. The historic struggle between communism and capitalism, he asserted, was of no particular concern to Jews. Cf. *Mein Weg,* P. 241.

45. Breuer, *Mein Weg,* p. 109.

46. Ibid., p. 107.

47. Ibid., p. 108.

48. For an account of the founding of Agudah and of the tensions between Western and Eastern elements, cf. Gershon C. Bacon, "The Politics of Tradition: Agudat Israel in Polish Politics, 1916–1939," in *Studies in Contemporary Jewry*, vol. 2 ed. Peter Y. Medding, (Bloomington: Indiana University Press, 1986), pp. 144–63.

I have suggested that Breuer's self-conception and activity are dialectically related to Theodor Herzl's. For an account of Agudah per se that develops this mirror-image thesis, cf. Ben Halpern, *The Idea of the Jewish State* (Cambridge: Harvard University Press, 1969), p. 86. Similarly, Eliezer Schweid has found that Breuer's theocratic utopianism is a mirror image of the secular utopianism of *Alt-Neuland*. Cf. Eliezer Schweid, "Medinat Ha-Torah bemishnato shel Yitzhaq Breuer," ("The Torah State in the Thought of Isaac Breuer,") in Rivka Horwitz, ed., *Isaac Breuer: The Man and His Thought* p. 130.

49. Bacon, "Politics of Tradition," p. 146. For Breuer's own account of the struggle over the "Frankfurt Principle" in the early Agudah, cf. his *Moriah* (Jerusalem: Ha-Merkaz le–ma'an Sifrut Haredit, be-Eretz Yisrael 1954), pp. 215–19.

50. Cf. Halpern, *Idea of the Jewish State*, p. 86. Herzl believed that the Zionist Organization embodied the sovereign will of the entire Jewish people, whether they acknowledged this supreme representative function or not. Schweid, in "The Torah State," p. 139, suggests that Breuer's messianic activism was realized by taking small institutional steps in the formation of Agudah. Institution building was equivalent to laying the foundation for the messianic Torah State. Herzl believed that when he founded the Jewish Agency at the First Zionist Congress, he was laying the basis for a future Jewish State.

51. Breuer, *Der Neue Kusari*, pp. 438ff., and *Mein Weg*, p. 118.

52. Breuer, *Mein Weg*, pp. 190–91. Jacob Levinger, "Hayav vepo'alo shel Yitzhaq Breuer," ("The Life and Work of Isaac Breuer"), in Rivka Horwitz, ed., *Isaac Breuer*, p. 22.

53. Cf. *Moriah*, p. 199, for Breuer's assessment of R. Sonnenfeld.

54. Cf. Horwitz, *Isaac Breuer*, pp. 181–88, for Breuer's memorial to Kook (in Hebrew translation). Breuer reports on his various meetings with Kook and the points of similarity and contrast between them. Significantly, Breuer believes that Kook was a solitary figure whose position was paradoxical and precluded a mass following. One cannot help but wonder whether Breuer felt humanly close to Kook because of this very trait.

55. Breuer, *Mein Weg*, pp. 150ff.

56. Ibid., pp. 222, 232.

57. Cf. Halpern, *Idea of the Jewish State*, p. 225.

58. "Edut lifnei va'adat ha-ḥaqirah ha-anglo-amerika'it le'inyanei eretz Yisrael," "Testimony of Isaac Breuer before the Anglo-American Committee of Inquiry", in Horwitz, *Isaac Breuer*, p. 206.

CHAPTER 2

1. Cf. Eliezer Goldman, "Responses to Modernity in Orthodox Jewish Thought," *Studies in Contemporary Jewry*, vol. 2, ed. Peter Y. Medding (Bloomington: Indiana University Press, 1986), p. 64.

2. The section on epistemology is located primarily in book 3, chapter 2, of *Der Neue Kusari*, pp. 253–321. In *Die Welt als Schöpfung und Natur* (Frankfurt am Main: J. Kauffman Verlag, 1926) (hereafter abbreviated in notes to *Die Welt*), comments on epistemology are scattered throughout, especially in chapters 8–12, pp. 55–84. The entirety of *Elischa* (Frankfurt am Main: J. Kauffman Verlag, 1928) is taken up by epistemology. This latter text was the principal "dress rehearsal" for the *Der Neue Kusari*. In *Naḥaliel* (Jerusalem: Mossad Ha-Rav Kook, 1982), Breuer begins his thesis on epistemology on pp. 4–10 and 20–29 and develops it at many other points in the work. In *Moriah: The Foundations of National Torah Education* (Hebrew), (Jerusalem: Ha-merkaz le-ma'an Sifrut Ḥaredit be-Eretz Yisrael, 1954), the thesis is enunciated on pp. 10–13; 46–49; and 168–74 inter alia. All references to *Moriah* in this study are taken from this second edition. A new, revised edition has recently been published by Mossad Ha-Rav Kook, 1982.

3. Breuer, *Lehre, Gesetz und Nation: Eine Historische-Kritische Untersuchung über das Wesen des Judentums* (Frankfurt am Main: Verlag des Israelit, 1910), pp., 3–8.

4. Breuer, *Moriah*, pp. 110–113.

5. Ibid., p. 113.

6. Ibid.

7. Hans Lewy, Alexander Altmann, and Isaak Heinemann, *Three Jewish Philosophers* (New York: Atheneum, 1969), p. 137. Cf. also Henry Slonimsky, Introduction to *Kuzari*, by Judah Halevi (New York: Schocken Books, 1964), p. 22.

8. Slonimsky, ibid., p. 28.

9. Heinz Moshe Graupe, *The Rise of Modern Judaism* (Huntington, New York: Robert E. Krieger Publishing, 1978), pp. 174–75.

10. Ibid. Cf. Hans I. Bach, *The German Jew* (New York: Oxford University Press, 1985), pp. 97–98.

11. Noah H. Rosenbloom, *Tradition in an Age of Reform* (Philadelphia: Jewish Publication Society of America, 1976), pp. 155–56.

12. Samson Raphael Hirsch, *The Nineteen Letters on Judaism*, ed. Jacob Breuer (Jerusalem: Feldheim Publishers, 1973), p. 32.

13. Hirsch's position seems to be that nature does indeed display itself as God's handiwork, but that we only appreciate nature in this manner given the tutelage of revelation. A representative quotation of this view can be found in Hirsch's commentary on Exodus 20:12: "Not on the results of our research into Nature, but on the actual events in the history of our people . . . did God found our Jewish knowledge and acknowledgement of Him." "Heaven and Earth had spoken in vain to mankind, worse, the sermon that they really preached had been twisted into polytheistic conceptions; and it was only the historical revelations of God in the history of the Jewish people, which brought back the monotheistic idea to mankind for their understanding of nature and history." (Samson Raphael Hirsch, *The Pentateuch*, trans. Isaac Levy, vol. 2 (London: Union of Orthodox Congregations of Great Britain, 1956), p. 274.) Breuer's fundamental ambivalence about creation and metaphysics as sources of revelation can be traced to Hirsch.

14. Breuer, *Mein Weg*, p. 55.

15. Ibid., pp. 56-57.

16. Ibid. Breuer kept a portrait of Kant over his desk in Frankfurt. He did not bring the portrait with him to Jerusalem in 1936, however.

17. Oskar Wolfsberg (Yeshayahu Aviad), Review of *Die Welt als Schöpfung und Natur*, by Isaac Breuer, *Monatschrift für Geschichte und Wissenschaft des Judentums* 9/10 (1926):426–28.

18. Zvi Kurzweil, *The Modern Impulse of Traditional Judaism* (Hoboken: Ktav Publishing Co., 1985), p. 44.

19. Niewöhner, "Isaac Breuer und Kant"; also his " 'Primat der Ethik.'"

20. Jacob S. Levinger, Introduction to Breuer's *Concepts of Judaism*, p. 23.

21. Zvi Kurzweil's *The Modern Impulse* pp. 44–47.

22. Baruch Kurzweil's essays on Breuer appeared in the Hebrew daily *Ha- Aretz* on December 17, 1943, and November 1, 1946, and a correction of the latter appeared on November 14, 1946. These have been gathered and reprinted in his *Lenokhaḥ Ha-Mevuchah* (Facing the Spiritual Perplexity of Our Time). These essays are now available in a collection of essays, *Isaac Breuer;* ed. Rivka Horwitz, pp. 149–61).

23. Judah Halevi, *Kuzari* 1.1. For a brief but insightful comparison of the original and Breuer's *Der Neue Kusari,* see M. Wiener, "Judah Halevi's Concept of Religion and a Modern Counterpart," *Hebrew Union College Annual* 23 (1950–51): 669ff.

24. Breuer, *Der Neue Kusari,* p. 9. "Was war ihm bisher Gott? Im Grunde genommen bestenfalls ein Grenzbegriff, der die Stelle kennzeichnete, über die menschliches Wissen nicht hinausdringen kann; meistens aber nur eine leere und abgegriffene Wortfloskel."

25. Ibid., pp. 15–33.

26. Ibid., p. 67.

27. Ibid., p. 84. "Erlebnis? Gewiss Erlebnis. Jedes Wunder ist ein Erlebnis. Auch das geschichtliche Wunder der jüdischen Nation in all seiner metageschichtlichen Geweissagtheit ist ein Erlebnis. Aber dieses Erlebnis vollzieht sich nicht von Innen nach Aussen, sonder von Aussen nach Innen."

28. The primacy of history or "metahistory" over metaphysics is an important theme in Breuer. For the Jew, the historical revelation at Sinai preempts the value of ahistorical, that is, metaphysical, religious experience. The nations, unlike Israel, are confined to metaphysically structured religious experience. That is to their detriment in Breuer's view. For they are unable to synthesize their metaphysical experience in a fulfilled, nontragic way.

The prefix "meta" that Breuer uses in relation to history has perhaps been borrowed from Rosenzweig, who uses it in conjunction with "metalogic," "metaethics," and "metaphysics." Nathan Rotenstreich explains Rosenzweig's usage of "meta" as designating an irreducible ontological reference, such that the sphere to which this designation is attributed cannot be subsumed under any other category. This definition accords well with Breuer's usage. "Metahistory" is unique. It is related to history, but not reducible to it. Cf. Nathan Rotenstreich, "Rosenzweig's Notion of Metaethics," in Mendes-Flohr, *Franz Rosenzweig,* pp. 69–71.

29. The figure of the young man who is searching for an intellectual grounding for his observance is based, I believe, on an acquaintance of Breuer's: cf. *Mein Weg,* p. 64. Breuer tells us that this acquaintance turned to observance with "fanaticism" but then foundered; he asked

Breuer to help him gain faith in the "divinity of the Torah." Breuer's response was to write *Lehre, Gesetz und Nation*. This was of no avail, and the acquaintance became completely nonobservant. He was killed in the First World War. Breuer says that his love for this man never died.

By the "divinity of the Torah" Breuer means a substantial, ontological connectedness between God and Torah. E.g. *Der Neue Kusari*, p. 263: "Zwischen der Göttlichkeit der Thora und Gott selber hat unser Volk niemals einen Unterschied gemacht. Die Thora ist wesentlich Eigenschaft Gottes. Wer sie leugnet, trennt Gott von seiner Eigenschaft; leugnet Gott."

30. Breuer, *Der Neue Kusari*, pp. 262–63.

31. Ibid.

32. Immanuel Kant, *Critique of Pure Reason*, trans. Norman Kemp Smith (New York: St. Martin's Press, 1965), pp 308–9. Breuer was not alone in relating the Kantian "das Unbedingte" to divinity. Martin Buber has a similar usage in his early lectures. See "Jewish Religiosity" in *On Judaism*, ed. Nahum N. Glatzer (New York: Schocken Books, 1977), p. 80. "Religiosity is his longing to establish a living communion with the unconditioned, his will to realize the unconditioned through his actions, transporting it into the world of man."

33. Breuer, *Der Neue Kusari*, p. 264.

34. Cf. Jeffrie G. Murphy, *Kant: The Philosophy of Right*, Philosophers in Perspective Series, ed. A.D. Woozley (London: Macmillian, 1970), p. 34.

35. Kant's "subtle line of attack" is to show that his premises are presupposed by his opponents, but that they are unaware of them. Breuer has a similar argument. In order to account for the world as it is, his opponents require categories like 'creation' and 'Sabbath'. They remain unaware of these categories, however, and so remain trapped in what is essentially a false form of consciousness.

36. Breuer, *Der Neue Kusari*, pp. 265–67.

37. Ibid., p. 265.

38. Ibid.

39. Arthur Schopenhauer, *The World as Will and Idea*, trans. R. B. Haldane and J. Kemp (Garden City, NY: Doubleday, 1961), pp. 86–100. (Hereafter cited as *World*.)

40. Post-Kantian idealism in general is a sustained attitude of impatience toward the *Ding an sich*. Schopenhauer, in particular, anticipates the neo-Romantics of Breuer's period by transforming the thing-in-itself

from a theoretical principle into an experience; an *Erlebnis*. For Breuer, following Schopenhauer, the "world in itself" is most definitely an object of experience.

41. Schopenhauer, *World*, para. 7, pp. 40–50.

42. Ibid., para 8, p. 50.

43. Ibid., para 4, pp. 23–29.

44. Ibid., para 9, p. 56.

45. Ibid., para 15, pp. 86–100.

46. Ibid., para 23, p. 128.

47. Ibid., para 18, p. 116.

48. Ibid., para 17, p. 115.

49. Ibid., para 19, p. 120.

50. Ibid., para 36, pp. 200–201.

51. Ibid., para 52, p. 278.

52. Ibid., para 68, pp. 388–408.

53. Friedrich Nietzsche, *The Birth of the Tragedy*, trans. Francis Golffing (Garden City, New York: Doubleday & Co. 1956), p. 35.

54. Cf. Paul Flohr, "From *Kulturmystik* to Dialogue: An Inquiry into the Formation of Martin Buber's Philosophy of I and Thou" (Ph.D. dissertation, Brandeis University, 1974), p. 55. This important study is available in German translation as *Von der Mystik zum Dialog: Martin Buber's geistige Entwicklung bis hin zu "Ich und Du,"* Paul R. Mendes-Flohr, trans. Dafna A. von Kries (Königstein/Ts.: Jüdischer Verlag, 1978). Page references in these notes are to the English version. Cf. George Mosse, *Crisis of German Ideology* (New York: Grosset & Dunlap, 1964), pp. 52–66.

55. Breuer, *Der Neue Kusari*, p. 84.

56. Herbert A. Hodges, *Wilhelm Dilthey: an Introduction* (New York: Howard Fertig, 1969), p. 117.

57. Joel, cited in Flohr, p. 6, n. 23 to Introduction (translation my own).

58. Mosse, *Crisis of German Ideology*, p. 60.

59. Breuer, *Der Neue Kusari*, p. 270.

60. Ibid.

61. Ibid.

62. Ibid. Cf. Schopenhauer, *World*, para 2, pp. 20–21: "That which knows all things and is known by none is the subject. Everyone finds himself to be a subject, yet only insofar as he knows, not insofar as he is an object of knowledge."

63. Breuer, *Der Neue Kusari*, p. 271.

64. Schopenhauer, *World*, para 18, passim.

65. Breuer, *Der Neue Kusari*, p. 273.

66. Ibid., p. 271.

67. Ibid., p. 270.

68. Ibid., p. 276.

69. Schopenhauer, *World*, para 5, pp. 29–34.

70. Breuer, *Der Neue Kusari*, pp. 282–83.

71. Ibid., p. 276. Charles Friedman traces Breuer's view of perception, as a unificatory experience in which subject and object merge, to Aristotle (*Metaphysics*, bk. 7, ch.7), filtered through Maimonides, *Guide*, pt. 1, ch. 68. Friedman notes that while Breuer was no Aristotelian, he was a lifelong reader of Maimonides, as the heavy dependence of *Naḥaliel* on the *Mishneh Torah* indicates. Although Friedman's suggestion has merit, I am inclined to think that Breuer's source is German idealism more than medieval Jewish Aristotelianism. In support of Friedman's view, Breuer does give to perception a theological coloration (it is a God-like act) that is found in both Aristotle and Maimonides *ad loc.* Cf. Charles (Shlomo) Friedman, *Ha-mishpat bemachshavato shel Rav Yitzḥak Breuer*, trans. Yehudit Kaufmann (Jerusalem: Ha-ma'ayan, n.d.), p. 23. This translated reprint was a chapter of an unfinished doctoral dissertation. It appeared originally in French in *Revue des Etudes Juives*, vol. 131 (1972): 127–59.

72. Breuer, *Der Neue Kusari*, pp. 283–84.

73. Gershom Scholem, *On the Kabbalah and its Symbolism*, trans. Ralph Mannheim (New York: Schocken Books, 1965), pp. 110–12.

74. Breuer, *Der Neue Kusari*, p. 284. One might compare Breuer's figurative description of these primal epistemic relations with Buber's descriptions of I/Thou, I/it ontological relations. Buber refers to the I/Thou

relation as one of love and asserts the inherent impermanence of that relation. Cf. *Ich und Du* (Heidelberg: Lambert Schneider, 1979), pp. 21–24.

75. Breuer, *Der Neue Kusari*, p. 294.

76. Ibid., pp. 295–96.

77. Ibid., p. 298.

78. Ibid.

79. Ibid., pp. 297–98.

80. Isaac Husik, *A History of Medieval Jewish Philosophy* (Philadelphia: Jewish Publication Society of America, 1948), p. 37.

81. Gershom G. Scholem, *Major Trends in Jewish Mysticism* (New York: Schocken Books, 1971), p. 240.

82. Ibid.

83. Maimonides, *Mishneh Torah*, Hilkhot Yesodei ha-Torah, 4:8–9.

84. *Zohar* cited in Yishayah Tishbi, *Mishnat Ha-Zohar*, 2 vols. (Jerusalem: Mossad Bialik, 1971), p. 11 (translation my own).

85. Ibid.

86. Ibid.

87. Breuer, *Der Neue Kusari*, p. 319.

88. Ibid.

89. Ibid., p. 320.

90. Ibid.

91. Ibid., p. 321.

92. Breuer, *Naḥaliel*, pp. 3–11; 20ff.

93. Schopenhauer, *World*, para 23, pp. 128–35.

94. This idea can be traced to Leibniz's *Discourse on Metaphysics*, cf. chapters 8 and 14.

95. Breuer, *Der Neue Kusari*, p. 351.

96. Ibid.

97. Ibid., p. 354.

98. Ibid., p. 356.

99. Ibid., p. 357.

100. Breuer, *Mein Weg*, p. 62.

101. Breuer, *Der Neue Kusari*, p. 359.

102. Ibid., p. 352.

103. Ibid., p. 357.

104. Ibid., p. 362.

105. Ibid., pp. 362–63.

106. Ibid., pp. 366–67.

107. Ibid.

108. Franz Rosenzweig, *The Star of Redemption*, trans. William W. Hallo (Boston: Beacon Press, 1972), p. 269. (Hereafter in notes referred to as *Star*.)

109. Breuer, *Der Neue Kusari*, p. 369.

CHAPTER 3

1. Cf. Moshe Idel, *Kabbalah: New Perspectives* (New Haven: Yale University Press, 1988), p. 139.

2. Breuer, *Die Welt*, p. 47.

3. Ibid., p. 6.

4. Breuer, *Concepts of Judaism*, p. 320 (note n.42).

5. Breuer, *Der Neue Kusari*, p. 393. R. J. Zvi Werblowsky, in his article ("Politics and Piety—Between Rationalism and Mysticism"), writes of his personal memory of Isaac Breuer's practice of studying Shelah on Sabbath afternoons, before *havdalah*. Cf. Horwitz, *Isaac Breuer*, p. 65. For the role of Shelah in spreading Kabbalah, cf. Heinz Moshe Graupe, *The Rise of Modern Judaism*, trans. John Robinson (Huntington, NY: Robert E. Krieger, 1978), p. 35.

6. Scholem, *On the Kabbalah*, p. 36.

7. Breuer, *Die Welt*, p. 48.

8. Breuer, *Der Neue Kusari*, p. 390.

9. The unintelligible hiddenness of the creation process is also a topic in the classical rabbinic literature. Cf. Jerusalem Talmud Chagiga 77c and Babylonian Talmud Chagiga 14a.

10. Breuer, *Die Welt*, p. 48.

11. Compare, e.g., *Der Neue Kusari*, p. 395, or *Naḥaliel*, p. 203.

12. Psalm translation from *The Book of Psalms* (Philadelphia: Jewish Publication Society of America, 1972), p. 105. For a discussion of the kabbalistic use of garment imagery, see Idel, *Kabbalah: New Perspectives*, pp. 237–38; 387.

13. Samson Raphael Hirsch, *The Pentateuch*, trans. Isaac Levy, vol. 1, 2nd ed. (Gateshead, England: Judaica Press, 1973), pp. 40–42. The source of the midrash is Genesis Rabbah 10:46.

14. Hirsch, *The Pentateuch*, p. 45.

15. Breuer, *Der Neue Kusari*, p. 394.

16. Ibid., p. 402.

17. Here, it seems, Breuer responds to Wolfsberg's negative review of *Die Welt*. Wolfsberg charged that his theory presents science as overly deductive. See infra, notes 28 and 29.

18. Breuer, *Der Neue Kusari*, p. 402.

19. Ibid., p. 392. For references within kabbalistic literature to the connection between the ten *ma'amarot* of creation and the ten *dibbrot* of Sinai, cf. Idel, *Kabbalah: New Perspectives*, p. 172. In Kabbalah, the connection between creation and Sinai becomes effective through the theurgic practice of the mitzvot. Idel quotes Recanati to the effect that the neglect of the commandments destroys worlds, while the practice of the commandments maintains them. Breuer's use of theurgic theory is explored below.

20. Cf. Genesis Rabbah 19:14, cited by Nachmanides in his commentary on Genesis. 2:3. Ibn Ezra's commentary is on Genesis 1:1 Cf. also Isaac Husik, *Medieval Jewish Philosophy*, p. 190. Breuer's own reference to Nachmanides is found in *Naḥaliel*, p. 53.

21. Breuer, *Die Welt*, p. 56.

22. Ibid., p. 57.

23. Ibid., p. 55.

24. Ibid., p. 51.

25. Kant, *Critique of Pure Reason*, p. 213.

26. It is interesting to note that Breuer seems to ignore the relevant discussion in the *Critique* of the first antinomy of pure reason. Kant demonstrated that the theses "The world has a beginning" and "The world is beginningless" are equally compatible with transcendental reason and are therefore equally objectionable. Although Breuer appears to break with Kant by holding that reason cannot predicate "beginning" of nature, he can also be read to agree with him. For Breuer is arguing that reason cannot, in general, accede to creation without revelation. Reason therefore is entrapped by nature such that any judgment reason comes to vis-á-vis creation must be arbitrary or erroneous. Cf. Kant, ibid., pp. 396–402.

27. Breuer, *Die Welt*, pp. 53–54.

28. The central passage of Wolfsberg's critique is worth quoting at length: "Schlimmer sind wesentliche Schwächen, mit denen das Schicksal des Buches verknüpft ist. Dieses Werk trägt nichts zu der grossen Auseinandersetzung zwischen dem Judentum der Überlieferung und der Philosophie bei. Wenn man es Breuer zum Verdienst anrechnen will, dass er keine schwächliche Eintagsapologetik betreibt, so vergesse man nicht dass er vielfach Kollisionen dadurch umgeht, dass er die Welt eben als Schöpfung und Natur darstellt und begreift. Dieser Lösungsversuch mag ernst gemeint sein—man kann sich aber des Eindrucks nicht erwehren, dass er auch ein prachtvoller Ausweg ist, der von vornherein vor allen Konflikten schützt. Der Gegensatz zum Weg moderner Wissenschaft allein wäre kein Grund zur Ablehnung von Breuer's Gedankengang. Aber Breuer will sich doch mit der Forschung auseinandersetzen und da ist immerhin auffällig, dass er nur in Terminologie und im Dialektischen sich ihr nährt. Seine durchaus deduktiv gerichtete Philosophie könnte von Bedeutung sein, wenn sie systematisch die grosse jüdische Traditionslehre und das Gesetz zu meistern suchte oder der Ausdruck der spezifisch jüdischen Religiösität—mit der Note starken eigenen Erlebens—wäre. Statt dessen wird die Begegnung mit der Wissenschaft besucht, aber sie wird in keinem Fall zu einer grossen Auseinandersetzung. Der Gefahr aller deduktiven Systeme, mit der empirischen Wirklichkeit—insbesondere der naturgesetzlichen— nichts anfangen zu können, erliegt auch Breuer; hierzu kommt aber die Arroganz des Dogmatikers, der beweislos alles besser weiss." Wolfsberg, review of *Die Welt*, pp. 426–27.

29. Breuer, *Die Welt*, p. 6.

30. A Kalam-like view of Providence does characterize the ontology of a recent Orthodox thinker, R. Eliyahu Dessler. Dessler rejects the scientific/secular Weltanschauung in toto, arguing that causality is a habit of mind, not an ontological property. Unlike David Hume, of course, he retreats to a medieval, Kalamist ontology as an alternative. Breuer would

have found this approach deeply muddled, I believe. Cf. Eliezer Goldman, "Responses to Modernity in Orthodox Jewish Thought," in *Studies in Contemporary Jewry*, vol. 2, ed. Peter Y. Medding (Bloomington: Indiana University Press, 1986) pp. 55–57.

31. Maimonides, *Guide for the Perplexed*, bk. 2, ch. 29.

32. Breuer, *Concepts of Judaism*, p. 123. Breuer's theory of miracles was developed in "Der Begriff des Wunders im Judentum," *Jüdische Monatshefte* 3 (1916): 258–71. It was reprinted in a German collection of his articles that appeared in 1923, *Wegzeichen*, (Frankfurt am Main: Kaufmann) under the title "Wunder, Prophetie und Schöpfung." That collection has been translated into Hebrew as *Tziyyunei Derekh*, trans. Moshe Speiser (Jerusalem: Mossad Harav Kook, 1982). "Mophet, Nevu'ah Uvri'ah," ("Miracle, Prophecy and Creation") is chapter 2, pp. 41–54, of that collection.

33. Levinger, *Concepts of Judaism*. p. 118.

34. Henry Slonimsky, Introduction to *Kuzari*, by Judah Halevi, p. 28. For a discussion of the role of this concept in Kabbalah, see Idel, *Kabbalah: New Perspectives*, p. 236.

35. Levinger, *Concepts of Judaism*, pp. 123.

36. Ibid.

37. Breuer, *Die Welt*, p. 57.

38. Ibid., p. 58.

39. Ibid.

40. "Nur die Lehre von der Welt als Schöpfung und Natur kann das Seiende mit 'mir' versöhnen." Ibid., p. 59.

41. Breuer, *Elischa*, pp. 15–42.

42. Ibid., p. 21.

43. Ibid., pp. 14–15.

44. While Breuer does not agree with Cohen that man is essentially a rational, moral, and therefore free being, there is a sort of agreement insofar as, in both, religion "discovers" individuality. For Cohen, ethics can only recognize man in his generality. The special contribution of religion is the discovery of the value of individual man as neighbor. Religion discovers individuality and also gives it a positive valuation. For Breuer, the value of individuality remains ambiguous. It is nonetheless ratified by the "religious" knowledge of creation. Cf. Samuel Hugo Berg-

mann, *Faith and Reason*, trans. Alfred Jospe (New York: Schocken Books, 1963), pp. 44–45. Breuer's rejection of an ethically generalizing discourse qualifies his Kantianism. It suggests a parallel to recent debates about Rawls' *Theory of Justice* and MacIntyre's *After Virtue*, regarding the sufficiency of rules versus virtue based moral philosophy.

45. Breuer, *Elischa*, p. 12.

46. Ibid., p. 15.

47. Ibid., p. 41.

48. Breuer, *Der Neue Kusari*, p. 314.

49. Breuer, *Elischa*, pp. 15–16. Cf. Rosenzweig, *Star*, p. 120, where he discusses creation in terms of the I discovering its own createdness. From man's point of view, unlike God's, creation means, for Rosenzweig, the assumption of a creature-consciousness. For Breuer, man's (or for that matter, the world's) point of view is the dominant perspective.

50. Cf. Frederick Copleston, S. J., *A History of Philosophy*, vol. 7 (Garden City, NY: Image Books, 1965), p. 62.

51. Breuer, *Elischa*, pp. 44–45.

52. Ibid.

53. "Gott ist nicht das Ich der Materie, sondern Ich schlechthin." Breuer, ibid.

54. Ibid., pp. 46–47.

55. Breuer, *Naḥaliel*, p. 44. *Kavod* is a term that figures prominently in the prekabbalistic mysticism of medieval Hasidism, where it signifies divine emanation. *Kavod* represents an embodiment of divine presence roughly equivalent to the rabbinic notion of the Shekhinah. The term also appears in this mediatorial sense in Saadiah and Abraham ibn Ezra's commentary on Exodus 33. Cf. Joseph Dan, *The Early Kabbalah*, trans. Ronald C. Kiener (New York: Paulist Press, 1986), pp. 19–20.

56. Breuer, *Naḥaliel*, p. 44.

57. Ibid., p. 47.

58. Breuer, *Elischa*, pp. 48–49.

59. Leibniz, *Discourse on Metaphysics*, ch. 14–29.

60. Breuer, *Elischa*, p. 50.

61. Ibid. "Das Formende im Ich ist das Subjekt.
   Das Geformtsein im Ich ist das Objekt.

Die formende Form stellt vor.
Die geformte Form wird vorgestellt.
Nur die Form ist vorstellbar.
Nur sie ist in der Vorstellung."

62. Lewy, Altmann, and Heinemann, *Three Jewish Philosophers*, p. 18.

63. *Sifre*, trans. Reuven Hammer, Yale Judaica Series, 24 (New Haven: Yale University Press, 1986), p. 70.

64. Cf. Scholem, *On the Kabbalah*, p. 36.

65. Cf. Rosenzweig, Star, pp. 160–61.

66. Breuer, *Der Neue Kusari*, p. 329.

67. Breuer, *Elischa*, p. 92.

68. Ibid., p. 94.

69. Breuer, *Die Welt*, p. 75.

70. Ibid. Cf. T. B. Avodah Zarah 3a: "The Holy One, Blessed be He, made a condition with the works of Creation and said to them, if Israel accepts the Torah you will endure; if not I will reduce you again to chaos." Cited in Idel, *Kabbalah: New Perspectives*, p. 171. Idel cites a number of rabbinic sources that clearly establish that a theurgic, "world-maintaining" view of the Torah was held by some early sages.

71. Breuer, *Die Welt*, p. 75.

72. Ibid., p. 76.

73. Ibid., pp. 64–65.

74. Ibid., p. 69.

75. Ibid.

76. Ibid., p. 79.

77. Ibid.

78. Ibid., p. 80.

79. Ibid.

80. Ibid., pp. 82–83.

81. Ibid.

82. Ibid., p. 84.

83. Breuer, *Naḥaliel*, p. 53.

84. Breuer, *Der Neue Kusari*, p. 325.

85. Ibid., pp. 330–31.

86. Ibid., p. 326.

87. Ibid. p. 327.

88. Cf. I. Grunfeld, "Taamei Hamitzvoth in the Jewish Legal Philosophy of Rabbi S. R. Hirsch," in *Rabbi Dr. Joseph Breuer Jubilee Volume*, eds. Marc Breuer and Jacob Breuer (New York: Feldheim, 1962), p. 95.

89. Breuer, *Der Neue Kusari*, p. 337.

90. Ibid., p. 327.

91. Ibid., p. 329.

92. Ibid., p. 331.

93. Ibid., p. 332.

94. Ibid.

95. Gershom Scholem, *The Messianic Idea in Judaism* (New York: Schocken Books, 1972), pp. 325–34.

96. Scholem, *On the Kabbalah*, p. 48.

97. Ibid., p. 50.

98. Breuer, *Der Neue Kusari*, p. 336.

99. Breuer, *Concepts of Judaism*, p. 331, note 29.

100. Joseph ben Abraham Gikatilla, *Sha'are Orah*, ed. Joseph ben Shlomo (Jerusalem: Mossad Bialik, 1970), p. 22.

101. Ibid., p. 36.

102. Ibid. Cf. Idel, *Kabbalah: New Perspectives*, p. 183, for a further account of Gikatilla's notion of cosmic tragedy and human sin.

103. Breuer, *Der Neue Kusari*, p. 336.

CHAPTER 4

1. The dissertation was not accepted, it seems on account of some personal animus on the part of one of his readers. Breuer remarks sarcas-

tically that this reader wrote angry corrections in the margins, not realizing that he was correcting Kantian citations as well as Breuer! His adviser was greatly embarrassed and accepted a paper he had written on patents, rushing it through the examination process. The essay was accepted by the *Kantstudien* series, the scholarly publication of the *Kant Gesellschaft*, to which Breuer belonged until he left Germany. Cf. *Mein Weg*, p. 85.

2. Breuer, *Mein Weg*, p. 85.

3. Breuer discusses the failure of Stammler, including his rather disappointing personal encounter with him, in *Mein Weg*, p. 86.

4. Breuer, *Der Rechtsbegriff auf Grundlage der Stammlerschen Socialphilosophie* (Berlin: Reuther, 1912), p. 8. (This volume is number 27 in *Kantstudien*, a series still in progress and currently published by Walter de Gruyter, Berlin.)

5. Carl Joachim Friedrich, *The Philosophy of Law in Historical Perspective* (Chicago: University of Chicago Press, 1963), p. 158.

6. Breuer, *Der Rechtsbegriff*, p. 4.

7. Ibid., p. 22.

8. Ibid., p. 26.

9. Friedrich, *Philosophy of Law*, p. 159.

10. Ibid., p. 160.

11. Ibid., p. 127.

12. Ibid.

13. Breuer, *Der Rechtsbegriff*, p. 46.

14. Ibid.

15. Ibid., p. 50.

16. Ibid.

17. Ibid., p. 53.

18. Charles Friedman argues that Breuer turns the tables on Kant, accusing him of a doctrine of heteronomy, not only from a Jewish apologetic standpoint, but from an internal Kantian one. Friedman cites Kant's *Opus Postumum* (citation from Jean Lacroix, *Kant et le Kantisme* (Paris: P. U. F., 1967), pp. 66–74) where Kant asserts that God is ultimately the legislator of practical reason and the moral law. Of course, that "fact" of origins is of no consequence to the moral agent, who must will the law

autonomously. Friedman sees Breuer as exploiting Kant's admission of the heteronomous origin of the moral law for his own purposes, including the critique of Kant. Cf. Friedman, *Ha-mishpat bemachshavato*, p. 16.

19. Breuer, *Der Rechtsbegriff*, p. 55.

20. Ibid., p. 63.

21. Ibid., p. 61.

22. Ibid., pp. 63–64.

23. Ibid., p. 87.

24. Ibid.

25. Ibid., p. 98.

26. Ibid., p. 65.

27. Ibid.

28. Ibid., p. 68.

29. George H. Sabine and Thomas L. Thorson, *A History of Political Theory*, 4th ed. (Hinsdale, Il: Dryden Press, 1973), p. 196.

30. Breuer, *Der Rechtsbegriff*, p. 74.

31. Ibid. Breuer uses this Schopenhauerian term as early as 1912, before his first exposure to Kabbalah. This suggests that the main influence upon him in regard to garment symbolism was philosophical rather then Jewish.

32. Ibid., p. 71.

33. Breuer's attitude toward halakhah, while strict and conservative, is occasionally critical. His criticism is directed toward the most human features of the halakhah, that is, *takkanot* for which the Jewish people themselves are responsible. For example, he is highly critical of commercial instruments such as *heter iska*, which seem to him to be a degeneration of the ideality of the law, brought on by the negative features of diaspora existence. The Torah requires, as we shall see, a Torah State in order for it to unfold to its maximal, ideal extent. Thus his criticism of specific Jewish laws is founded on the ideal stature of the law, not on any values extraneous to the law. Cf. *Naḥaliel*, pp. 328–30.

34. Cf. Breuer, *Weltwende*, (Jerusalem: Mossad Jizchak Breuer, 1979) pp. 28–33, and Breuer, *Concepts of Judaism*, p. 60. In *Mein Weg*, (p. 85) Breuer refers to *Der Rechtsbegriff* as his way of discharging a debt of gratitude to "Edom's" (that is, gentile) law. This illustrates the persistence

of his sense of incipient *Gerechtigkeit* in gentile institutions. There is an ambivalence toward *Kultur*, which, it seems to me, Breuer never resolved. He continued to read and so to participate in *Kultur* literally until his death. (He died reading Thomas Mann's letters.) On the other hand, the preponderant weight of his philosophy leaves little or no independent axiological room for non-Jewish spiritual expression. Breuer was truly suspended between "Kant and Kabbalah," a fact of some importance in trying to extrapolate where Breuer might fit along today's Orthodox scale. Breuer's attachment, highly qualified though it was, to Western culture after the Holocaust rules out, it seems to me, including him within the ranks of Jewish fundamentalists. Cf. Eliezer Schweid, "Medinat Ha-Torah", in Horwitz *Isaac Breuer*, p. 126. Schweid suggests that "fundamentalism" represents one pole of Breuer's complex intellectual disposition. I do not think that this usage is strictly correct. The sense of the term "fundamentalism" within the Jewish context is itself controversial. I would suggest that a certain disingenuous or inappropriate naiveté in the face of the real challenges of modern secularism might be a criterion for fundamentalism. Breuer's highly nuanced and dialectical relationship to philosophy and *Kultur* preclude this. His naiveté is hard-won, so-called "zweite Naivität."

35. Breuer, *Moriah*, p. 3.

36. Ibid., p. 6.

37. I shall argue below that Breuer's strictly causal understanding of nature has given him an impoverished and inadequate conception of the natural world. Breuer rejects any sort of teleology inherent in nature, thus rendering nature essentially static and flat. Nature may be "slumbering Spirit," but the gulf between man, who awakens the Spirit to self-consciousness, and nature is absolute. It is not bridged by any inherent vitalistic progression. Man, although partly natural, comes to self-consciousness through the dialectic of *Sein-Sollen*, and *Sollen* is nonnatural.

38. Breuer, *Moriah*, p. 10.

39. Ibid. In *Weltwende* (pp. 25–26), Breuer elaborates slightly on the Ideas. They require, he claims, no special revelation. The process of human culture gives expression to them. The Creator has given the Ideas an initial impetus on their journey through history and culture through setting His image on the human soul. The Ideas appear to represent unique, albeit historically ineffective, artifacts of creation in the midst of nature. Once again, the ambivalence toward culture is marked.

40. Schweid, in "Medinat Ha-Torah," p. 131, argues that Breuer's dichotomization of polities (i.e., the Torah State vs. all natural sociopolitical orders) derives from Maimonides' distinction (*Guide*, bk. 2, ch. 40) between polities ordered by genuine prophetic revelation and polities or-

dered by the *nomoi* of statesmen. There are suggestive parallels between Breuer and Maimonides, and the two versions of types of state are, with qualifications, compatible. Nonetheless, while Breuer depends on the *Mishneh Torah* in *Naḥaliel*, he nowhere explictly reveals his dependence on the *Guide*. He does in *Mein Weg* (p. 151) acknowledge his dependence on German thought, Ihering from example, for his distinction between natural and Torah-ordered polity. I believe that Kantian and neo-Kantian notions exercised, therefore, a more profound effect on his thought than the Maimonidean view.

41. Breuer's *Die Rechtsphilosophischen Grundlagen* originally appeared in the *Jahrbuch der Jüdisch-Literarischen Gesellschaft* 8 (Frankfurt am Main: n.p., 1911): 35–64. It also appears in Hebrew translation as "Mishpat ha-Eshah, ha-Eved veha-Nokhri" in Isaac Breuer, *Tsiyyunei Derekh*, trans. Moshe Speiser (Jerusalem: Mossad Ha-Rav Kook, 1982). References in this study are to the English translation of Jacob Levinger. "The Philosophical Foundations of Jewish and of Modern Law," in Breuer, *Concepts of Judaism*, pp. 53–81.

42. For a discussion of the role of internal and external points of view in the description of a legal system, cf. H. L. A. Hart, *The Concept of Law* (New York: Oxford University Press, 1978), pp. 79ff.

43. Breuer, *Concepts of Judaism*, p. 63.

44. Ibid., p. 67.

45. It is striking that Breuer makes no room for public discourse in his social and legal theory. It is as if the law is worked out in the private conscience of the legislator or judge or in some ideal *Begriffshimmel* not shaped in the give-and-take of the public realm. Breuer's idealism has given his theory an otherworldly cast. He does envision, in his theocratic model in *Naḥaliel*, a Sanhedrin where debate will take place about halakhic and other matters of State. This notwithstanding, he lacks any positive appreciation for democracy, a problem that we shall presently investigate.

46. Breuer, *Concepts of Judaism*, p. 73.

47. Ibid., p. 74.

48. Ibid.

49. Ibid., p. 79.

50. Ibid., p. 81. Breuer has in mind here the rabbinic belief that "causeless hatred" between Jews brought God's punishment upon them.

51. Nathan Rotenstreich, *Philosophy, History and Politics: Studies in Contemporary English Philosophy of History*, vol. 1 of Melbourne International Philosophy Series (The Hague: Martinus Nijhoff, 1976), p. 132.

52. Breuer, *Messiasspuren* (Frankfurt am Main: Verlag Rudolph Leonhard Hammon, 1918), pp. 10–13. In *Weltwende*, Breuer treats nationalism as a political religion of post-Christian paganism (cf. chapter 1). Christianity's putative withdrawal from authentic Jewish legal-national existence created a vacuum in European civilization that was filled by the old gods under new names. Jesus preached the fatherhood of God, which the Christian nations accept, but not kingship of God. Christianity is a privatized, apolitical religion that has abandoned history to Caesar. This reading of Christianity was not uncommon. Compare Joseph Klausner's *Jesus of Nazereth* (1922), Ahad Ha-am's *Al shtei se'epim* (1910) or Leo Baeck's "Romantische Religion" (1938).

53. Scholem, "The Crisis of Tradition in Jewish Messianism," in *The Messianic Idea in Judaism*, p. 57. Cf. David Biale's discussion of Scholem's treatment of messianism in his *Gershom Scholem Kabbalah and Counter-History* (Cambridge: Harvard University Press, 1979), pp. 148–70.

54. Hermann Cohen, *Religion der Vernunft aus den Quellen des Judentums* (Weisbaden: Fourier Verlage, 1978), ch. 14, para 37, p. 341. Behind Cohen's view lies at least a century of liberal Jewish secularization of messianic thought. One must be cautious in construing the character of this "secularization," however. Hans Bach has suggested that German Jews in the early nineteenth century transformed their messianic expectations into an immanentist eschatological reading of their contemporary experience on religious grounds. On his reading, it is not the attenuation of the messianic idea, but its intrinsically religious transformation, that produced the modern Jewish return to history. Cf. Bach, *The German Jew*, p. 75.

This reading may stretch the concept of messianism a bit too far, but it does seem to fit Breuer's case. One sees strong continuity with both rationalistic and mystical messianic concepts as well as secularization in Breuer's view. While the messianic process is political, this-worldly, and historical, it is also contingent on the theurgic practice of the mitzvot and will culminate with the return of the Shekhinah to the rebuilt Temple.

55. Breuer, *Messiasspuren*, p. 16.

56. Cohen, *Religion der Vernunft*, ch. 14, para 25, p. 328. Cf. para 27, p. 330.

57. Ibid., ch. 14, para 27, p. 333.

58. Breuer, *Weltwende*, pp. 46–48.

59. Ibid., pp. 33–36. This shift toward "survivalism," perfectly understandable in 1938, represents something of a move away from Samson Raphael Hirsch, who gave the Jews a cathartic function within the dias-

pora. The Jews were to think the thoughts of the nations from within their midst and so to raise them up before God in a redemptive manner. Cf. Hirsch, *Horeb*, trans. I. Grunfeld (New York: Soncino Press, 1981), bk. 5, ch. 96, pp. 460–62. Breuer retains this view in *Messiasspuren*.

60. Breuer, *Messiasspuren*, p. 15.

61. Breuer is at his most "modern," it seems to me, in passages of this kind. He reveals that one of his fundamental orientations remains a kind of Kantian cosmopolitan internationalism, informed by socialism. While this thrust gets translated into a more traditional framework in *Naḥaliel*, it does not disappear. Breuer's messianic picture is thus a mix of rationalism, classical supernaturalism, and modern secularism.

62. Breuer, *Messiasspuren*, p. 15.

63. Cf. George Foot Moore, *Judaism in the First Centuries of the Christian Era*, vol. 1 (Cambridge: Harvard University Press, 1954), pp. 226–27.

64. Breuer, *Moriah*, p. 24.

65. Murphy, *Kant*, pp. 147–49.

66. Breuer, *Messiasspuren*, p. 20. Cf. *Naḥaliel*, pp 54-58. In *Naḥaliel*, Breuer hypostatizes Abraham's differentiation from the nations. To Abraham's descendants is attributed a different hereditary, physical substance from other human beings, such that their wills are capable of greater inherent unity and autonomy than others' wills. Deviation from the life of mitzvot, for instance, by eating nonkosher foods, actually diminishes the unique hereditary substratum of Jewish physical being. This "gnostic" dualism and hypostatization reflects Breuer's kabbalistic inclination, pushing his Kantianism to the limit, if not over the edge.

67. In *Naḥaliel*, ibid., Breuer argues this case through an exegesis of the Akedah.

68. Breuer, *Messiasspuren*, p. 37.

69. Ibid., p. 81. For the notion of Israel's special *Schicksalslast* in Hermann Cohen, cf. *Religion der Vernunft*, ch. 14, para 31, p. 333. Israel's burden is to bear all of the sins of the nations among which it dwells.

70. Breuer, *Die Welt*, p. 18. For other German critiques of bourgeois values and consciousness from this period, cf. H. S. Hughes, *Consciousness and Society* (New York: Alfred Knopf, 1958), pp. 40, 46, 50.

71. Breuer, *Moriah*, pp. 36–41.

72. Breuer, *Die Welt*, p. 19.

73. Ibid., p. 20.

74. Ibid., p. 22.

75. Sabine and Thorson, *History of Political Theory*, p. 599.

76. G. W. F. Hegel, *Grundlinien der Philosophie des Rechts* (Stuttgart: Reclam, 1970), p. 406 (translation my own).

77. Breuer's explicit critique of democracy is found in *Weltwende*, pp. 62–64.

78. Cf. *International Encyclopedia of the Social Sciences*, s.v. "Gierke, Otto von." There is an additional perspective Breuer might have gained from Gierke. The idea of rejecting the conceptual apparatus of Roman law and of discovering and rebuilding a Germanic jurisprudence has a distinct resemblance to Hirsch's methodological bias. Breuer heard Gierke's lectures in Berlin. Cf. *Mein Weg*, p. 77.

79. Breuer, *Die Welt*, pp. 95–96.

80. Ibid., p. 30.

81. Breuer, *Moriah*, p. 94.

82. Breuer, *Nahaliel*, pp. 379–81.

83. Breuer, *Moriah*, p. 115. God enabled the *Shulhan Arukh* to be written so that the Jews would able to withstand the coming trials of modernity.

84. Breuer, *Nahaliel, p. 378.*

85. Ibid., p. 381.

86. Breuer, *Moriah*, p. 224. The greater part of *Mein Weg* is taken up by sharp critiques of Agudat Israel, particularly its president, Jacob Rosenheim, and by Breuer's many struggles within the World Executive for his point of view.

87. Cf. Nathan Rotenstreich, *Jews and German Philosophy: The Polemics of Emancipation* (New York: Schocken Books, 1984), pt. 2. I do not think that Breuer was fighting the nineteenth century battle against Hegel and Bauer, as was Rosenzweig. Anti-Hegelian premises underlie his whole appraoch to Jewish history, however.

88. Cf. Paul Tillich, *Perspectives on 19th and 20th Century Protestant Theology* (New York: Harper and Row, 1967), pp. 30–34.

89. This helpful phrase was coined by David Biale in *Gershom Scholem* p. 11.

90. Rosenzweig, *Star*, p. 302.

91. Cf. Paul R. Mendes-Flohr, "To Brush History Against the Grain: The Eschatology of the Frankfurt School and Ernst Bloch," *Journal of the American Academy of Religion* 51 (December 1983): 631–33.

92. Rosenzweig, *Star*, p. 302.

93. This remark was quoted by Professor Rivka Horwitz at a conference on Isaac Breuer, Yeshiva University, December 26, 1983.

94. Rosenzweig, *Star*, p. 267.

95. Breuer, *Der Neue Kusari*, p. 111. Cf. Hirsch, *Horeb*, p. 461. For Hirsch, the Torah does not exist for the State, but the State for the Torah. Both Hirsch and Breuer absolutize the Torah, making it independent of Israel's sovereignty. The effect of this dichotomy in Hirsch is to depoliticize Jewish existence. Breuer, I am arguing, achieves precisely the opposite effect. While undoubtedly rooted in Hirsch, Breuer performs a far-reaching and radical transvaluation of values on the Hirschian schema. Breuer thus represents a systematic reformulation of the Hirschian framework; a reform from within. Cf. Eliezer Schweid, "Medinat Ha-Torah," pp. 127–28.

96. Breuer, *Der Neue Kusari*, pp. 107–8. The reference to "as if" refers to the philosophy of Hans Vaihinger (1852–1933). Vaihinger was the president of the Kant Society to which Breuer belonged and the editor of its series, *Kantstudien*. Breuer wrote a review of Vaihinger's *Philosophie des Als Ob*, on his invitation, from a jurisprudential angle. It appeared in *Gerichtssaal* 80 (1913) as "Die Lehre vom Unrichtigen Recht," pp. 395–404. Cf. *Mein Weg*, p. 86.

97. Breuer, *Mein Weg*, p. 156.

98. Breuer, *Der Neue Kusari*, p. 216.

99. Ibid., p. 224.

100. Ibid., p. 225.

101. Ibid.

102. Joseph Ben Abraham Gikatilla, *Sha'are Orah*, p. 35.

103. Ibid., p. 38.

104. Use of a hypostatized concept of *knesset Israel* need not always entail a kabbalistic orientation. Cf. Pinchas Hacohen Peli, "Repentant Man—A High Level in Rabbi Soloveitchik's Typology of Man," *Tradition* 18 (Summer 1980): 135–59, for Soloveitchik's use of the concept.

105. Breuer, *Naḥaliel*, p. 308.

106. Ibid., p. 312. Eliezer Schweid detects in this rejection of the concept of theocracy an implicit critique of Spinoza and a defense of Maimonides, whom Spinoza "misunderstood," Cf. Schweid, "Medinat Ha- Torah," p. 136.

107. Breuer, Naḥaliel, p. 313.

108. Ibid., p. 315.

109. Ibid., pp. 318–19.

110. Ibid., p. 391.

111. Ibid., p. 407. Breuer points to the Cherubim as the locus at which the Shekhinah will dwell (p. 385). He interprets these, at the same time, as symbolic of a purified humanity engaged in atonement and turned toward the neighbor. The Talmud, T. B. Baba Batra 99a, imagines the Shekhinah to dwell between the Cherubim. Idel cites a wealth of ancient texts, rabbinic and nonrabbinic, on the theurgy of drawing the Shekhinah down to the Temple. Cf. Idel *Kabbalah: New Perspectives*, pp. 166–67.

112. Breuer, Naḥaliel, p. 426.

CHAPTER 5

1. Cf. M. Breuer, *Jüdische Orthodoxie*, p. 358.

2. John Hick, ed. *Classical and Contemporary Readings in the Philosophy of Religion*, 2nd ed. (Englewood Cliffs: Prentice-Hall, 1970), pp. 282–301.

3. Isaiah Berlin, *Four Essays On Liberty* (New York: Oxford University Press, 1971), pp. 118–72.

4. B. Kurzweil, *Lenokhah Ha-Mevuchah*, p. 122.

5. Ibid., p. 118.

6. Alexander Altmann, "Franz Rosenzweig on History," in Mendes—Flohr, *Franz Rosenzweig*, pp. 130–31.

7. Gershom Scholem, "Franz Rosenzweig and His Book, *The Star of Redemption*," in Mendes-Flohr, *Franz Rosenzweig*, p. 20.

BIBLIOGRAPHY

Bach, Hans I. *The German Jew*. New York: Oxford University Press, 1985.

Bacon, Gershon C. "The Politics of Tradition: Agudat Israel in Polish Politics, 1916-1939." In *Studies in Contemporary Jewry*. Vol. 2. Edited by Peter Y. Medding. Bloomington: Indiana University Press, 1986.

Berlin, Isaiah. *Four Essays on Liberty*. New York: Oxford University Press, 1971,

Biale, David. *Gershom Scholem: Kabbalah and Counter-History*. Cambridge: Harvard University Press, 1979.

Isaac Breuer. *Concepts of Judaism*. Edited by Jacob S. Levinger. Jerusalem: Israel Universities Press, 1974.

———. *Der Neue Kusari: Ein Weg zum Judentum*. (The New Kusari: a Way to Judaism) Frankfurt am Main: Rabbiner Hirsch Gesellschaft, 1934.

———. *Der Rechtsbegriff auf Grundlage der Stammlerschen Sozialphilosophie*. (The Concept of Law on The Basis of Stammler's Social Philosophy) Berlin: Reuther, 1912.

———. *Die Idea des Agudismus*. (The Ides of Agudism) Frankfurt am Main: L. Sänger Verlag, 1921.

———. *Die Rechtsphilsophisden Grundlagen des Jüdischen und des Modernen Rechts*. (The Legal-Philosophical Foundations of Jewish and of Modern Law) In *Jahrbuch der Jüdisch-Literarischen Gesellschaft*, Vol. 8. Frankfurt am Main: n.p., 1911.

———. *Die Welt als Schöpfung und Natur*. (The World as Creation and as Nature) Frankfurt am Main: J. Kauffmann Verlag, 1926.

———. "Edut lifnei Va'adat ha-Ḥaqirah ha-Anglo-Amerika'it le'inyannei Eretz Yisrael." (Testimony Before The Anglo-American Committee Concerning the Land of Israel, 1946) In *Yitzḥaq Breuer: Iyunnim be-Mishnato* (Isaac Breuer: The Man and His Thought). Edited by Rivka Horwitz. Ramat Gan: Bar Ilan University Press, 1988.

———. *Elischa*. Frankfurt am Main: J. Kauffmann Verlag, 1928.

————. *Lehre, Gesetz und Nation: Eine Historische-Kritische Untersuchung über das Wesen des Judentums*. (Doctrine, Law and Nation: A Historical-Critical Investigation of the Essence of Judaism) Frankfurt am Main: Verlag des Israelit, 1910.

————. *Mein Weg*. (My Way) Jerusalem/Zürich: Morascha Verlag, 1988.

————. *Messiasspuren*. (Traces of the Messiah) Frankfurt am Main: Verlag, Rudolph Leonhard Hammon, 1918.

————. *Moriah*. Jerusalem: Ha-Merkaz lema'an Sifrut Haredit be-Eretz Yisrael, 1954.

————. *Naḥaliel*. Jerusalem: Mossad Ha-Rav Kook, 1982.

————. *Programm oder Testament: Vier Jüdisch-Politische Aufsätze*. (Program or Testament: Four Jewish-Political Essays) Frankfurt am Main: J. Kauffmann Verlag, 1929.

————. *Tsiyunnei Derekh*. (Way Signs). Translated by Moshe Speiser. Jerusalem: Mossad Harav Kook, 1982.

————. *Wegzeichen*. (Way Signs). Frankfurt am Main: J. Kauffmann Verlag, 1923.

————. *Weltwende*. (World Turn) Edited by Mordechai Breuer, Jerusalem: Mossad Jizchak Breuer, 1979.

Breuer, Mordechai. *Jüdische Orthodoxie im Deutschen Reich 1871- 1918*. Frankfurt am Main: Jüdische Verlag bei Athenaeum, 1986.

————. *Review of Tradition in an Age of Reform*, by Noah H. Rosenbloom. *Tradition* 16 (Summer 1977), 142-43.

Buber, Martin. *Drei Reden über das Judentum*. Frankfurt am Main: Literarische Anstalt Rutten und Loening, 1961.

————. *Ich und Du*. Heidelberg: Lambert Schneider, 1979.

———— "Jewish Religiosity." In *On Judaism*. edited by Nahum N. Glatzer. New York: Schocken Books, 1977.

Cohen, Hermann. *Religion der Vernunft aus den Quellen des Judentums*. Wiesbaden: Fourier Verlag, 1978

Copleston, Frederick. *A History of Philosophy*. Vol. 7. Garden City, N.Y.: Image Books, 1965.

Dan, Joseph. *The Early Kabbalah*. Translated by Ronald C. Kiener. New York: Paulist Press, 1986.

Ehrmann, Saloman. "Isaac Breuer." In *Guardians of Our Heritage*, pp. 619-46. Edited by Leo Jung. New York: Bloch Publishing Co., 1958.

Flohr, Paul. "From *Kulturmystik* to Dialogue: An Inquiry into the Formation of Martin Buber's Philosophy of I and Thou." Ph.D. dissertation, Brandeis University, 1974. (Available as *Von der Mystik zum Dialog*. Translated by Dafna A. von Kries. Königstein/Ts.: Jüdischer Verlag, 1978.)

Friedman, Charles (Shlomo). *Ha-Mishpat bemachshavato shel Rav Yitzḥaq Breuer*. (The Law in the Thought of Rabbi Isaac Breuer.) Translated by Yehudit Kaufmann. Jerusalem: Ha-Ma'ayan n.d.

Friedrich, Carl Joachim. *The Philosophy of Law in Historical Perspective*. Chicago: University of Chicago Press, 1963.

Gikatilla, Joseph ben Abraham. *Sha'are Orah.* Edited by Joseph ben Shlomo. Jerusalem: Mossad Bialik, 1970.

Goldman, Eliezer. "Orthodoxy in Historical Perspective." In *Studies in Contemporary Jewry.* Vol. 2., Edited by Peter Y. Medding. Bloomington: Indiana University Press, 1986.

Graupe, Heinz Moshe. *The Rise of Modern Judaism: An Intellectual History of German Jewry, 1650-1942.* Translated by John Robinson. Huntington, N.Y.: Robert E. Krieger Publishing, 1978.

Grunfeld, Frederic V. *Prophets Without Honour.* New York: Holt, Rinehart and Winston, 1979. Philadelphia: Jewish Publication Society of America, 1979.

Halevi, Judah. *The Kuzari.* Foreward by Henry Slonimsky. New York: Schocken Books, 1964.

Halpern, Ben. *The Idea of the Jewish State.* Cambridge: Harvard University Press, 1969.

Hegel, G. W. F. *Grundlinien der Philosophie des Rechts.* Stuttgart: Reclam, 1970.

Hick, John. *Classical and Contemporary Readings in the Philosophy of Religion.* Englewood Cliffs: Prentice-Hall, 1970.

Hirsch, Samson Raphael. *Horeb.* Translated by I. Grunfeld. New York: The Soncino Press, 1981.

———. *The Nineteen Letters on Judaism.* Edited by Jacob Breuer, Jerusalem: Feldheim Publishers, 1969.

———. *The Pentateuch.* Translated by Isaac Levy. Gateshead, England: Judaica Press, 1973.

Hodges, Herbert A. *Wilhelm Dilthey: An Introduction.* New York: Howard Fertig, 1969.

Horwitz, Rivka. *Yitzhaq Breuer: Iyunnim be-Mishnato.* (Isaac Breuer: The Man and His Thought) Ramat Gan: Bar Ilan University Press, 1988.

———. "Voices of Opposition to the First World War among Jewish Thinkers." *Leo Baeck Institute Yearbook.* Vol. 33. New York: Leo Baeck Institute, 1988.

Hughes, H. S. *Consciousness and Society.* New York: Alfred Knofp, 1958.

Husik, Isaac. *A History of Medieval Jewish Philosophy.* Philadelphia: Jewish Publication Society of America, 1948.

Idel, Moshe. *Kabbalah: New Perspectives.* New Haven: Yale University Press, 1988.

International Encyclopedia of the Social Sciences. Ed. s. v. "Gierke, Otto von."

Kant, Immanuel. *Critique of Pure Reason.* Translated by Norman Kemp Smith. New York: St. Martin's Press, 1965.

Katz, Jacob. "German Culture and the Jews." *Commentary* 77 (February 1984).

———. "Orthodoxy in Historical Perspective." In *Studies in Contemporary Jewry.* Vol. 2., Edited by Peter Y. Medding. Bloomington: Indiana University Press, 1986.

Kurzweil, Baruch. *Lenokhaḥ Ha-Mevuchah Ha-Ruḥanit Shel Doreinu.* (Facing the Spiritual Perplexity of Our Time) Edited by Moshe Scwarcz. Ramat Gan: Bar Ilan University Press, 1976.

Kurzweil, Zvi. *The Modern Impulse of Traditional Judaism.* Hoboken: Ktav Publishing Co., 1985.

Leibniz, G. W. F. v. *Discourse on Metaphysics.* Translated by George Montgomery. In *The Rationalists.* Garden City, N. Y.: Anchor Books, 1974

Lewy, Hans: Altmann, Alexander; Heinemann, Isaak. *Three Jewish Philosophers.* New York: Atheneum, 1969.

MacIntyre, Alisdaire. *A Short History of Ethics.* New York: Macmillan Co., 1973.

Maimonides, Moses. *Mishneh Torah.* (Part I.) *Hilkhot Yesodei Ha-Torah.* New York: Abraham Isaac Friedman, N.D.

Medding, Peter Y. *Studies in Contemporary Jewry.* Vol. 2. Bloomington: Indiana University Press, 1986.

Mendes-Flohr, Paul, ed. *The Philosophy of Franz Rosenzweig.* Hanover: Brandeis University Press, 1988.

———. "To Brush History Against the Grain: the Eschatology of the Frankfurt School and Ernst Bloch." *Journal of the American Academy of Religion* 51 (December 1983): 631-47

Mosse, George L. *Crisis of German Ideology.* New York: Grosset & Dunlap, 1964.

———. *The Nationalization of the Masses.* New York: New American Library, 1975.

Murphy, Jeffrie G. *Kant: The Philosophy of Right.* Philosophers in perspective Series. edited by A. D. Woozley. London: Macmillan & Co. 1970.

Nietzsche, Friedrich. *The Birth of the Tragedy.* Translated by Francis Golffing. Garden City, N.Y. : Doubleday, 1956.

Niewöhner, Friedrich. "Isaac Breuer und Kant." *Neue Zeitschrift für Systematische Theologie und Religionsphilosophie.* 17 (1975), 142-150.

———. "Primat der Ethik' oder 'Erkenntnis-theoretische Begründung der Ethik'? Thesen zur Kant-Rezeption in der jüdischen Philosophie." In *Judentum im Zeitalter der Aufklärung. Wolfenbuetteler Studien zur Aufklärung.* Vol. 4. Wolfenbuettel: Jacobi Verlag, 1977. pp. 119-161.

Peli, Pinchas Hacohen. "Repentant Man—A High Level in Rabbi Soloveitchik's Typology of Man." *Tradition* 18 (Summer 1980): 135-159.

Rosenbloom, Noah H. *Tradition in an Age of Reform.* Philadelphia: Jewish Publication Society of America, 1976.

Rosenzweig, Franz. *Kleinere Schriften.* Berlin: Schocken Verlag, 1937.

———. *The Star of Redemption.* [1921] Translated by William Hallo. Boston: Beacon Press, 1972.

Rotenstreich, Nathan. *Jews and German Philosophy: The Polemics of Emancipation.* New York: Schocken Books, 1984.

————. *Philosophy, History and Politics: Studies in Contemporary English Philosophy of History. Melbourne International Philosophy Series.* Vol. 1. The Hague: Martinus Nijhoff, 1976.

Sabine, George H., and Thorson, Thomas L. *A History of Political Theory.* 4th Edition. Hinsdale, Ill.: Dryden Press, 1973.

Scholem, Gershom G. *Major Trends in Jewish Mysticism.* New York: Schocken Books, 1971.

————. *On Jews and Judaism in Crisis.* Edited by Werner J. Dannhauser. New York: Schocken Books, 1976.

————. *On the Kabbalah and its Symbolism.* Translated by Ralph Mannheim. New York: Schocken Books, 1965.

————. *The Messianic Idea in Judaism.* New York: Schocken Books, 1972.

Schopenhauer, Arthur. *The World as Will and Idea.* Translated by R. R. Haldane and J. Kemp. Garden City, N.Y.: Doubleday & Co., 1961.

Schwab, Hermann. *A World in Ruins.* London: Edward Goldston, 1946.

Stammler, Rudolph. *Die Lehre vom Richtigen Recht.* Halle: Buchhandlung des Waisenhauses. 1926.

Tal, Uriel, "Theologische Debatte um das 'Wesen' des Judentums." In *Juden in Wilhelminischen Deutschland 1890-1914.* pp. 599-632. Edited by Werner Mosse. Tübingen: J. C. B. Mohr, 1976.

Tillich, Paul. *Perspectives on 19th and 20th Century Protestant Theology.* New York: Harper and Row, 1967.

Tishbi, Yishayah. *Mishnat Ha-Zohar.* 2 vols. Jerusalem: Mossad Bialik, 1971.

Waxman, Meyer. *A History of Jewish Literature.* 4 vols. New York: Bloch Publishing Co., 1943.

Wiener, M. "Judah Halevi's Concept of Religion and a Modern Counterpart." *Hebrew Union College Annual.* XXIII (1950-1951): 669ff.

Wolfsberg, Oskar. Review of *Die Welt als Schöpfung und Natur,* by Isaac Breuer. *Monatschrift für Geschichte und Wissenschaft des Judentums* 9/10 (1926), pp. 426-27

————. "Popular Orthodoxy." *Leo Baeck Institute Yearbook.* Vol. 1. New York: Leo Baeck Institute, 1956.

INDEX

A

Abraham, and alienation, 155, 156
Agudat Israel, 10, 19, 23–24, 163;
  founding of, 18
Amalek, 162
Anarchism, 140
Apologetics, and philosophy, 32
Asceticism, 65

B

Balfour Declaration, 163, 164; and
  messianism, 19
Bamberger, R. Seligmann, 5
Bible Criticism, 114, 117, 118
Bourgeoisie, critique of, 7, 11, 18,
  22, 34, 156
Breuer, R. Salomon, 3, 6, 19
Buber, Martin, 9, 164
Bund Jüdischer Akademiker, 6,
  15–16

C

Calker, Fritz van, 14
Causality, 106, 177

Childhood. *See* Parenthood, and
  Childhood
Christianity, 157, 158, 164, 166
Circumcision, and creation, 171
Cohen, Hermann, 12, 35, 91; and
  messianism, 152–53, 155
Coercion, 141, 148
Congregation of Israel. *See* Knesset
  Israel
Conscience. *See* Law, and
  Conscience
Consciousness, 108–11
Consensus, 140–41
Creation, 55; and chaos, 105, 161;
  and law, 82; and nature, 74, 76–
  90, 106, 109; and science, 80–81,
  83–84; and sefirot, 102; and tele-
  ology, 92; and thing-in-itself, 82;
  and Torah, 104; commands, 106;
  of man and woman, 96–97; process of, 94–97; rabbinic
  doctrines of, 81, 102, 103; two
  concepts of, 100

D

Diaspora. *See* Exile
Dignity, 144–45
Duties, distribution of, 147, 149

Dilthey, Wilhelm, 50

E

Empiricism, 55
Epistemology (Theory of Knowledge), 12, 51–62; and revelation, 74; foundational character of, 26, 34
Equality, 142, 144–45
Erlebnis, 36, 37, 38, 42, 49–50
Essence of Judaism, 26
Ethics. *See* Law, and Ethics
Exile, 152, 155–56, 167

F

Feeling, 58–59
Fichte, J. G., 76, 98–99
Frankfurt Principle (of separatism), 5, 7, 168, 171; and Zionism, 10; redefinition of, 21, 23
Freedom, 59, 148; and causality, 73; and love, 71, 72; of God, 68, 77; of will, 67

G

Gierke, Otto von, 159–60
Gikatilla, R. Joseph ibn, 122, 170, 171

H

Halevi, R. Judah, 28, 35, 86–87
Hegel, and the State, 158–60
Herod, 161
Herzl, Theodor, 9–10
Hirsch, Mendel, 5
Hirsch, R. Samson Raphael, 3, 4, 30; and Halevi, 28; and rationalism, 29; conception of Sabbath,

79; doctrine of revelation, 116, 119; ontology of, 92
History, and States, 156, 160. *See also* Metahistory
Holocaust, 162
Horowitz, R. Isaiah (Shelah), 77

I

Ibn Ezra, R. Abraham, and creation, 81
Idealism, 55, 99, 100
Ideas, doctrine of, 47, 112
Individuation, 154; and creation, 89; and embodiment, 61; problem of, 33, 46, 47–49
Israel, creation of people, 161. *See also* Knesset Israel
Israelitische Religionsgesellschaft, 3, 22, 38, 131; founding of, 4

J

Johanan ben Zakkai, 162
Judgment, 133–34
Justice, Idea of, 141

K

Kabbalah, and hermeneutics, 114; neo-Orthodox view of, 8. *See also* Sefirot, Theurgy
Kant, Immanuel, 12, 53; and categorical imperative, 68–69; and freedom, 45; and international order, 154; and law, 127, 129; and substance, 83; and the unconditional, 39–40; and transcendental deduction, 40–41; Breuer's attitude toward, 30–31
Kingdom of Ends, 132, 134–35
Kingdom of God, 168, 169
Knesset Israel, 185; and individuation, 33–34, 89–90; and meta-

history, 124, 165, 179; and
redemption, 149; and sefirot,
120, 171; and Torah, 169; non-
identity with empirical Israel,
166; relationship with empirical
Israel, 170
Kohn, R. Pinchas, 8, 19, 75
Kook, R. Abraham Isaac, 21–22
Kurzweil, Baruch, 184

L

Laband, Paul, 14
Law, ahistorical nature of, 143; and
conscience, 147, 148; and creation. *See* Creation, and law;
and ethics, 132–33, 137–38, 144,
146–147, 149; and obedience, 33,
137; and State, 14; and teleology,
128–29; comparative, 142, 172;
discovery of, 136; German philosophy of, 14
Leibniz, G. W., 98–99, 105
Lenel, Otto, 13
Liberal Judaism. *See* Reform Judaism
Liberalism, political, 183
Liberty, negative and positive,
181–82
Love, 97; and freedom, 71–72
Luria, R. Isaac, 57

M

Maccabees, 161
Maimonidean Controversy, 27
Maimonides, 35; and Aristotle's
doctrine of soul, 63–64; and creation, 81; and messianism, 151–
52; and miracles, 86–87;
harmonization of philosophy and
Torah, 27; *Mishneh Torah*, 171,
173
Marx, Karl, 22, 126

Materialism, 65
Mathematics. *See* Proof
Mensch-Yisroel, 29, 132
Messianism, 17, 150–52
Metahistory, 37, 149–50, 161,
166–74
Miracle, 37, 86–88
Mission, 153
Mitzvot, 76, 107, 170–72
Monism, 47, 62, 77. *See also*
Schopenhauer, Arthur

N

Nachmanides, and creation, 81,
95–96
Nationalism, 157, 187
Nations, origin of, 153–54, 160
Natural Law Theory, 127, 128, 135
Nature, and creation, 74, 76–90;
and Torah, 30
Neo-Kantianism, 12, 125–26
Neo-Romanticism, 49–51; and
Schopenhauer, 57
Nietzche, Friedrich, 48–49, 50
Nobel, R. Nehemiah, 8
Nothingness, 96, 99

O

Objects, facticity of, 99
Oral Torah, 119, 120–22, 137

P

Parenthood, and Childhood, 91–93;
and Sabbath, 94
Peoplehood, sacral, 176
Perception, 44. *See also* Represen-
tation
Poalei Agudat Israel, 20
Poalei Ha-Haredi, 22
Prayer, and historical activism, 174

Primal Ground, 119, 121–22
Privacy, 158–59
Proof, and mathematics, 41; and Torah, 40; of divine existence, 38, 39
Prophecy, 87
Providence, 105

R

Reason, 33, 44–45, 46, 83, 85, 101, 176
Rebellion, against God, 74. *See also* War
Recanati, R. Menachem, 75, 107
Reform Judaism (Liberal Judaism), 4, 36, 152
Redemption, and eschatology, 124, 136, 165; and Torah, 125
Repentance, 72
Representation, 44, 47, 98; and science, 46; and thing-in-itself, 58. *See also* Perception
Revelation, and creation process, 94–97; givenness of, 115–116; intelligibility of, 113; language of, 115. *See also* Torah
Rights, 182
Rosenheim, Jacob, 18–19
Rosenzweig, Franz, 9, 34–35, 184–87; and creation, 74, 101; and exile, 165; and history, 164; and love, 71; and revelation, 103–104, 105
Rules, 130, 134, 135, 137

S

Saadiah Gaon, and doctrine of soul, 63–64; and revelation, 100
Sabbath, 21, 107; and creation, 76, 78, 97; robes, 78, 109, 110
Sacrifice. *See* Temple
Sanhedrin, 172–73
Schelling, F. W. J., 9

Scholem, Gershom, 2, 20, 102, 120, 164
Schopenhauer, Arthur, 42, 179; and alienation, 45; and body, 61; and determinism, 66, 70; and epistemology, 43; and Fichte, 55–56; and individuation, 46, 89; and monism, 47, 53, 76; and science, 45; and sufficient reason, 44–45; and understanding, 44–45; and veil of Maya, 78; and will, 45; Platonic idealism of, 47, 141
Scroll of Esther, 162
Secularity, neo-Orthodox attitude toward, 27
Secularization, 2, 150
Sefirot, 75, 95, 120, 122, 170, 186; and creation, 102
Self-limitation, of God, 107
Self-perception, 53
Shekhinah, 18, 170, 173; and meta-history, 162
Simmel, Georg, 134
Slavery, 143, 149
Society, and interests, 143, 146; and morality, 126, 131; ground of, 139; of animals, 139; order of, 140
Sollipsism, 118
Sonnenfeld, R. Joseph Chaim, 20, 21
Soul, doctrine of, 62–63, 108–11
Stammler, Rudolf, 125–27, 131, 134–35, 146; and right law, 128, 130; and the social ideal, 129
State, ontology of, 158, 160
Subject, and object, 55, 73, 98; in-itself, 59–60; perceiving, 60

T

Talmud, study of, 13
Temple, and sacrifice, 173–74
Theory of knowledge. *See* Epistemology

Theurgy, 102, 104, 120; and mitzvot, 107

Thing-in-itself, 43, 44, 53, 56, 58–61, 79, 88, 90, 99, 117; and creation. *See* Creation, and thing-in-itself; and science, 46; and will, 45

Torah, and freedom, 69–70; and science, 84; and will, 113, 117; as constitutional law, 125; as cosmic law, 68, 70; creation account in, 80, 83; divinity of, 38, 103, 113, 118; in-itself, 114, 118, 119, 121, 122, 137; methodology in study of, 116, State, 22, 160, 167–68, 170, 173, 181–82; totality of, 2, 5

Totalitarianism, 181

Transcendental Deduction, 42, of law, 126, 135

Truth, jurisprudential, 126–27; unconditional, 39

Tsimtsum, 57

U

Understanding, 33, 44–45, 82, 87, 117

V

Values, 112, 140

W

War, as rebellion against God, 17

Will, and feeling, 97; and perception, 52; and self, 46, 92; and self-maintenance, 51, 53, 54, 60; and thing-in-itself, 45; and Torah, 132; and truth, 51, 52; as activity, 66–68, 70; as passivity, 66–68, 70; conditionality of, 93; conflict of, 47; contraction of, 57–58; diverse senses of, 178–80; renunciation of, 47–48; three aspects of, 65

Wittgenstein, Ludwig, 185

Wolfsberg, Oscar, 75, 84

World War I, 15, 17, 138

Y

Yom Kippur, 174

Z

Zionism, 10–11, 19–20, 150; as historical activism, 10; Breuer's critique of, 36

Zohar, doctrine of the soul, 63–64